D1115012

Anatomy of English

An Introduction to
the Structure of
Standard American English

Anatomy of English

An Introduction to the Structure of Standard American English

DOROTHY SEDLEY
West Virginia University

ST. MARTIN'S PRESS
New York

Senior editor: Mark Gallaher
Project editor: Beverly Hinton
Editorial assistant: Robert Skiena
Production supervisor: Alan Fischer
Text design: Leon Bolognese & Associates
Graphics: G & H Soho, Ltd.
Cover design: Ben Santora

Library of Congress Catalog Card Number: 88-63039

Copyright © 1990 by St. Martin's Press, Inc.
All rights reserved. No part of this publication may be reproduced, stored in a retrieval system, or transmitted by any form or by any means, electronic, mechanical, photocopying, recording, or otherwise, except as may be expressly permitted by the 1976 Copyright Act or in writing by the Publisher.

Manufactured in the United States of America.
432
fedc

For information, write:
St. Martin's Press, Inc.
175 Fifth Avenue
New York, NY 10010

ISBN: 0-312-02687-0

PREFACE

Anatomy of English began as a series of classroom activities at West Virginia University for a course called "The English Language," which attracts not only English majors and prospective teachers of English, but journalism students and others who are interested in using language for pleasure as well as for profit. In addition, quite a few foreign-language majors, struck by the realization that they know more about the workings of Japanese or French than they know about their own native tongue, and even a smattering of international students who want to supplement what they have learned in their EFL or ESL courses, are prompted to enroll. All these students are seeking nontechnical information about the structure of English, not a course in linguistics or grammatical theory.

I was faced with the same problem encountered in teaching introductory material to laypersons in any discipline: how to simplify fundamental concepts and principles without distorting the facts. I wanted a book that is accurate yet readable, a book that is not filled with confusing "exceptions" yet does not give the false impression that systematicity is equivalent to complete and rigid regularity. I wanted instructional materials that manage to suggest the complexity of the grammatical system without *being* complex, materials that are simple without being simple-minded.

Over the years I have used many different texts, and I have read and rejected many more. Most of them try to cover too much ground—always a mistake in an introductory text. Many are not in fact introductory grammars of English, but introductory linguistics texts, intent on teaching about grammar in general, not about English as a unique system. Some have adequate exposition but insufficient or uninspired activities and exercises. Others are not only cluttered and confusing, but worst of all, they are dull. Exercises are repetitive, unimaginative, and simply boring. Because of endless, mechanical fill-in-the-blank monotony, even conscientious students find it difficult to keep their minds on the principles supposedly being taught.

So I began writing materials of my own. According to students, the activities I created turned out to be not only instructive, but easy to use and interesting, if not exactly "fun." Moreover, students began to tell me that their textbooks were superfluous, because working through the activities had taught them what they needed to know. Each semester I used more of these "Discovery Activities," and finally I dispensed with textbooks altogether. After a while, however, I began to distribute handouts containing conclusions, comments, and summaries of class discussions, so that absentees could be assured that they had indeed grasped the point of the Activities. Moreover, two of my colleagues were now using the Activities, which were at that time not always as transparent as I now believe them to be, and even they sometimes asked for assurance.

The exposition in *Anatomy of English*, which evolved from this feedback, is not intended to be comprehensive or definitive, but rather to provide confirmation of the discoveries and to address some of the incidental questions that arise out of the Activities but are not resolved in or by their solution. I did not put an answer key in the book because I do not want to encourage the notion that filling the blanks with the "right" answers (that is, the ones the author has in mind) is the goal of any Discovery Activity (although I have prepared an *Instructor's Manual* for *Anatomy of English* that suggests an appropriate range of responses). And I have limited the exposition purposely to encourage students to supplement the explanations with data from their own experience and to allow the dynamics of each new class to determine what needs to be discussed at greater length.

My students, along with those of six of my colleagues, have used successive revisions of *Anatomy of English* since the late 1970s. More recently, the book has been field-tested in classrooms outside my home institution. In written evaluations, students credit the book with making English grammar make sense, and even with making grammar interesting—no doubt because *Anatomy of English* does not just tell them the facts about English, but requires them to discover the facts for themselves. Unlike exercises in ordinary texts, which often require nothing more than simple recall or which ask learners to do nothing more challenging than "circle the prepositional phrases," the approximately 85 Discovery Activities in *Anatomy of English* are designed so that students must work toward discovery of grammatical facts, using what they already know about how the language works. These Activities are carefully constructed in incremental steps to lead to valid conclusions about English structure—conclusions that are then confirmed by the reading. Students like the fact that the exposition is kept brief and comes as reinforcement *after* they've attempted the problems.

Moreover, *Anatomy of English* does not overwhelm students with details they cannot absorb in a semester or are unlikely to find useful. It describes in detail only the most productive morphological processes and basic syntactic functions, and provides a very brief introduction to the sound system. Yet the open-ended Activities and the questions at the end of each chapter excite curiosity, so that students *want* to go beyond the bare fundamentals. I have found that the mere mention of matters that are beyond the scope of the book actually encourages my students to raise questions about those matters, even though the students know they may not fully understand the issues without further, more advanced, study. Thus, *Anatomy of English* allows for a good bit of classroom spontaneity and permits students to decide what topics they want to discuss, another feature that they have praised.

Among the most appreciated features of *Anatomy of English* is its reliance on observing syntactic and morphological behavior, rather than on definition alone, as a way of learning. Students are delighted to have such concrete criteria as inflectional potential and syntactic substitutability as yardsticks of class membership and grammatical function. But perhaps more than anything else, they're thankful that *Anatomy of English* is not overloaded with jargon. In general, I have adopted traditional terminology, even though I point out its shortcomings and report terminological differences among scholars. Most technical terms are redefined in the glossary, often with references sending the user back to relevant Discovery Activities, and important concepts are summarized at the end of each chapter.

Anatomy of English begins, as do most current books, by distinguishing between the constitutive rules of grammar and the prescriptive rules of usage. Instructors are divided, however, over what constitutes a beginning point for the study of the grammatical structure itself. I usually begin with the sound system (Chapter 9) and work through morphology and the structure of phrases (Chapters 2 through 6) to the syntax of larger structures (Chapters 7 and 8). But because colleagues have chosen to start with morphology, work through syntax, and study the sound system last, I arranged the chapters accordingly. I think the book is flexible enough for either sequence. At one point I considered dropping the phonology chapter, but students—believe it or not—asked that it be retained.

Some time ago, at the request of students themselves, I added the chapters on spelling and using the dictionary, as well as the one covering the problems students encounter with the usage conventions of academic writing. Although the usage chapter departs somewhat from the avowed goal of description, I believe you will find it compatible in spirit and method with the rest of the book. I justify its inclusion on the grounds that students themselves asked for it. You may want to assign it as an optional supplement, perhaps only to those students who show the need.

In response to suggestions from colleagues, I recently added a chapter on the history of English as well as one on variation in contemporary English. Some students consider their own speech inferior to that of other people; some think their speech is not merely "correct," but superior to that of others. For both groups, learning that variation is a linguistic fact and not something to be either smug about or ashamed of can be a liberating experience. I hope that everyone using *Anatomy of English* will not only agree, but will use the entire book to that end.

ACKNOWLEDGMENTS

I wish I could say I did it all myself. Fortunately for the students and teachers who will use *Anatomy of English*, I've had help and advice not only from students and colleagues who have used the book, but also from the reviewers selected by St. Martin's Press. Colleagues at West Virginia University who have used the book—Professors Rudy Almasy, Nick Evans, Pat Conner, Phyllis Morris, Margo Racin, and Beth Daniell—all provided valuable suggestions for improvement. Professor Daniell, now at Clemson, not only goaded me into publication but secured student evaluations at crucial points in the revision process, enabling me to correct weaknesses that my own students had not seen or were reluctant to point out. Professor R. Baird Shuman of University of Illinois, Urbana, tested the book for St. Martin's and also offered excellent criticism. I also want to thank Wanella Huddleston of Western Kentucky University, Muriel Schulz of California State University—Fullerton, and Eugene Smith of the University of Washington; and special thanks to Professor Franklin Horowitz of Columbia University

Teachers College, who read the entire manuscript twice and not only submitted insightful suggestions but with unfailing tact and kindness kept me from making some embarrassing errors. My heartfelt appreciation to all of them.

TO THE STUDENT

If you were born and raised in the United States, you are in a very real sense already an expert in this subject. As a native speaker of English, you are expected to challenge every statement in the book and to test every conclusion against your own experience with the language. If you are a non-native speaker of English, perhaps you will feel reluctant to challenge the book, but you too will be able to use what you already know about English to learn even more. In short, all students using this text are expected to become active participants in their own course of instruction. Have fun!

Dorothy Sedley
West Virginia University

CONTENTS

1 | Grammar vs. Usage

Before we can investigate American English grammar, we ought to have some notion of what it is we're investigating—and what it is not. Unlike language scholars, who use the word *grammar* in very restricted and specialized ways, you are probably accustomed to applying the word, as most laypersons do, to cover matters that properly belong to the field of usage. This chapter will help you arrive at a definition and understanding of the word *grammar* as it will be used throughout this book.

EVERYONE KNOWS GRAMMAR

A **grammar** is something like a set of blueprints for building a structure. The words you know are simply the bricks, boards, or other building materials. To prove to you that your knowledge of English grammar is excellent, I'll provide the materials for a sentence. Your grammar—your knowledge of how to combine these materials—will tell you what order to put them in. In a few minutes, and without much trial and error, you will be able to turn an apparently random collection of words into an English sentence. Here's the list.

very, cave, looking, six, out, tigers, the, mean, of, came

Your sentence: _____

It's a safe bet that you wrote one of the following sentences:

Six very mean looking tigers came out of the cave.

Six tigers came out of the cave, looking very mean.

Six tigers, looking very mean, came out of the cave.

You didn't write *six very tigers* or *mean very looking*; you knew you had to write *out of the cave*, not *out of cave* or *out cave of*; and it's highly unlikely that you wrote *tigers six*. These facts prove that you know English grammar, even though you may not be able to articulate exactly what it is that you know or how you know it.

GRAMMAR AS SYSTEM AND GRAMMAR AS DESCRIPTION

When you learned English, you didn't simply learn a bag of words, nor did you simply learn to repeat or imitate the utterances you heard. You actually learned English grammar—that is, the system of operations for creating an indefinitely large number of sentences out of a finite number of elements. Your ability to create and understand new and unique utterances that are recognized as English sentences—even though they've never been heard before—is evidence of your unconscious knowledge of the rules of English grammar. Similarly, every adult speaker of Russian knows the rules for making Russian sentences, which other native speakers recognize as Russian and not something else. The same can be said for Japanese, Basque, or any language. That's grammar.

DISCOVERY ACTIVITY 1-1

Examine the following sentences, half of which deviate from ordinary structure. Then answer the questions that follow.

Many apples were in the basket.	Much apples were in the basket.
How many students came?	How much students came?
Too many cooks spoil the broth.	Too much cooks spoil the broth.
There are many reasons for . . .	There are much reasons for . . .
Many energy was expended.	Much energy was expended.
How many money do you have?	How much money do you have?
Too many salt spoils the soup.	Too much salt spoils the soup.
There is many sense in what you say.	There is much sense in what you say.

1. Grammarians use an asterisk (*) to mark sentences that are ungrammatical—that is, those that deviate from ordinary structure in such a way as to be unlikely in the speech of adult native speakers except perhaps as false starts, slips of the tongue, or

intentional deviation for artistic or shock effect. Put an asterisk in front of the preceding sentences that are deviant.

2. What do the grammatical sentences with *many* have in common?
3. How are the grammatical sentences with *much* different from those with *many*?
4. Make up four sentences using *much* correctly and four using *many* correctly.
5. Now, formulate a generalization or rule (i.e., a description of what native speakers do) that accurately describes the use of *much* vs. *many*. (What is it that governs your choice between the two words? When do you choose *much*, when *many*? How do you decide which form to choose?)
6. Were you ever consciously aware of this generalization before?
7. Do you think your generalization might be a rule of English grammar?
8. Why or why not?

You just discovered a rule of English grammar that requires the use of *many* with a noun that can be pluralized because it names something countable (**count noun**) but *much* with one that names something perceived as an undifferentiated mass or collection rather than a countable unit (**non-count noun**). You were probably unaware that you knew that rule or even that there was such a rule.

As Discovery Activity 1-1 implies, most people cannot tell you what the rules of their language are, and for many languages (especially those spoken in nonliterate cultures) nobody has written them down. If you want to learn the grammar of an unwritten language, you might live among the speakers of that language, observe what they do, and infer the rules from the evidence around you in somewhat the same way that children learn a language. If you can figure out what the rules are and can describe them accurately, your description might be put into a book called "a grammar," because sometimes the word *grammar* is used to refer to a written description of the rule system that is the grammar of the language or dialect in question. This book, *Anatomy of English*, is called "a grammar" because it describes the rules (like the one about *much* and *many*) that speakers of English unconsciously know and conform to when they use one particular variety of English. The book couldn't be called *The Grammar of English* or even *A Grammar of the English Language* because such titles suggest a homogeneity that doesn't exist. The grammar is the system itself, and each variety, or dialect, of English has a separate system of rules, that is, its own grammar. It's more precise to speak of "the grammars of the varieties of English" and to give textbooks on grammar such titles as *A Grammar of Standard English* or *The Grammar of Appalachian English*.

Yet despite superficial differences, speakers and writers of all varieties agree that they're speaking the same language, because their grammars "overlap" or duplicate one another. The grammars of all varieties of English share a large number of rules. For example, all English speakers unconsciously observe the rule that distinguishes between *much* and *many*. But some of the rules you may have been taught as "grammatical rules" are not, strictly speaking, English **grammar rules**, which describe what speakers and writers actually do. Rather, they are **usage rules** that prescribe what someone thinks speakers and writers should do.

DISCOVERY ACTIVITY 1-2

Some people make the same count vs. non-count distinction between *amount* and *number*, as well as between *less* and *fewer*, that is made between *much* and *many*. They maintain that the following examples are unacceptable, incorrect, even "ungrammatical."

Less students came than I expected. (You're told to use *fewer.*)
He ate *less* apples than I did. (You're told to use *fewer.*)
I couldn't determine the *amount* of students. (You're told to use *number.*)
There was a large *amount* of students. (You're told to use *number.*)

1. Do you and your peers regularly say *less students* and *less apples*?
2. Do you and your peers say *a large amount of students*?
3. Are you and your peers native speakers?
4. Is the rule prohibiting the use of *less* and *amount* in the examples a description of what you and your peers say?
5. Do you think the rule prescribing *fewer* and *number* and outlawing *less* and *amount* is a rule of English grammar?
6. Why or why not?

"GOOD GRAMMAR," "BAD GRAMMAR," AND RULES

Almost all of us can remember being reprimanded at some time or other by teachers or parents who told us that "using double negatives is ungrammatical," or "bad grammar." They probably meant that if you say *I don't have no choice* you'll be considered uncouth. You may even have been told that *a large amount of students* is "bad grammar." People who talk about "bad grammar" are usually referring to a particular usage they disapprove of, or to ways of speaking that indicate lack of education, status, and prestige.

But it's misleading to talk of "good grammar" or "bad grammar," when what we have are just *different* grammars. All varieties of English conform to grammatical rules. The notion that there could be grammatical rules for a nonstandard variety of English may seem bizarre to you if you are accustomed to thinking of grammar rules only as those written in books, and you may find it hard to imagine rules for what you've been told is "bad English." But grammars are in people's heads, not just in books. People who say things like *it don't make no sense* and *me and Eddie was throwed out of there*—that is, those who appear to be making grammatical mistakes or "breaking the rules"—are in fact conforming to a different set of grammatical rules from those of standard English, just as people who use *less* and *amount* are conforming to a different set from those who use *fewer* and *number*.

Confusion on this matter probably stems from the fact that the grammatical rules of the prestige varieties of American English are perceived, and hence prescribed, by teachers, employers, purists, and pop grammarians as the only "real" or legitimate rules. Thus, *de*scriptions of standard English usage become *pre*scriptions for all usage. That is, instead of saying "Speakers and writers of standard English use *thrown*," which would be a description, hence a grammatical rule of standard English, many writers and teachers say, in effect, "You must use *thrown*, which is the only correct form." Instead of saying "Some speakers and writers use *fewer*, not *less*, with count nouns like *apples*," they say "You ought to say *fewer apples* because it's more precise (or logical, or whatever) than *less apples*." Obviously, telling you what to do is not describing what you do do. Rules that dictate a particular usage are just that—usage rules—not grammar rules.

Moreover, the conventional usage rules governing standard *written* English are often taught as if they were applicable at all times and for all purposes, including speaking. As a result, many people believe that they are "making mistakes" when their own usage deviates from what is taught in school. But although it may be a *social* mistake to say *me and Eddie was throwed* because it may mark you as uneducated and limit your upward mobility, it isn't a grammatical mistake. Although some people may condemn *less apples*, it isn't a grammatical mistake. Table 1-1 should help clarify the distinction between grammar rules and usage rules.

DISCOVERY ACTIVITY 1-3

Some of the following sentences exemplify nonstandard, hence stigmatized, usage; that is, although they are grammatical for the speakers who regularly use them, they deviate from the usage that is prescribed for standard English. However, others are ungrammatical, in that they are not structures that are used by adult native speakers of any contemporary variety of American English. Identify those that you think are ungrammatical, and mark them with an asterisk.

1. He asked where to put.
2. Eddie and him drove home real slow.
3. It just ain't none of his business.
4. Give me twelve of.
5. Who do you want to talk to?
6. Whither thou goest, I will go.
7. The trees will bear oysters.
8. The trees will oysters bear.
9. Came he not home last night?
10. He won't take it serious because he don't believe in ghosts.
11. Throw mama from the train a kiss.
12. Hambones for dinner are.
13. The baby needs changed.
14. According to the papers, a truck run him down.
15. We thought you had drank all the lemonade.

WHAT IS UNGRAMMATICAL?

Although you had no difficulty deciding about some of the sentences in Discovery Activity 1-3, you may have had to puzzle over others. Perhaps you are so familiar with Naomi's pledge, *Whither thou goest . . .* , that you had difficulty labeling it ungrammatical. But a moment's reflection will make it clear that although such speech was normal when it was written, it would not occur spontaneously in anyone's speech today. No current variety of English calls for us to use forms like *goest*. On the other hand, because you believe it unlikely that trees will bear oysters and hence highly unlikely that anyone would say such a thing, you might want to call sentence 7 ungrammatical. But if you substitute *fruit* for

TABLE 1-1   Grammar Rules vs. Usage Rules

GRAMMAR RULES	USAGE RULES
1. Constitute a description of what adult native speakers actually do. "English speakers use *many* with count nouns like *apples*, and *much* with non-count nouns like *energy*."	Constitute a prescription of what some group or person thinks speakers or writers should do. "Use *fewer* with count nouns like *apples*, *less* only with non-count nouns like *energy*."
2. Are based on objective observation and are free of value judgment. The statement in (1) is a neutral and factual report; it expresses neither approval nor disapproval.	Are often based on individual taste and imply a value judgment. The instruction to "use *X*, not *Y*," is not a report; it reflects the opinion that *X* is preferable to *Y*.
3. Are learned without formal instruction. People are not taught about *much* vs. *many*, yet they know the difference.	Must (often) be taught through formal instruction. Many people first encounter the *less* vs. *fewer* distinction in school.
4. Are automatically followed and require no conscious thought. People never even know they are following the *much* vs. *many* rule, yet they are unlikely to make the wrong choice.	Often require conscious effort to remember and apply. Some people might have to remind themselves to use *fewer* because *less* comes to them spontaneously and unbidden.
5. Are learned completely and applied consistently and predictably. People who have the *fewer* vs. *less* distinction in their grammar will consistently apply the rule just as they apply the *much* vs. *many* rule.	Are often learned incompletely and applied sporadically or randomly. People who are taught about *fewer* as a rule of usage sometimes forget to apply it, because it isn't fully absorbed into their grammar.

oysters, you will probably see that the sentence, though silly, is grammatical, in that it violates none of the rules for structuring English sentences. Yet even though such inversions as *oysters bear* do occasionally occur, sentence 8 is ungrammatical because it is a deviation from what native speakers consider the normal order.

You probably recognized sentence 5 as grammatical and sentence 4 as ungrammatical. But unless you are familiar with a dialect spoken in western Pennsylvania, you probably did not recognize *the baby needs changed* as grammatical structure. Most people in that region regularly omit *to be* after *need* or *needs*, and for them this sentence is grammatical. Similarly, when someone from Great Britain says *I felt a complete idiot*, we can translate this into American English as "I felt *like* an idiot" or "I felt *idiotic*," realizing that *felt* isn't being used as it is in *I felt a slight breeze* or *I felt a rough surface*. For most Americans *I felt an idiot is ungrammatical for the intended meaning, even though it's grammatical for British speakers.

If children say *I saw some gooses* or *mommy teached me*, we correct them. The forms *gooses and *teached are ungrammatical—that is, they do not occur in adult speech of any dialect. If, like *the baby needs changed*, *less apples*, *me and Eddie was throwed*, and *it don't make no difference*, *gooses and *teached were in the adult version of some variety, they would be grammatical for that dialect and children wouldn't be corrected, because the forms wouldn't be perceived as deviant.

When someone who has learned English as a second language deviates from typical English structure, native speakers can usually interpret the ungrammatical sentences despite their peculiarities because such speakers generally get enough of the structure right to provide the information we need. Because we know the grammar, we can mentally supply the missing elements or rearrange those that are out of order or otherwise correct the things we know to be inconsistent with English pronunciation, word form, and word order. Because we know the rules we can recognize an utterance as deviant, that is, as ungrammatical, yet still understand it. Thus, intelligibility or interpretability is not, at least by itself, a good criterion of grammaticality. There are many ungrammatical or ill-formed utterances that you understand perfectly well, and many grammatical ones that you might not understand. (Do you really understand *Ontogeny recapitulates phylogeny?*)

The extent to which a native speaker can understand an utterance is not as good a criterion of grammaticality as is the extent to which adult native speakers might be expected to use such a structure. Those who regularly use *he don't*, for example, are conforming to a rule in a grammatical system in which *don't*, like *can't* and *won't*, remains unchanged whether the subject is *I*, *you*, *he*, *we*, or *they*. Thus, even though it may be socially stigmatized, *he don't* is grammatical, not because we know what it means, but because it is governed by the same sort of rules as those that operate in the standard varieties. On the other hand, **Why we no go for walking?*

is ungrammatical, even though we may know what it means, because the rules of no American dialect (so far as I know) will predict *why we no* as an alternate of *why don't we* or *for walking* as an alternate of *for a walk.*

DISCOVERY ACTIVITY 1-4

1. You should be able to recognize the following as an English sentence, even though you may not be able to say what all the words mean:

   Froobling greebies were smarmishly zarbing some granflons.

   a. Who are the zarbers? (Who zarbs?)
   b. How do you know the answer to (a) without knowing the meanings of the words?
   c. Who are the victims, and how can you tell?
   d. What are two clues that there was more than one zarber?
   e. Did the zarbing happen instantaneously, or take time, and what makes you say so?
   f. What makes it an English sentence?
   g. What kind of sentence is the following, and how can you tell?

   were the froobling beesters zarbing some granflons

2. Why is the following string of words not an English sentence, even though it is made up entirely of English words?

   The singing was the were birds shining and sun.

3. *Signal words* (also called *function words* or *structure words*) make a difference in meaning. Notice that the following is ambiguous: *Ship sails today.* Addition of a signal word, *the*, shows which is the noun phrase: *The ship sails today* or *Ship the sails today.* Disambiguate the following newspaper headline by supplying some appropriate function word(s):

   Neighbors Help Burn Victims

4. Arrange each of the following ungrammatical strings of words into a grammatical phrase.

   Indians ten little the
   five those boys small
   tiny your kittens three

   a. Each *noun phrase* you wrote has a noun, a numeral, an adjective pertaining to size, and a noun phrase signal word (*the*, those, your) called a *determiner*. Using the same types of words, write five or six more of this type of phrase.

b. Make a general statement describing the normal order of the words in such phrases.

c. Do you think your statement is a rule of English grammar? Why or why not?

d. Were you aware of knowing that rule before doing this activity?

e. Here is a rule that some people follow. "Don't say *It's me* because *me* is an object pronoun and *is* can't have an object. The correct form is *It is I.*" Why is that not a rule of grammar? What kind of rule is it?

5. Look over the outline in Table 1-2. Try not to be intimidated by the terms, and don't try to memorize them. They will be reintroduced and explained in the next few chapters. From the outline, supply the information requested below about this sentence:

The smarchivity must crandalize those very snabrous cleefers.

a. What *morphological (formal) characteristic* enables you to identify *smarchivity* as a noun even though you don't know what it means? That is, what is there about the form of the word *smarchivity* that tells you it's a noun?

b. What *syntactic evidence* is there that *smarchivity* is a noun? That is, what else in the sentence (besides the word itself) points to its being a noun?

c. What formal or morphological characteristic tells you that *crandalize* is a verb?

d. What syntactic evidence tells you that *crandalize* is a verb?

e. What formal or morphological characteristic tells you that *snabrous* is an adjective?

f. What syntactic signal tells you that *snabrous* is an adjective?

g. What tells you that the cleefers are going to be the victims and not the perpetrators of the crandalization? Is it something about the form (a morphological fact about *cleefers*) or some syntactic evidence?

GRAMMATICAL FEATURES AND MEANING

In Discovery Activity 1-4, you saw that you could extract some meaning from a sentence whose vocabulary was largely unfamiliar. You were able to "understand" because you unconsciously know, in addition to the dictionary meanings of words, a system of grammatical devices or features that are also meaningful in themselves. Such meaningful features make up the grammar of English.

TABLE 1-2   Grammatical Devices That Convey Meaning

A. Morphological (Formal) Characteristics (Contrasts in form)
  1. Inflection
    a. A contrast in form for plurality identifies nouns: *mouse/mice*.
    b. A contrast in form for tense and aspect identifies verbs: *eats/ate/ eating/eaten*.
    c. A contrast in form for degree identifies adjectives: *tall/taller/tallest*.
  2. Derivational Affixes:
    a. Suffixes such as *-ity*, *-ness*, and *-age* create nouns: *active/activity; happy/happiness; break/breakage*
    b. Suffixes such as *-ify*, *-ize*, and *-en* create verbs: *object/objectify; visual/visualize; length/lengthen*
    c. Suffixes such as *-able*, *-full*, and *-ous* create adjectives: *love/lovable; care/careful; fame/famous*

B. Syntactic Devices
  1. Signal words (or function words or structure words) combine with inflectional words to make functional phrases.
    a. Some signal words combine with nouns:
      determiners: *the/a/an/some/those/many/your/my* . . . .
      prepositions: *of/into/over/during* . . .
    b. Some signal words combine with verbs:
      modal auxiliaries: *will/can/may/must/shall* . . .
      other auxiliaries: *have/be/do*
    c. Some signal words combine with adjectives:
      qualifiers: *very/rather/somewhat/too* . . .
      prepositions: *. . . than/as . . . as*
  2. Word order and syntactic position determine function.
    a. Order distinguishes statements from questions:
      She is a doctor./Is she a doctor?
    b. Position of phrases distinguishes agent from affected:
      The snake killed the mouse./The mouse killed the snake.

You can see from Activity 1–4 that morphology deals with the structure of words and smaller units of meaning. Inflection and derivation, which we will study in Chapter 2, are morphological processes or devices. In this activity, for example, the derivational *-er* and the inflectional *-s* on *cleefers* are two indicators of "noun-ness," as is the *-ity* of *smarchivity*. This is just another way of saying that the form of the word *smarchivity* tells you that it's almost certainly a noun, even though you don't know what it names—if, indeed, it names anything.

Syntax, as you can also see from Discovery Activity 1–4, deals with relationships between and among words, that is, with the structure of phrases and their arrangement in clauses and sentences rather than with the structure of individual words. You will be learning about English syntax beginning with the discussion of noun phrases in Chapter 3. You will see, for example, that a signal word like *the* is part of a syntactic structure called a noun phrase and is thus a good indication that *smarchivity* is a noun. Any statement dealing with the arrangement or order of words or phrases is a matter of syntax. It is a syntactic fact that auxiliaries generally come first in certain kinds of questions, instead of after the subject, as they do in most statements. Because you know that syntactic fact, you were able to identify *were the froobling beesters zarbing some granflons* as a question, even without a question mark. And because you know other syntactic facts, you were able to identify the very snabrous cleefers as the victims of crandalization. Not bad for someone who doesn't even know what cleefers are or what's happening when something is being crandalized.

Table 1-2 gives a sketchy overview of some of the important grammatical devices of contemporary English that the following chapters will cover in greater detail. In addition to the morphological and syntactic devices listed in Table 1-2, certain features of the sound system (certain *phonological devices*) also convey meaning. For example, a rising pitch can signal or "mean" that you're surprised: "You did????" Stress placement, another feature of the sound system, can make the difference between nouns and verbs: *OBject*, with stress on the first syllable, is a noun; *obJECT*, with stress on the second syllable, is a verb. There are hundreds of such pairs in our language; *CONtract/conTRACT* and *PROduce/proDUCE* are but two more examples. All of these devices are governed by rules, and all are part of your knowledge of English grammar, even though you may not have been aware of them before now.

IMPLICATIONS: SITUATIONAL APPROPRIATENESS

Having read that nonstandard expressions like *me and Eddie was throwed* and *he don't* are perfectly grammatical, you may need to be cautioned against misinterpreting such remarks to mean or imply that "everything is correct" or that "anything goes." *Grammatical* is not an evaluative term and cannot be equated with *correct, acceptable,* or *appropriate.* Judgments about correctness depend on variable factors such as audience, purpose, and whether you're speaking or writing. Just as you would not ask Miss Manners

"Is a tuxedo correct?" without specifying what for, you cannot ask whether this or that locution is correct without specifying what for. Just as a tuxedo would be wrong for a picnic or a hike in the mountains, so might standard English be perceived as wrong—that is, inappropriate—for some audiences or purposes. The choice of "correct" language cannot be made without considering the context and circumstances, because it often depends on social or rhetorical options rather than what is possible within the grammatical system.

SUMMARY

1. Knowing grammar is knowing a set of operations for creating and understanding an indefinitely large set of novel sentences from a finite inventory of elements.
2. All varieties of English are governed by grammatical rules, but some varieties enjoy less prestige than others.
3. Grammar rules neither prescribe nor proscribe. That is, they never take the form "You should . . ." or "You shouldn't . . . ," as usage rules do.
4. Many of the usage rules taught in school are based on the grammar of a variety of English (standard edited English) used in *writing* and may not accurately reflect the speech patterns of even the educated.
5. The grammatical features (or the grammar) can be subdivided into morphology (the structure of words and meaningful segments of words), syntax (the relationships between two or more words, or the structure of phrases, clauses, and sentences), and phonology (the sound system).
6. Grammatical features convey meaning. This book attempts to describe the meaningful features or devices of standard American English.
7. Correctness is not merely a matter of grammar; it depends on the situation or context of what someone says or writes.

STUDY QUESTIONS

1. What evidence is there for the existence of a grammar of a language?
2. Explain in your own words why the expression *the grammar of English* is inaccurate or inadequate.
3. List at least three items that you were told were ungrammatical or "bad grammar" that you now know are grammatical English even though

they may be stigmatized as nonstandard usage. What do you think is the best test for distinguishing a grammar rule from a usage rule? Write a paragraph that explains to someone unfamiliar with this course the distinction between grammar and usage rules.

4. What is the domain of morphology? of syntax?
5. Based on what you've read and the activities you've done, suggest some reasons why we must write new grammars (descriptions of languages) from time to time. Hint: Look at items 6 and 9 of Discovery Activity 1-3.

FURTHER STUDY AND DISCUSSION

Write a paragraph that defends or attacks the position that standard English could be considered wrong (inappropriate, unacceptable, incorrect) for some audiences or purposes. Be sure to support your position with specific details, concrete examples, and particular instances.

2 | Morphology

A list like "toothpaste, phone, cleaners, ice trays" makes sense only to the person who wrote it, and uttering "blue" out of the blue might cause some confusion. Without a context, the meaning of a one-word utterance or of a set of syntactically unrelated words can only be guessed at. Yet it is clear that individual words have distinct meanings. After all, we do look them up in dictionaries to find their definitions, so it is obvious that most of us think of words as the forms that embody our meanings. But if you think about it a little, you will realize that forms even smaller than words (prefixes and suffixes, for example) are independently meaningful. In this chapter, we will look at English **morphology**, that is, at the structure of meaningful linguistic forms smaller than the phrase or sentence.

If you were studying introductory botany, you would not study all plants at once. Botanists divide and subdivide the plant kingdom into small groups on the basis of similarities and differences in physical form. They subdivide trees, for example, into at least two categories—those that drop their leaves and those that don't. Then they subdivide the evergreens into the subsets pine, spruce, cedar, and so on. We can do something like that to make the study of linguistic forms manageable. We first divide English words into two large groups, called *form classes* and *structure classes*. Then, on the basis of similarities and differences in form, we can subdivide the form classes into subsets, the traditional "parts of speech": nouns, verbs, adjectives, and adverbs. In this chapter you will discover the characteristics that enable us to separate members of one class from members of all other groups.

FORM CLASSES vs. STRUCTURE CLASSES

Here's a list of invented words, all of which are possible English words, in that they violate none of the morphological rules governing the construction of English words: *murgatrists, murgatrized, zery, murgatrous, slavinize, ott, slavinist, slavinous, thon*. If asked to sort these words into groups on the basis of form alone, you would be likely to put the *murgatr-* words in one group and the *slavin-* words in another (and to assume that they are also likely to have some feature of meaning in common). Or you might group *murgatrists* with *slavinist, murgatrized* with *slavinize,* and *murgatrous* with *slavinous*. But what would you do with the others? There is nothing about the forms of *zery, ott,* and *thon* that would make you want to group them together. Without any other criterion you have no choice, at least for now, but to put them in a bag labeled *miscellaneous*.

Those words in the language that we can group together on the basis of a *shared meaningful form* (such as *-ist, -ize,* or *-ous*) we call *form class words*. These words can often be analyzed into meaningful subparts, like *murgatr-, -ize,* and *-ed* or *murgatr-, -ist,* and *-s*. We can then subdivide form class words into smaller groups on the basis of the specific formal features (like *-ed* as opposed to *-s*) that distinguish one subset from another. Words like *very, too,* and *than,* having no formal characteristics in common, must be subdivided according to some criterion other than form. We'll return to them later in this chapter. For now, let's look at form class words and the formal features and contrasts that enable us to subclassify them.

SOMETHING ABOUT FORM: MORPHEMES

Everyone agrees that meaning must be embodied in some form, and although "words" may be the first thing that comes to mind, there are units of meaning that are not necessarily equivalent to words. Sometimes these meaningful units, called **morphemes**, do coincide with the units we call words, but sometimes they don't. The following Discovery Activity is designed to permit you to discover for yourself how to define the term *morpheme*. The activity also illustrates that morphemes can be subdivided into various types.

DISCOVERY ACTIVITY 2-1
Say the following words aloud:

1. taller, shorter, greener, higher, lower, sweeter, smarter
2. mower, teacher, sailor, farmer, caller, operator

3. never, cover, finger, either, river, candor, other
   a. For each word in group 1, does the first syllable constitute a single, meaningful unit? Does the second syllable of the group 1 words constitute a separate unit of meaning? If so, what is its meaning?
   b. For each word in group 2, is the first syllable a single unit of meaning, incapable of further breakdown? Does the second syllable of the group 2 words also have a meaning? If so, what is its meaning?
   c. Does the first syllable of any word in group 3 constitute a unit of meaning? Does the second syllable of group 3 mean anything?
   d. If you take off the second syllable, which group of words fits into this frame: "He/she/it seems . . ."
   e. If you take off the second syllable, which group of words fits into this frame: "He/she/it will . . ."
   f. Without the second syllable, which group fits neither frame?

It should be obvious from this activity that although all the words in the three groups are superficially alike, they are fundamentally different in structure. You can see that the words in group 3 cannot be analyzed into smaller meaningful forms. (A *river* is neither "one who rivs" nor something that is "more riv than" something else.) The words in group 3 are themselves minimal units of meaning; that is, despite having two syllables, each constitutes a single morpheme, which cannot be analyzed into smaller meaningful parts. Separated from one another, the syllables of the group 3 words are not individually meaningful.

The words in groups 1 and 2, on the other hand, contain a **base** morpheme and an **affix**; that is, they consist of two morphemes each, two separate units of meaning, the base and the -er, each of which retains its meaning even when separated from the other. But you must note that the -er of group 2 (and its variations -or, as in *operator* and *sailor*, and occasionally -ar, as in *liar*) is not the same -er as the one that appears in group 1. Since they do not have the same meaning in both environments, the two -er's are not the same morpheme, but homophonous forms, like the words *bare*, *bear* (meaning "to carry"), and *bear* (referring to the animal), which sould alike but have different meanings. Note that because the -or of *candor* and the -er of *other*, *never*, and *finger* are not meaningful in their own right, they are not considered morphemes at all.

Obviously, there are significant morphological differences between the words in one group and those in the other. Those in group 1, for example, will fit the "*seems* frame" with or without the

-er morpheme (which, in this context, means "more of" or "to a greater degree"). The suffix, in other words, does not affect the grammatical function or syntactic behavior of the base morphemes, *tall*, *short*, and *sweet*. The words in group 2, however, behave quite differently. Because their base morphemes "work" in the "*will* frame" we know that those particular bases are verbs. But when you add *-er* (or *-or* or *-ar*), the resulting words no longer fit the syntactic frame; they become nouns meaning "the person (or thing) that does" whatever the verb specifies.

SOMETHING ABOUT FORM: INFLECTION

The words in group 1 of Discovery Activity 2-1 illustrate the morphological process of **inflection**, wherein a change in form does not result in any change in the classification of the affected word. (We will discuss the one exception in Chapter 3.) Most, but not all, English **inflectional changes** (contrasts between various forms of the same word) take the form of suffixes. The contrasts created by the eight inflectional suffixes provide an objective criterion on which to base the subdivision of words into three of the major "parts of speech," or **form classes**. In later chapters you'll learn more details about the words in these classes, but for now let's just see how inflection makes it possible for us to define the categories themselves.

DISCOVERY ACTIVITY 2-2

Here are three sets of words to illustrate how inflectional changes can help us classify English words. Study these sets; then complete the activity as instructed.

1.	cat	cats	cat's	
	dog	dogs	dog's	
	horse	horses	horse's	
2. (will)	walk	walks	(is) walking	walked
	brag	brags	bragging	bragged
	rush	rushes	rushing	rushed
	decide	decides	deciding	decided
3.	tall	taller	tallest	
	smart	smarter	smartest	

a. Sort the following words into three sets on the basis of whether they ordinarily undergo the series of changes illustrated by set 1, set 2, or set 3:

follow, pave, haircut, girl, lively, realize, situation, friendly, explosion, qualify, hat, bathe, deny, healthy, quartet, angry, sweet

b. Although we have the word *follower*, its base, *follow*, does not belong in set 3. Why? Do not refer to meaning in your response. Look instead for some related formal characteristic. Which set does the word *follower* belong to?

The point of Discovery Activity 2-2 is that membership in any given class of words is based on whether a word accepts specific inflections, that is, has particular contrasts in its form. *Lively*, *friendly*, *healthy*, *angry*, and *sweet* all belong to the adjective class because they all have contrasting *-er* and *-est* forms. You can see that although we have a contrast between *follow* and *follower*, we do not have the additional contrasting form, **followest*, to complete the series. Therefore, *follow* does not belong with words like *tall*, *lively*, and *angry*, which have all three forms shown in the **comparative paradigm**, the name given to this particular series. It is not the occurrence of *-er* itself, but its occurrence in contrast with *-est*, that is significant in assigning a word to a comparative class.

The series of formal contrasts exhibited by the members of any one of the sets enables us to distinguish between them and words belonging to any other class. But there are many words that will fit more than one paradigm. Take the word *show*, for example. In addition to the contrasts in the **verb paradigm** exhibited in the series *show*, *shows*, *showing*, *showed*, we also have the forms *show*, *shows*, *show's* (as in *the show's producers*) of the **noun paradigm**. In such instances (and they are quite numerous), we simply stipulate that we have a verb, *show*, as well as a noun, *show*. Despite the large number of words which, like *show*, will turn out to have double identities, the paradigms are useful because they provide objective criteria and establish definable limits on class membership.

DISCOVERY ACTIVITY 2-3

Refer to Discovery Activity 2-2 to complete this activity.

1. List the affixes of set 1, that is, the noun inflections: _____
2. List the affixes of set 2, that is, the verb inflections: _____

3. List the affixes of set 3, that is, the inflections for degree: _____
4. Test the following words for inflection or formal contrasts. Specify which set or sets each belongs to—or that it doesn't belong to any of the sets established by these paradigmatic tests. In the case of words of more than one morpheme, test the whole word, not just the base. Label those that fit set 1, N for *noun*, those that fit set 2, V for *verb*, and those that fit set 3, A for *adjective*. Put a question mark by those that fit none of the paradigms.

shiny_____	sister_____	sick_____	play_____
mystify_____	complete_____	healthy_____	book_____
fluctuate_____	somewhat_____	friendly_____	buy_____
fluctuation_____	very_____	carpenter_____	nearly_____
open_____	groupie_____	fort_____	mainly_____

5. Which of the words fit more than one paradigm?
6. Even though there is no *buyed*, would you argue that *buy* fits the verb paradigm? Why or why not?

SOMETHING ABOUT FORM: DERIVATION

You may have realized that there are some words that certainly belong to one or the other of the classes we have established yet will not pass the paradigmatic test. You may know, for example, that *cut* belongs to the same class as *walk*, even though *cut* does not accept the *-ed* and there is no such form as *cutted*. In Chapter 5 we'll revise the paradigms and refine the tests so that they will "recognize" *cut* and verbs like *fly*, *break*, *eat*, and *write*, which have a fifth form as well as an irregular past tense.

Consider, also, a word like *careless*, which you may recognize as a member of the class that includes *angry*, *happy*, and *tall*, even though you may balk at accepting such forms as *carelesser* and *carelessest*. There are quite a few words that don't pass the inflectability tests at all and many that pass for some speakers but not for others. That is, not everyone will agree that a form does or does not occur: for example, Smith uses and accepts as unremarkable such forms as *foolisher* and *foolishest* but her neighbor, Jones, claims never to have heard of any such thing and rejects them an non-English. It doesn't matter that equally competent speakers disagree about whether a particular word belongs in the set; everyone agrees that a set exists and can offer prototypical or exemplifying members like *tall*, *taller*, *tallest*. But applying the paradigmatic test would exclude words like *splendiferous* and *famous* from the adjective class—because nobody seems to inflect them—even though we know they belong there.

Such cases are no cause for concern because **derivation**, another important morphological process, provides additional sets of contrasting forms that will enable us to assign uninflectable words to their appropriate classes. You may recall that in Discovery Activity 2-1, we attached the morpheme -*er* (sometimes spelled *or*, sometimes *ar*) to a series of verbs: *ride, operate, lie.* The derived forms *rider, operator,* and *liar* proved to be nouns, because they accept the inflectional affixes from the noun paradigm. The consistent derivation of **agent nouns** by the affixation of -*er* to a base (which, as you can see from *astronomer*, need not be a verb) suggests that there may be other **derivational affixes** that can be relied on to produce nouns, verbs, and adjectives. As it turns out, that is indeed the case. We can, for example, trust *reflection, option, investigation, repetition, motion, nation, production,* and thousands of other words with the -*tion* affix to be nouns, without bothering to put them to the paradigmatic test. Their -*tion* form guarantees it.

Not all derivational affixes are as reliable as -*tion*. Some, like -*ate* and -*ly*, for example, participate in the derivation of more than one class of words. Nevertheless, analysis of the structure of -*ly* words for specific formal characteristics enables us to assign them correctly to separate groups, as we will soon see. In addition, there are syntactic tests like the "*seems* frame" that can be used to supplement the morphological information and confirm class membership.

DISCOVERY ACTIVITY 2-4

1. Submit the following words to paradigmatic tests and divide them into two sets, nouns and adjectives:

   friend, quick, beast, quiet, narrow, world

2. Add the derivational -*ly* to the words. Test them again in the paradigms. What class did the nouns move into after the addition of -*ly*?
3. Test the following words: *manner, heaven.*
4. If you add -*ly* to the nouns listed in 3, the resulting words may not pass the paradigmatic test for adjectives. Do they pass the "*seems* frame" test?
5. Complete this generalization: If you add -*ly* to nouns, you get

   _____.

6. Analyze the structure of the following -*ly* words. That is, take them

apart and identify what class their bases belong to. Then say which of these -*ly* words are adjectives:

cowardly, lovely, quarterly, masterly, queenly, timely, wifely, fatherly, motherly.

Derivational Series

You have just seen that we can derive adjectives from nouns by adding -*ly*. When we add -*ly* to existing adjectives, however, the resulting words no longer qualify as adjectives; they no longer fit the "*seems* frame." This second -*ly* derives a class of words for which we have provided no paradigm. But they constitute a major class of words in English, and we can use the fact of their derivation from adjectives as the basis for their classification. We can say that adding -*ly* to nouns creates adjectives, but that adding -*ly* to existing adjectives creates a subset of adverbs (like *quickly* and *carefully*) called *manner adverbs*. In Chapter 6 we will discuss the differences between adjectives and adverbs in greater detail.

You should see that inflection works internally, within a given class of words, and in fact constitutes the defining feature of a given class. Derivation, on the other hand, works as a kind of passageway, allowing a base morpheme to enter a series of different classes. This morphological process enables us to establish **derivational series** to supplement the inflectional paradigms used to establish the three major classes and to assign membership on the basis of form alone. Thus, series like *glory/glorious/gloriously* give us a rationale for putting -*ous* words into the adjective class even though they don't inflect for degree. Syntactic facts will confirm this assignment, but you can often identify classes by their formal characteristics and contrasts alone, sometimes even without recourse to syntax or appealing to meaning. If you encounter an unfamiliar word ending in the -*ous* morpheme, it's a pretty safe bet that the word's an adjective (even though you may also find nouns like *mucus*, *callus*, and *phosphorus* spelled as -*ous*, no doubt because they sound exactly like their adjective forms and it's easy to mix them up). Let's look at some familiar derivational affixes.

DISCOVERY ACTIVITY 2-5

1. Test the following words for inflectability. Which paradigm do they fit?

specify, beautify, solidify, diversify, purify, simplify

a. What does the affix -*ify* (or -*fy*) mean?

b. To what inflectional class does *complexify* belong?

c. What does *complexify* mean?

d. Although your dictionary probably has an entry for *simplify* it may not have one for *complexify*; nevertheless, you can guess its meaning. Would you find this word useful? Does it matter that it's not in the dictionary?

e. What derivational affix(es) can you add to the -*ify* words?

f. To what inflectional class(es) do the newly derived words belong?

2. a. Which paradigm do the following words fit?

visualize, satirize, realize, sterilize, criticize, civilize

b. Can you think of any -*ize* words that don't fit the verb paradigm? What do you call think of the predictive value of -*ize*? That is, can you count on -*ize* as a fairly certain marker of "verb-ness"?

c. What derivational affix(es) can you add to the -*ize* words? To what inflectional class(es) do the newly derived words belong?

3. What do you call someone who plays the piano? _____

What if he or she plays guitar? _____ clarinet? _____

trumpet? _____

AFFIXATION: DIFFERENCES

As you have seen, derivation is a more complex process than inflection. Inflectional affixes are a small set—only eight members. Derivational affixes number in the hundreds, but some are more productive than others. We see -*tion* far more often than -*tude*, though both make nouns. That observation points up another difference between the two morphological processes: inflection is restricted, and highly predictable; derivation is open ended, and less predictable. We can be sure, for example, that if a word is a verb, there will be formal contrasts like those of *run/runs/running, talk/talks/talking, fly/flies/flying*. In short, all verbs take the -*s* and -*ing* inflections but they don't all take the same derivational affixes, and there is no easy way to predict which stems will take which affixes. Compare, for example, *relax* + -*ation* and *adorn* + -*ment*. Why not **relaxment* and/or **adornation*? And why is a person who plays the trumpet a *trumpeter* rather than a *trumpetist*? Note, too, the peculiar asymmetry of these series: *man/manish/manly, woman/womanish/womanly*, but *child/childish/*childly, boy/boyish/*

boyly, and *girl/girlish/*girlly* (different from the noun *girly* or *girlie*). But the availability of the affixes and the openness of the system allow us to create new words on the spot to fill a lexical gap—hence, *complexify*—whether or not the word is in a dictionary.

Another difference between the two processes and the sets of affixes is that, whereas inflections can attach only to stems that are already complete words, derivational affixes can be attached to morphemes that are not. In other words, both inflectional and derivational affixes are called **bound morphemes** because they must be attached, or bound, to something. (**Free morphemes**, of course, are words: *mother, fame, eleven, bother*.) But there are also morphemes that are not affixes but must nevertheless be bound to something: *-ceive* and *leg-* (referring to law) come to mind. Although they are base morphemes with lexical content, they cannot stand alone as words. An inflectional affix cannot attach to such a bound base alone: we do not have **ceives* or **ceived*. Although we can inflect the word *leg*, we cannot inflect the bound morpheme *leg-*. But a derivational affix can attach to a bound base, and the result will be words made entirely of bound morphemes: *receive* and *conceive*, as well as *legal, legitimate*, and *legislate*. Similarly, we have no word *hor*, but what appears to be a bound lexical base, *hor-*, becomes *horror, horrid, horrify*, or *horrendous* when another bound morpheme is added.

Still another difference between inflection and derivation is that we can add whole strings of derivational morphemes one after another, but usually only one inflection. The derivational process will yield behemoths like *antidisestablishmentarianism*, but inflection will not yield anything like **talkseding*. An exception is the so-called possessive inflection, which can be added to a small number of already inflected nouns—specifically, to irregular plurals like *women*—hence, *women's*. Occasionally, an inflected form moves into a different class and accepts the inflections of that class on top of the one it's already carrying. For example, in the expression *your elders and betters*, the inflected adjectives, *elder* and *better*, have moved into the noun class and now accept the plural affix in addition to what was originally a comparative inflection. So, although more than one inflection is occasionally possible, a stem usually takes only one inflection from any given paradigm, and inflection usually precludes further derivation. Thus, we can have *problem/problems* or *problem/problematic*, but not **problemsatic*. But perhaps the most striking difference between the two types of affixes is in their effect on the morphemes they're attached to, as you will see in the following Discovery Activity.

DISCOVERY ACTIVITY 2-6

1. What result do you get when you add the derivational affix -th to wide? What if you add -th to deep?
2. Say the words wide/width and deep/depth aloud. Also pronounce these pairs: crime/criminal, divine/divinity, cave/cavity. What effect does adding a derivational affix have on some stems?
3. What are the effects of adding -tion to receive, conceive, deceive, and perceive? What about the addition of -tion to redeem?
4. What happens when you try to add -tion to divide or collide?
5. What happens when you try to add -tion to remit, commit, admit, submit?
6. Can you think of some words whose pronunciation is changed by the addition of an inflectional rather than a derivational affix?

The preceding activity was designed to make several points. The obvious one, of course, is that with the exception of the plural affix on a small set of words ending in an "f" sound, that is, on words like *knife, elf, hoof,* and *wolf,* inflectional affixes usually do not "deform" the morphemes to which they are attached the way derivational affixes so often do. Less obvious, and therefore more difficult to grasp, is the notion that members of pairs like *wide/wid-* and *deep/dep-* are in some sense just different manifestations or realizations of a single morpheme. It may sound nonsensical or paradoxical to say that *-ceive* and *-cept,* such visibly different forms, are "the same," but it's so. Since the alternation between these pairs is so predictable, the difference in form is actually a difference without a distinction: the two realizations are equivalents. As a matter of fact, some scholars now argue that it is just such alternations in form, and not meaning, that enable us to isolate and identify morphemes.

DISCOVERY ACTIVITY 2-7

For each of the following, indicate how many morphemes are in the word and whether the affix (if any) is derivational, inflectional, or both/either.

tanner____   friers____   smother____   showers____
murder____   faker____   murmur____   tower____
drier____   friars____   smoother____   order____

The preceding activity demonstrates that it is sometimes diffi-cult, without a syntactic context, to assign a particular word, especially in written form, to one class or another. *Tanner* and *drier* could be derived nouns or inflected adjectives. Pronounced one way, *tower* refers to a tall edifice; pronounced another way, it refers to someone or something that tows. In isolation, a word like *stranger* could be an adjective bearing the comparative inflection, ready to be used in *truth is stranger than fiction*, or it could be a derived noun. If it is a noun, it can take plural form: *I saw three strangers coming down the road*. Similarly, a word like *clipping* might be a verb, inflected for progressive aspect: *The barber was clipping my hair*. But it could just as easily be a derived noun, as you can see by inflecting it: *He sent me some newspaper clippings about the event*.

Potential ambiguities abound, but they are more apparent than real, and they cause no problems. Inflectional *-en*, illustrated by forms like *eaten*, *broken*, and *written*, might at first glance be confused with the derivational *-en* that derives verb stems from adjectives and nouns, as illustrated by pairs like *bright/brighten*, *length/lengthen*. But even without a context we can tell whether *-en* is inflectional or derivational by submitting the word to the test for inflectability. If the word is a derived verb stem, we can inflect it: *brighten/brightens/brightened*. If the word is already inflected, we can't usually add anything: *eaten/*eatens/*eatened*. Even the *-ed* affix is ambiguous. It is typical of participles (verb forms) to move into the adjective class; for example, *devoted* could be an inflected verb (*He had devoted his life to God*) or an adjective (*He seems very devoted*). The fact that *-ly* can be added to derive the adverb *devotedly* demonstrates that *devoted* is an adjective as well as a verb. There is, in addition, a derivational *-ed*, a remnant of an Old English form that meant "filled with" or "provided with," that we use to derive adjectives like *gifted*, *freckled*, and *domed*, usually from concrete nouns. Working in tandem, the two morphological processes, derivation and inflection, make it possible to say and write an infinite variety of things with a limited number of gram-matical elements, the morphemes.

DISCOVERY ACTIVITY 2-8

1. List the noun inflections: _____
   List the verb inflections: _____
   List the comparative inflections: _____

2. Test the word *friend*. To what class does it belong? Add the derivational *-ly* to *friend*. Test the result. To what class does the derived word *friendly* belong?
3. What evidence can you give that *matronly* is an adjective, but *quickly* is an adverb?
4. Using a series of contrasting forms, give proof that the word *cut* is a verb. Use evidence of the same kind to prove that *cut* is a noun.
5. Give formal evidence that the word *cutting* might be a noun. Give some reasons for calling the *-ing* on the noun *cutting* a derivational affix rather than an inflection.
6. Give syntactic evidence that the word *cutting* might be a verb.
7. Copy a line from this chapter and say how many morphemes are in each word.

DISCOVERY ACTIVITY 2-9

For each of the following words decide whether the *last* affix is derivational, inflectional, or ambiguous and what class(es) the word potentially belongs to.

filling inflected, V	walked inflected, V	drier inflected, Adj.
derived, N	————	derived, N
sails inflected, V	brotherly derived, Adj.	logically derived, Adv.
inflected, N		
happened _____	narrowly _____	surprised _____
growth _____	clipping _____	lover _____
dropping _____	creates _____	gratitude _____
operator _____	steps _____	famous _____
aged _____	failure _____	logical _____
blessing _____	magnify _____	ripen _____

lighten _____	proclivity _____	cutter _____
_____	_____	_____
depth _____	stronger _____	lower _____
_____	_____	_____
strangely _____	princess _____	broken _____
_____	_____	_____
princes _____	gifted _____	smiles _____
_____	_____	_____
acts _____	length _____	crooked _____
_____	_____	_____
activity _____	pictures _____	pictured _____
_____	_____	_____

WHERE WORDS COME FROM

There's more to English morphology, of course, than the inflectional and derivational processes described in this chapter. In English we frequently invent new words by compounding words already in use. Thus, we get nouns like *babysitter*. Then, by a process called "back formation," we get the verb *babysit* by removing the derivational *-er*. In addition, we "create" new words by a process known as **conversion**, which allows us to use a word from one class with the inflections from another without benefit of a derivational affix, a change in pronunciation, or any other alteration in the form of the original. Thus, the adjective *empty* has become both a verb and a noun.

We often invent words, too, such as the names of new products, like *nylon* and *mylar*. Many new words, called *acronyms*, result from reading initials or parts of a string of words as if they were words in their own right. For example, we recognize *NATO* (*North Atlantic Treaty Organization*) and *NASA* (*National Aeronautics and Space Administration*) and some common nouns, including *radar* (*radio detecting and ranging*) and *laser* (*light amplification by stimulated emission of radiation*). We now have a verb, *lase*, a backformation from *laser*.

For centuries, we have been adding to our inventory of morphemes and words by borrowing from other languages. *Graffiti,* for example, is a recent loan word from Italian. As the years go by, borrowed forms become so much a part of the English language that we even make new words with parts that originally came from different languages: We got *mini-,* for example, from Latin and *skirt* from Old Norse, but that didn't stop us from creating *miniskirt.* In Chapters 11, 12, and 14 you will learn more about the sources of our word stock.

DISCOVERY ACTIVITY 2-10

1. Using only the morphological facts, not grammatical function, identify the form class of each italicized word in the following sentences.
   a. The *poor* are always with us.
   b. He has a *broken* arm.
   c. The house was surrounded by a *stone* fence.
   d. Get a *moving* van.
   e. The *young* need love and attention.
   f. *Swimming* is my favorite sport.
2. In the following sentences, the italicized words, normally members of another class, have become *de facto* nouns. What is the rationale for saying so?
   a. Put your *empties* in the garbage.
   b. The red ones are my *favorites.*
3. In which of the following is the -'s an inflection?
   a. the *show's* the thing
   b. the *show's* producer

FORM vs. FUNCTION

This chapter has concentrated on the characteristics that enable us to classify words. Thus far, we have said nothing about the grammatical functions those words perform because in English, grammatical function is not a matter of morphology but of syntax. Here, you may need to be cautioned against confusing form class (membership in noun, verb, adjective, or adverb class) with grammatical functions such as subject, object, modifier, complement, and others. Discovery Activity 2-10 makes this point: in (1a) and (1e), adjectives, not nouns, are functioning as the head words of phrases which in turn are functioning as subjects; in (f), a verb form is in the subject function; in (b) and (d), verbs, not adjectives, are modifying nouns; in (c) a noun, not an adjective, is modifying a noun. Belonging to a particular class doesn't guarantee what job you get to do. And that's how English works, too.

DISCOVERY ACTIVITY 2-11

The following sentence is ambiguous. Can you give paraphrases that reflect two different meanings?

He found her a good conversationalist.

STRUCTURE CLASS WORDS

As you have seen, membership in the noun, verb, adjective, and adverb classes (the form classes) is assigned mainly on the basis of form, with inflection and derivation providing the criteria. They are open sets, to which new members may be added by borrowing from other languages, by coining wholly new words, or by deriving a form where none previously existed.

Unlike form class words, **structure class words**, also called *function words* or *signal words*, usually have invariant or fixed forms; that is, there are no inflectional paradigms or derivational possibilities for words like *the* and *very*. Unlike form class words, structure class words constitute small, closed sets. (Unless you consider *via* a fully naturalized form, no structure class words have been added for centuries.)

Structure class words are restricted to a narrow range of positions: *must go, must be going, must have gone, must have been going* are all grammatical verb phrases; **go must, *be must going, *gone have must* are all ungrammatical. The structure word, *must*, always has to come first. Structure class words are therefore subdivided into determiners, prepositions, auxiliaries, qualifiers, conjunctions, and many other subsets on the basis of the positions they occupy relative to the particular form class words they accompany or the type of phrase they usually contribute to. Because they typically accompany specific form classes, particular structure class words make effective signals of noun phrases, verb phrases, and adjective phrases. They also serve to join phrases and clauses, subordinate some structures, and establish logical relationships between the parts of a sentence.

TABLE 2-1   Distinguishing between Form Class and Structure Class Words

FORM CLASS WORDS	STRUCTURE CLASS WORDS
1. Can often be identified by form alone, and display changes or contrasts in their forms: 　a. Inflection: 　　eat/eats/ate/eating/eaten 　b. Derivation: 　　art/artist/artistic/ 　　artistically	1. Not members of inflectional or derivational series or paradigms; do not share formal features that make them identifiable as members of the class(es) they belong to. For example, nothing about the *form* of prepositions *at*, *of*, *by*, *in*, and *for* identifies them as prepositions.
2. Open sets. New members can be added by borrowing, compounding, backformation, conversion, or coinage.	2. Closed sets. New members are rarely added to the existing stock.
3. Have lexical content in addition to grammatical function.	3. Some, whose "meaning" is primarily their grammatical function, have little lexical content.
4. Occur in a variety of phrase types and/or grammatical constructions. Function shift is common; for example, in The <u>*aged* deserve respect</u> an adjective heads a noun phrase.	4. Fixed positions relative to the form class words they signal: *the* furniture not *furniture the*; rocks *and* rills not *and rocks rills*; *very* smooth not *smooth very*.
5. Do not always require the services of structure class words. For example, a verb phrase does not always require an auxiliary; noun phrases do not all require a determiner.	5. Must accompany form class words; cannot function alone: I'm *very* tired not *I'm very*; I saw *the* accident not *I saw the*.

    In some ways, structure class words are like inflectional affixes. They don't work unless they're "attached" to a form class word: *you look very* and *we saw the* are not grammatical units. Structure classes include many meaning-bearing words like *under*, *because*, *before*, and *after*, yet others are like inflections in that they seem to have little lexical content. If you look up *the* or *of*, for example, you will find descriptions of grammatical functions rather than definitions, and that's why they're known as **function words**

TABLE 2-2   Characteristics of Inflectional Affixes

1. A closed set of only eight members; limited in number and distribution:
    - I. Noun inflections:
        - A. plural -*s*: *cats*
        - B. possessive (also known as genitive) -'*s*: *Mary's*
    - II. Verb inflections:
        - A. Tense inflections
            1. third person singular present -*s*: *swims*
            2. past -*ed*: *walked*
        - B. Aspect inflections
            1. past participle (also known as perfective) -*en*: *written*
            2. present participle (also known as progressive) -*ing*: *writing*
    - III. Comparative inflections for adjectives and adverbs:
        - A. comparative -*er*: *taller, later*
        - B. superlative -*est*: *tallest, latest*

2. Highly predictable. If a new verb enters the language, it will take the regular -*ed* ending for past tense. All verbs take the third person singular present inflection (-*s*) and the -*ing* inflection: *smargs*/*is smarging.*

3. With one exception, do not change the part of speech or syntactic function of the stem to which they're attached. (The exception is the possessive inflection, which does change the function of the stem to which it's attached.)
    cat (noun) + -*s* = *cats* (still a noun: *I see the cat/cats.*)
    eat (verb) + -*en* = *eaten* (still a verb: *I eat/have eaten.*)
    tall (adj.) + -*er* = *taller* (still an adjective: *He seems tall/taller.*)

4. Typically come last, after all derivation is finished: *crime, crimes, criminal, criminals*; but not **crimesinal.*

5. Don't "accumulate." With the exception of noun plural + possessive, there is only one inflection per word. One verb stem cannot be inflected for both aspects or both tenses, or for aspect and tense: *walks, walking, walked; eat, eats, ate, eating, eaten*, but **walksed, *walkeding, *walksing, *eatsatening.*

6. Cannot be added to a single bound morpheme: **ceives, *ified*; must be attached to complete words: *receives, amplified.*

7. Often have little lexical content. The -*en* of *eaten* doesn't refer to anything outside of language; it signifies grammatical aspect. The -*s* of *swims* doesn't refer, either; it simply signifies grammatical status (third singular, present tense).

and as *syntactic* as opposed to *lexical* morphemes. Yet they are indispensable to meaning, and the more complex a sentence, the more important they seem. The *good conversationalist* sentence in Discovery Activity 2-11, a fairly simple case, can be rendered unambiguous with their help: *found her to be* one or *found one for her.*

TABLE 2-3   Characteristics of Derivational Affixes

1. Large number; not really a closed set. While coining or borrowing new members is unusual, it is not entirely out of the question. For example, -*nik*, borrowed from Russian and/or Yiddish to make words like "peacenik," "beatnik"; -*aholic* or -*holic*, from *alcoholic* ("workaholic"); -*thon* or -*athon* from *marathon* ("telethon"); -*gate* from *Watergate* ("Koreagate").

2. Unpredictable distribution. It is difficult to predict which words in a particular class will accept which affixes. For example, there's no sure way to predict *boyly when *manly* is perfectly all right. Also we have *ferocious/ferocity* but not *gorgeous/*gorgeocity*.

3. Frequently, but not invariably, alter the part of speech or syntactic function of the stem to which they're attached:
    child (noun) + -*ish* = *childish* (adj.); *quick* (adj.) + -*ly* = *quickly* (adv.)
    but: *child* (noun) + -*hood* = *childhood* (still noun); *law* (noun) + -*er* = *lawyer* (still noun); *dead* (adj.) + -*ly* = *deadly* (still adj.)

4. Can come at the beginning as well as at the end: *de*criminalization; *be*head; *en*liven; *un*happy; *a*sleep.

5. Can accumulate almost indefinitely: *anti*disestablishmentarianism.

6. Can be attached to a bound base to form a word: *de-* + -*ceive* = *deceive*; *stult-* + -*ify* = *stultify*.

7. Often help us recognize or identify class membership: -*ify* is characteristic of verbs; -*ity* is characteristic of nouns; -*able/-ible* is characteristic of adjectives.

And although *the* doesn't appear to contribute any independent meaning or additional information, it makes a big difference in what something might mean. Inserting it into the ambiguous headline, *Neighbors Help Burn Victims*, in Discovery Activity 1-4 enables us to tell what goes with what. By specifying the noun phrase, the determiner clarifies the grammatical relationships, hence forcing interpretation of *burn* as a noun modifier rather than a predicating verb. Beyond such purely grammatical functions, words like *the* have a wide range of roles (called *pragmatic functions*) in written and spoken discourse, but those are matters that are outside the limited scope of this book. In the coming chapters, as we take up the major form classes one at a time, along with the structure of the phrases they enter into, and then the syntactic relationships between and among phrases themselves, we will discuss further the grammatical functions of particular sets of structure words. For now, it is enough to know that form class words are identified by form and structure class words by position. The relevant information is summarized in Tables 2-1, 2-2, and 2-3.

SUMMARY

1. Morphology generally refers to the structure of words.
2. A morpheme is a (1) meaningful form (2) which cannot be subdivided or analyzed into smaller meaningful parts and (3) which has a relatively stable meaning wherever it appears.
3. Morphemes can be subdivided:
   I. Lexical morphemes:
      A. free (words): *woman, boy, green*
      B. bound
         1. bases: *-ceive, stult-, leg-*
         2. derivational affixes:
            a. prefixes: *un-, mini-*
            b. suffixes: *-ous, -ify*
   II. Syntactic (or grammatical) morphemes:
      A. free (words): *the, of, to, and, if*
      B. bound: all the inflectional affixes
4. Major groups of words are subdivided into form classes or "parts of speech" on the basis of their characteristic forms and the contrasts reflected in inflection and derivation.
5. Structure class words are identified by their syntactic position rather than by their form, since they do not participate in derivational or inflectional morphology. (See Table 2-1.)
6. The major morphological processes are inflection and derivation. (See Tables 2-2 and 2-3.)

STUDY QUESTIONS

1. Explain why *capsize* consists of only one morpheme.
2. What are the three criteria for establishing a unit of language as a morpheme?
3. Name the eight inflectional suffixes.
4. Summarize the differences between inflectional and derivational affixes.
5. What's the difference between an inflectional paradigm and a test frame like the "*will* frame" or the "*seems* frame"?
6. If a word can be pluralized, that is, if you can add a plural morpheme to it, to what form class must it belong? If a word has *-s*, *-ed*, and *-ing* forms, to what form class must it belong? If a word has comparative and superlative degree forms, to what form class does it probably belong?

7. On what basis are words subdivided and assigned to classes such as noun, verb, and adjective?

8. The series consisting of a stem, the plural, and the possessive is called *the noun paradigm* and the series consisting of a stem, the third person singular present, the past, the perfect, and the progressive is called *the verb paradigm*. Why is the series with the comparative and the superlative not named *the adjective paradigm*? Related question: Why do the first two questions in (6) ask what class the words *must* belong to, while the third question asks what class the words *probably* belong to?

9. What criterion is used for subclassifying structure words?

10. The words *my*, *your*, *a*, *some*, *the*, and *these* all belong to one subset of structure class words, the determiner class. Why? That is, what do they have in common?

11. How are structure words and inflections alike?

12. In English we can't add a derivational affix to an inflected form. Does this statement constitute a rule of English grammar? Why or why not?

FURTHER STUDY AND DISCUSSION

Words like *salesperson*, *newscaster*, and *sportswoman* appear to be exceptions to the rule that requires inflections to come at the end, in that they apparently have a plural inflection in the middle. Can you think of additional words of this kind? Can you show that these words do not in fact violate the rule?

3 | Nouns, Determiners, Prepositions, and Pronouns

If you asked an ordinary person on the street to tell you what a rose is, the answer might be that it's a flower, sometimes red, sometimes yellow, occasionally white, that has a pleasant smell, that grows on a bush, and so on. If you asked a botanist the same question, the answer would be quite different. The botanist's definition, based on observation and classification of many different plants, would be far more objective than the layperson's, and much more precise. The definition would not invalidate the layperson's definition, but it might be far more useful in helping you to identify a rose (even if it grows where you don't expect roses) and to distinguish it from all non-roses. In the field of English grammar, if you ask a layperson to tell you what a noun is, the answer will probably be that it's a word that names something. A grammarian, however, would offer far more precise guidelines for identifying nouns. The grammarian would not refute what the layperson said nor call it "wrong," but the grammarian might question its usefulness. The fact is that you know *murgatrist* to be a noun not because it names something; rather, you assume it names something because you have recognized it as a noun. This chapter will help you discover some objective criteria for identifying nouns and other classes of words.

PARADIGMS REVISITED—AND REVISED

Chapter 2 introduced the concept of the inflectional paradigm as a way of identifying the words of English that belong to the **noun** class. But you don't have to look far to find words that you feel certain are nouns but which do not meet the requirements imposed by the paradigm as given in Chapter 2. Instead of abandoning the paradigm, however, we will revise it so that words which at first appear not to conform to it can still be included in the noun category. But first, let's take another look at the paradigm and test some words to see what the paradigm tells us about them.

DISCOVERY ACTIVITY 3-1

The noun paradigm displays the following forms, potentially available to all nouns. Because usage varies from one person to another, however, it is not possible to know for certain how many forms a particular noun can take. The question mark implies uncertainty about whether anyone uses such a form.

Singular	Plural: -s	Possessive: -'s	Plural + Possessive
girl	girls	girl's	girls'
woman	women	woman's	women's
lens	lenses	?	?
series	series	?	?
knowledge	?	?	?
?	surroundings	?	?
Aristotle	———	Aristotle's	———

1. Check each of the following words against the paradigm and indicate in the blank how many forms it has in your speech.

Einstein____	mouse____	athletics____	scissors____
(panty)hose____	child____	Susan____	apparatus____
police____	chaos____	news____	tennis____
vermin____	cattle____	hardware____	furniture____
equipment____	fun____	species____	thanks____
foot____	clothes____	clothing____	bread____
(chicken) pox __	data____	suds____	Chicago____

2. Read through all the following questions before attempting to answer any. Don't worry if your judgments differ from those of other native speakers of English. If these are words you use, your judgments are valid.

   a. In Chapter 1 we distinguished between count nouns (one chair, many chairs) and non-count nouns (much furniture, not *one furniture, *many furnitures). Using the "much/many test," decide which nouns in question 1 fall into the non-count category.

   b. What is peculiar about the noun police? Is cattle like police? Can you think of any other words that behave like one or the other of these two?

c. The L. L. Bean catalog refers to a pair of pants as a *pant*. Have you adopted this usage? If so, have you extended it to *panties*, *trousers*, *scissors*, *pliers*? That is, do you say *a panty* or *a scissor*?

d. How are the words *clothes* and *suds* different from the words in (c)?

e. In your speech is *data* a non-count noun, like *information*, or a count noun like *fact*? In your speech, is *media* singular, plural, or both?

f. Would you use a possessive form of any of the words in the list that do not have a singular/plural contrast? Which ones? For which words does a possessive form seem odd, if not impossible, for you?

g. Which words have only one form in your speech and thus do not pass the paradigmatic test for you?

h. Can you think of some words not listed above that do not pass the paradigmatic test for you (because you don't inflect them either for plural or for possession) but which you *know* are nouns? On what do you base your decision? That is, how do you know they're nouns?

3. Compare your responses to question 2 with those of your classmates. On which questions do you find disagreement? Compare the various means suggested in response to (h) for proving membership in the noun class for words that don't inflect and thus don't pass the paradigmatic test.

You can see from Discovery Activity 3-1 that many words you know to be nouns do not exhibit all the formal contrasts in the paradigm. If we insist that nouns must have all the forms, what will we do with proper nouns like *Chicago* and *George Zywalefski*, which normally take the possessive, but not the plural? Of course we can pluralize them when necessary (for example, *there are two George Zywalefskis in the phone book*) but the very defining characteristic of proper nouns is that under ordinary circumstances they cannot be pluralized because they name unique entities. Therefore, to say that all nouns must take plural forms is too strong a requirement, not only because of proper nouns, but because some common nouns also "reject" the plural affix.

Words like *sheep*, as well as the names of many game animals, have no plural form even though we can refer to more than one and specify a number: *ten sheep*. Some nouns, like *clothes*, surprisingly have only a plural and no singular: *many clothes*, but *a clothe.

And unlike *trousers*, which can lose its *-s* in phrases like *trouser leg*, *clothes* cannot. Can you imagine a **clothe closet* or a **clotheline*? At first glance, *suds* may look like *clothes*, because there's no such thing as **a sud*, but most people probably say *too much suds*, not **too many suds*. Then, too, there are words like *linguistics* and *news*, which, as nouns, have only one form—a form that looks plural but acts singular. That is, we say *linguistics is* (not *are*) *his field* and *the news is* (not *are*) *good*. (The stems, *linguistic* and *new*, by the way, are not nouns.)

On the other hand, to insist that all nouns must have a separate contrast for possessive is also too much to require. In speech, there is no contrast in the possessive form of most nouns that is any different from the contrast for plural. That is to say, *boys*, *boy's*, and *boys'* are all pronounced the same and are distinguished not by form but by context. In speech we have only two "forms," the stem, *boy*, and one contrasting form, pronounced "boys" regardless of the spelling conventions that require the *'s* or *s'*. One spoken form serves for plural, possessive, and plural + possessive.

We will therefore revise the paradigmatic test by stipulating that *any word that exhibits at least one of the possible contrasts of the noun paradigm (i.e., has at least two forms) is a member of the noun class.* The revision will accommodate *George Zywalefski* and *deer*, which have only one contrast because they have a possessive but no plural; *boy* and *girl* and thousands of others that have only one contrast because their plural and possessive forms are the same in speech even though they're distinguished in writing; and those, like *crisis*, that have a contrasting plural but are unlikely to take the possessive. Then we will have to establish some other criteria for membership in the noun class for those words (for example, *thanks*, *haste*, or *chaos*) that have no inflectional contrasts at all.

As Discovery Activity 2-1 implies, it is not necessary for all speakers to agree that a particular word does or does not inflect. You may use a phrase like *haste's result*, to the consternation of a friend who does not inflect *haste* and uses *the result of haste* instead. For your friend, *haste* does not pass the test because it has neither a plural nor a possessive form. But as you saw in Chapter 2, another formal criterion, participation in derivational series like *haste/hasty/hastily/hastiness*, can establish membership in the noun class for *haste*, and syntactic evidence can be offered in support as well, as you will soon see.

The second revision of the paradigmatic test applies specifically to the contrast between singular and plural forms. Regular noun plurals in English are pronounced in three different ways depending on the final sound of the stem. We have, in fact, not one but three plural affixes: the syllabic "iz" of *churches*, the "s" of *hats*, and the "z" of *shoes*. Yet it seems counterintuitive to maintain that we have three different plural affixes when they all have the same use—are, in fact, alternating versions of one morpheme. What we have is actually one morpheme with three different pronunciations, depending on the preceding sound. The expression *the plural morpheme* is an abstraction, a kind of shorthand for "whatever you do to a noun stem in English to indicate the notion of plurality." With this understanding, we can introduce the second revision, which will allow not only *churches*, *hats*, and *shoes*, but will also account for words like *man* and *mouse*, where plurality is manifested as an internal vowel change rather than an affix. That is, *mice* is to *mouse* what *houses* is to *house*. Therefore, we will stipulate that not only the -*s*, but *any contrast in form for plurality counts as a manifestation of the plural morpheme*. Moreover, if we simply stipulate a singular-plural contrast without specifying a particular form, we can include such contrasts as *crisis/crises*, *datum/data*, *focus/foci*, and all other such pairs that conform to the morphological rules of the languages from which we borrowed them rather than to English rules.

DISCOVERY ACTIVITY 3-2

1. The following words are determiners, divided into several subsets. Using the list of words in Discovery Activity 3-1, check each word to see whether you can make a noun phrase of it with any one or more of these words.

Example
the equipment, some equipment, but *a/an equipment

   a. the, some, a/an
   b. this, that, these, those
   c. my, your, his, her, its, our, their, whose
   d. Sue's (or any name with the possessive inflection added)
   e. three, four

2. Do any words from Discovery Activity 3-1 "work" with words from all the subsets?
3. What do those words seem to have in common?
4. Are there any words that do not work with any of the determiners?

5. Think of some other words which, like those in your answer to question 4, do not "work" with determiners. Do they have something in common? Do they fall into groups that have something in common? What is it?
6. Here is a list of the most frequently used *prepositions*.

   of, in, to, at, by, for, from, on, with

   Do the words you listed in response to questions 4 and 5 work with any of these prepositions?
7. Do the following words form acceptable noun phrases (when preceded by a determiner) or prepositional phrases (when preceded by a preposition)?

   carelessness, indebtedness, happiness, loneliness, kindness, sweetness

8. Can you think of any -ness words that don't work with prepositions or determiners?
9. Do you think that -ness is a good indicator of "noun-ness"?
10. List as many words as you can that end in each of these derivational affixes. Write at least five words for *each* affix.

    -ist, -ism, -hood, -acy, -tion/-sion, -ance/-ence, -ment, -ity, -dom, -ship

    Do the words you listed participate in noun phrases and/or in prepositional phrases? What can you surmise about an unfamiliar word that ends in one of these affixes?

The point of Discovery Activity 3-2 is that we can supplement formal criteria with syntactic information to identify nouns. Whether or not a word passes the paradigmatic test, we can be fairly certain that it belongs in the noun class if it regularly appears in the same kinds of grammatical structures, called **phrases**, that the inflectable nouns regularly appear in. In a way, this is like saying that nouns can be defined, roughly, as the words that fit in the blank and thus make a working unit of this structure: "my ____ (-s) ."

BEYOND PARADIGMS: NOUN PHRASES AND PREPOSITIONAL PHRASES

Syntactic identification relies on the stability of structure class words. By themselves, many structure class words have little meaning; their main job is to accompany words from specific form classes, thus creating various kinds of phrases. A word like *the*, the prototypical **determiner**, usually accompanies common nouns to form noun phrases: *the chair, the activity, the apparatus*. You are unlikely to find **the quickly, *the collide*, or **the tantamount*. So, if an uninflectable word appears exclusively or even consistently in the company of determiners, it is likely to be a noun in spite of its lack of inflectional contrasts. The resulting unit is a **noun phrase**, like *some fun, your haste*, or *those vermin*. Because it is the main element, giving its name to the type of phrase, the noun is called the **headword** of the noun phrase.

When using a structure word as a diagnostic, we're looking for typical syntactic behavior, not unusual or extraordinary circumstances. Moreover, we use structure word tests only in the absence of formal criteria or to confirm formal criteria, but not to override formal criteria. Thus, a word like *young* is not a noun even though we find it in a phrase like *the young* (equivalent to "young people"). Since it doesn't inflect for plural (**the youngs*) but for degree (*the younger/youngest*) it's an adjective despite its nounlike syntactic behavior here. Remember what you learned in Discovery Activity 2-8: membership in a particular form class does not guarantee or predict a specific syntactic function, and many form class words can move freely in and out of the territory of others.

As Discovery Activity 3-2 shows, members of another structure class, **prepositions** (*of, in, at, by, for, from*, and *with*), also regularly team up with nouns; so even if a questionable word doesn't enter into acceptable noun phrases, you can still identify it as a noun if it shows up as the "working partner," or **object, of a preposition**. Thus, *linguistics* proves to be a noun because it regularly appears in phrases like *of linguistics* even through it doesn't work with determiners (**the/*some/*my linguistics*). Note also that pronouns and whole noun phrases, not just nouns, serve as objects of prepositions: *of them, in the closet, by a river*.

In fact, it is this kind of syntactic evidence that enables us to certify particular derivational affixes as supplementary formal indicators of "noun-ness," that is, to establish specific derivational affixes as characteristic of nouns rather than some other class. As Discovery Activity 3-2 shows, words ending in *-ness, -ist, -ity, -ism*, and certain other derivational affixes all work with determiners and/or prepositions. Thus, whether or not they are inflectable, we know that those words belong firmly in the noun class because they consistently serve as headwords in noun phrases and as objects in prepositional phrases.

Notice that although whole prepositional phrases can be used as modifiers, determiners and prepositions themselves are not modifiers. When they occur, they are essential to the structure of their phrases. Without them, we would have an entirely different kind of phrase, or an ungrammatical one. If we delete *of* from *the study of linguistics*, we get *the study linguistics*; if we delete both *the* and *of*, what's left is verb-plus-object or a command, *study linguistics*, not a noun phrase with an embedded prepositional phrase.

DISCOVERY ACTIVITY 3-3

1. Make a grammatical arrangement of each of the following strings of words:
   a. the, the, the, of, of, study, biochemistry, human, brain
   b. the, the, the, about, at, news, accident, airport
   c. a, a, a, by, in, house, river, dark, forest
2. In each case, what kind of phrase did you create?
3. For each complete string, what is the headword?
4. For each noun phrase that is the object of a preposition, what is the headword?

Discovery Activity 3-3 shows that noun phrases and prepositional phrases are radically different kinds of structures even though they both incorporate nouns. The basic structure of a noun phrase is determiner + noun: *a forest*. Of course it is possible to "expand" this basic structure by inserting strings of modifiers: *a cool, dark forest*. The basic structure of a prepositional phrase, on the other hand, is preposition + noun phrase: *of the human brain*. You can see that each type of phrase can be embedded inside the other: *the study of the biochemistry of the human brain*. Typically, noun phrases and prepositional phrases not only have different internal structure, but also have entirely different grammatical jobs to do, as we will see in later chapters. In order not to confuse them, it will help to remember that you can substitute a pronoun for a noun phrase, but not for a prepositional phrase. You could substitute *it* for *the study of the biochemistry of the human brain*: *It is his field*; for *the biochemistry of the human brain*: *the study of it*; or for *the human brain*: *the biochemistry of it*; but you can't substitute *it* for *of the biochemistry of the human brain* or for *of the human brain*: *the study it* and *the biochemistry it*. Because of this lack of syntactic equivalence, neither a prepositional phrase nor the noun,

noun phrase, or pronoun serving as its object can usually assume such noun phrase functions as subject or object of a verb, as Chapter 7 makes clear.

DISCOVERY ACTIVITY 3-4

Which italicized words in the following sentences can be replaced by a complete noun phrase, and which by only a determiner?

Yours is better looking than *hers*.   She rejected *him*
Its wheels are stuck.   He liked *her* ideas; she rejected *his*.

Your life is in danger, not *mine*.   I like *your* style, but not *theirs*.
He kissed *her*.   Where is *she*?
He kissed *her* hand.   Where is *hers*?
That book belongs to *me*.   *That* is *mine*.
                                             Where are *those* pens?

PRONOUNS

When you worked through Discovery Activity 3-2, you may have been surprised to find *my, your, his, her, its, our, their, whose,* and proper names bearing the possessive inflection among the determiners, especially if you've been taught to call them pronouns or adjectives. But we stipulated that structure words are grouped according to their positions relative to form class words, and all these words assume a position "reserved" for determiners—immediately before nouns: *the book, some books,* as well as *my book, your book,* and *Sally's book*. While a word is in the determiner position, it assumes the determiner's identity and function. You can see that *my, your,* and *Sally's* constitute only part of a noun phrase, the same part that *the* or *a* does. Unlike **pronouns**, which are equal to whole noun phrases, these possessive words cannot work alone; like all other determiners, they need nouns in order to make complete working units. That is, we can say *Give me mine* and *Mine fell off,* but not **Give me my* or **My fell off.*

Clearly, we are dealing with two different classes of words, because *my* does not work like *mine*. It is true that some of the words show up in both classes, and the occurrence of *Sally's* as both a determiner (*Sally's book*) and a pronoun (*Sally's* [= "Sally's book"] *was lost*) isn't remarkable. In some dialects *them* is both a pronoun (*I'll take two of them*) and a determiner (*I'll take two of them cakes*) whereas in standard English it is *those* that belongs to both sets (*I'll take two of those* and *I'll take two of those cakes*) and *them* that belongs only to the pronoun class.

Discovery Activity 3-4 shows that pronouns take the positions that complete noun phrases take and are syntactically equivalent to determiner + noun: *mine* = "my life." Pronouns do not in fact "replace nouns," but noun phrases. That is, we can say *The wheels are stuck, Its wheels are stuck*, or *They are stuck*, but not **The they are stuck* or **Its they are stuck*. We can have *She rejected Bo Jones, She rejected the man with the halo*, or *She rejected him*, but not **She rejected the him with the halo*. In fact, pronouns can replace long, heavily modified, expanded noun phrases, proper nouns, plurals, and nouns like *chaos*, which work without determiners, but they cannot usually replace a singular common noun alone: *she* = "Susan" or "*the girl*," not "the she." Thus, proper nouns, nouns without determiners, and pronouns themselves can all count as noun phrases, even though they consist of only one word, because they are syntactic equivalents of noun phrases; thus, pronoun substitution is a good test for noun phrases and noun phrase functions (but not for prepositional phrases and their functions).

DISCOVERY ACTIVITY 3-5

1. Fill in the blanks with appropriate forms.

Example
If I have X, X belongs to <u>me</u>, and X is <u>mine</u>.

a. If *you* have X, X belongs to ____ and X is ____.

b. If *she/he/it* has X, X belongs to ____ / ____ / ____ and X is
   ____ / ____ / ____.

c. If *we* have X, X belongs to ____ and X is ____.

d. If *all of you* have it, it belongs to ____ and it is ____.

e. If *they* have it, it belongs to ____ and it is ____.

2. Using your responses to (1) as a source, complete this chart of pronoun forms:

	Subject	Object	Possessive
1st person singular	I	me	mine
2nd person singular			

3rd person singular   _____ _____ _____

1st person plural   _____ _____

2nd person plural   _____ _____

3rd person plural   _____ _____

3. Fill in the rest of the inventory of names for the pronoun forms.

Example

I is the first person singular subject pronoun.
Me is the first person singular object pronoun.
Mine is the first person singular possessive pronoun.

a. *You* is the second person singular and plural subject pronoun.

_____ is the second person singular and plural _____ pronoun.

_____ is the _____.

b. *He, she,* and *it* are the third person singular _____ pronouns.

_____, _____, and _____ are the third person _____.

_____, _____, and _____ are _____.

c. *We* is the first person plural _____.

_____ is the first person _____.

_____ is _____.

d. *They* is the third person plural _____.

_____ is the _____.

_____ is the _____.

4. In the blanks below, write either *its* or *it's*, as appropriate.
   a. _____ a nice car; I like _____ style.

   b. Although _____ illustrations are fine, I don't think _____ a great book.

   c. I love my cat, but _____ a pain to look after _____ needs all the time.

You can see from item 3 in Discovery Activity 3-5 that pronouns exhibit striking formal contrasts that correlate not only to grammatical functions like subject and object, but also to person, number, and sometimes even to gender. When speaking of *our friend Fosnick*, for example, we might say *She likes tripe but it doesn't like* _her_. Both _she_ and _her_ refer to the noun phrase _our friend Fosnick_, but unlike that noun phrase, which remains the same regardless of its syntactic position, the pronoun changes. Furthermore, we would have chosen _he_ and _him_ if _Fosnick_ referred to a man. On the basis of these inflectional contrasts, some scholars consider pronouns a subset of the noun class. But others count pronouns as a structure class despite their inflectional contrasts because they do not participate in derivational morphology. Nor do they behave like individual members of the noun class, but like complete noun phrases, as you have seen. Moreover, form classes are open sets, but pronouns constitute a small closed set whose membership has remained constant for hundreds of years, although the functions of some of those members have changed radically over the centuries.

In contemporary American English, some of the contrasts in pronoun form have ceased to be functional and are ignored by many speakers in some contexts. For example, _between you and I_ and _between you and me_ are linguistically equivalent, and both versions are widely used even though purists condemn _between you and I_. In some parts of the country, there is widespread use of object pronouns in compound subjects and of subject pronouns in compound objects. Despite condemnation of such usage in the academic community, many college students say _her and I are friends_ and _it took she and I two hours to get here_. We will not address these usage issues now but will return to them after we have had a closer look at the syntactic functions involved.

The fourth item in Discovery Activity 3-5 was designed to call attention to a matter of usage: namely, the conventional spelling of the possessive _its_ never calls for an apostrophe, which is used only in the contracted forms of _it is_ and _it has_. It may help to remember that the notion of possession associated with _'s_ is already built into the possessive determiners. It is no more necessary to use an apostrophe with _its_ than with _his_.

FORM AND MEANING

We have said a good deal about the forms that nouns can take and the names used for the forms: singular, plural, possessive. Although very little has been said about the uses and meanings of the various forms, by now you should be aware that the names can be quite misleading if taken literally, as the following activity will further demonstrate.

DISCOVERY ACTIVITY 3-6

1. *Little Bo Peep has lost her sheep.* Was it one or more? How do you know?

2. Use each of the following in a phrase or sentence that clearly indicates whether the word is grammatically singular or plural (for example, by choice of *this* vs. *these*, *is* vs. *are*, replacement by *it* vs. *they/them*).

   hair, news, summons, ethics, police, vermin, scissors, politics, grouse

3. The collective nouns lack inflection in both sentences of the following pairs. Nevertheless, it is obvious from the verb forms and choice of possessive determiners (*its* vs. *their*) that *clergy* and *faculty* are being treated as grammatically singular in one context and as grammatically plural in the other. Does the difference imply a difference in meaning for you?

   a. The clergy retain their neutrality in this matter.
      The clergy gets involved when its assistance is appropriate.
   b. The faculty work well on their research when supported.
      The faculty works well with its new dean.

The preceding activity shows that we don't always use a plural form when more than one of something is involved; nor do we always use a singular form for "only one." Grammatical number does not invariably reflect real-world number. You might expect confusion to arise with words like *sheep*, which have only one form, but other devices reflecting number are at hand. Sometimes a pronoun provides information about number and can thus clarify intended meaning, as *leave them alone* does for Bo Peep's sheep. If you refer to aircraft with the pronoun *it*, you must be talking about one plane; if you refer with *they* or *them*, it's obvious you're speaking of more than one. Actually, there is no logical reason to require an inflection meaning "more than one" when you have at your disposal words like *many*, *few*, and *several*, and names like *ten* and *a thousand* for specific numbers that logically entail "more than one" and thus make an inflection for plural a redundancy. Some languages omit the plural marker when a number larger than one is specified, but standard English generally keeps it: *ten books*, not **ten book*.

Paradoxically, it seems, we refuse to use a plural when logic might appear to require it. Take *hair*, for example. Although we might say something like "there's a hair on your collar" or "I hate to see hairs in the bathroom sink," we do not refer to how nice "your hairs" look when you've just come from the salon, although some languages do just that. Unlike other languages, English treats the hairs on one's head as an undifferentiated mass of stuff, as if it (not "they") were an indivisible or amorphous volume of gas or liquid, or something abstract, like honesty. We also use non-count nouns, which are always singular, to talk about baggage, furniture, and many other things that consist of more than one: *the baggages/ furnitures/equipments and *your hairs (compare piece of baggage/ furniture/equipment and strand of hair).

Actually, it isn't precise to refer to "non-count nouns," because there isn't a specific set of particular nouns that refer to non-countable items and always occur in the singular. Rather, what we have is a grammatical device for implying, in a given context, that we perceive something as a mass rather than as countable units, as the examples with hair are intended to show. In some contexts we talk of foods as opposed to food. But some words, furniture, equipment, and luggage, for example, seem to resist moving into the countable realm.

Perhaps the strangest noun forms are **collective nouns**, words like clergy, faculty, crew, team, and family. In many contexts they are inflected for plural: ten teams are in the league. But in some cases these nouns are treated as plurals (perhaps with a slight change in meaning) even without the inflection (although it is less common to do so in American English than in British, where, for example, the government are . . . is standard). But we do have the choice, if we want to exercise it, of saying either the faculty are united where the word faculty, though not inflected, is plural or the faculty is united, where it is singular, as the are/is contrast shows.

THE GENITIVE "INFLECTION"

And finally, there is the affix usually called the **possessive**. This inflection, also known as the **genitive**, is unique not only because it can attach to a few already inflected stems (children's, women's, men's) but also because it changes the grammatical function of the word to which it's added. It temporarily changes a noun to a determiner: Helen's book is the same kind of structure as her/the book. In addition to these peculiarities, the genitive is grammatically and semantically complex, in that it indicates a broad range of concepts and relationships, some of which are only tenuously or indirectly related to the notion of possession.

DISCOVERY ACTIVITY 3-7

Look at the following expressions and think about the meaning of the inflection:

John's coat	Shakespeare's plays	men's wear
a day's work	your money's worth	Reagan's performances
Cynthia's gift	the city's destruction	Reagan's critics

1. What meaning is expressed by the inflection in *John's coat*?
2. What about in *Shakespeare's plays*? What about in *men's wear*?
3. Is the meaning expressed in *a day's work* and *your money's worth* the same?
4. Paraphrase *a day's work*: _____
5. Does *Reagan's performances* imply that Reagan performed?
6. Does *Reagan's critics* imply that Reagan criticized?
7. Is *the city's destruction* anything like *Reagan's critics*?
8. Does *Cynthia's gift* necessarily refer to a gift she possesses? What other meaning could it have?

DISCOVERY ACTIVITY 3-8

1. Some people will not use expressions like *the table's leg*, preferring instead *the leg of the table* or *table leg*. Note also *door knob* (but the highly improbable *door's knob*), *kitchen floor*, *hat brim*, *college president*, *course content*, and so forth. Are the relationships between the two words the same in all these expressions? Think of some others like these. Are various meanings expressed? Is there a prevalent one?
2. Is there any good reason why *teachers' lounge* shouldn't be *teacher lounge*? Would you ever say *the lounge of the teachers*?
3. Do you find anything self-contradictory or something unintentionally humorous in the following? What is it?

    Barber's Union Local No. 192

4. The following are ambiguous. Provide at least two different interpretations for each:

    Gordon's photograph; John's punishment

Discovery Activities 3-7 and 3-8 suggest some of the many meanings and functions of the genitive inflection. In the case of *John's coat* it almost certainly does signify possession or ownership, but in the case of *Shakespeare's plays* it means something like "originator." In *men's wear* it implies "intended for." Sometimes the genitive has functions that can only be determined in context by the semantic content of the noun following the inflected stem. For example, in *Reagan's performances* it implies a subject-predicate relationship like that of "Reagan performed," but in *Reagan's critics* it implies a verb-object relationship like that expressed in "They criticized Reagan," where Reagan was the object of criticism, not the one who criticized.

Because of its many peculiarities, *-'s* is difficult to classify and is the center of much controversy. Some grammarians consider it a "grammatical word" and argue that it can hardly be a noun inflection, since it often attaches to words from other classes, as it does in such phrases as *somebody else's* and *the boy over there's*. Sometimes it doesn't attach to the stem it "belongs to," but to an entire phrase, as it were. That is, the phrase *the Shah of Iran's death* refers to the death of the Shah and not the death of the country, yet the *-'s* is attached to *Iran*; we don't find **the Shah's death of Iran* or **the Shah's of Iran death*.

A WORD ABOUT INDEFINITES

Among the most peculiar forms in English are **indefinite pronouns** (*somebody, everyone*, and the like) which act like pronouns in that they do not pair up with determiners (**the everybody*) but unlike them in that they do not refer to specific persons. Nor does an indefinite pronoun have an **antecedent**, that is, a previously named noun phrase to "replace." Like many indefinite noun phrases (*a person, the average citizen*), indefinite pronouns select the third person singular verb form even though they often refer to more than one person. That is, we say *everyone is*, not **everyone are*. Since these indefinites are singular when it comes to verb choice their frequently plural or collective meaning is disregarded by some writers of standard English, who insist that they be replaced by *he, him*, and *his*, a strategy that may conflict with the rule that pronouns must agree with their antecedents in gender as well as number.

Conservative writers and feminists appear to be at odds: the former recommend *Everyone is entitled to his opinion*; the latter object on the grounds that although *everyone* may be singular, not everyone is masculine. And although the National Council of Teachers of English has approved the more natural *everyone . . . they/them/their* that most of us use in speaking, some people still do not accept that usage; hence the adoption of *his/her*. But many rhetoric teachers object to the *his/her* solution on stylistic grounds and ask students to consider a wider range of options, which you can find in Chapter 13, where this usage issue is addressed.

SUMMARY

1. Nouns are identified on the basis of their ability to accept at least one of the characteristic inflections, plural or possessive.
2. Nouns can be identified by characteristic derivational forms like *-ness, -ity, -ance, -ist*, and others.
3. Function words like *much/many, one/two, a/some* create noun phrases and enable us to divide nouns into subsets including (but not limited to) groups that:
   a. have contrasting forms for singular and plural: *one mouse, two mice*
   b. have the same form for singular and plural: *one species, five species; one deer, five deer*
   c. have singular forms that look plural and are not counted: **a new, *two news, news is, *news are; *a politic, *two politics, politics is, *politics are*
   d. have no plural and are not counted: *the furniture, some furniture; *five furniture, *a furniture, *five furnitures*
   e. name unique entities: *Chicago, *the Chicago, *the Chicagos*
4. Determiners precede nouns to create noun phrases. Words that take the position of *the*, the prototypical determiner, are determiners.
5. Prepositions accept nouns, pronouns, and noun phrases as objects, to create prepositional phrases: *in school, in the park, for him, for her sake*.
6. Nouns are called heads or headwords in noun phrases, but nouns and noun phrases are called objects in prepositional phrases.

STUDY QUESTIONS

1. Of what use are inflectional paradigms? Review Chapter 2 for an explicit statement if you can't infer an answer from this chapter.

2. What is the maximum number of inflectional forms for nouns?
3. What revisions does this chapter make in the noun paradigm and the paradigmatic test, and why?
4. What is the function of determiners?
5. If a word fails the inflectional test, does that necessarily mean it's not a noun? What other morphological (not syntactic) characteristic can you use as a criterion of "noun-ness"? (Structure words and pronoun substitution constitute syntactic, not morphological, evidence.)
6. List at least five noun-forming derivational affixes.
7. Why are *my*, *your*, and so on classed as determiners and not as pronouns?
8. Why is a name bearing the possessive inflection classed as a determiner?
9. Give evidence that each of the following underscored words constitutes a phrase. *Susan laughed*; *Furniture is expensive*; *Poppies grow wild*.
10. List two kinds of morphological and two different syntactic proofs of membership in the noun class, and give examples.
11. Despite formal contrasts, pronouns are not included in form classes. Why?
12. List the subject pronouns in the conventional order, specifying person and number; then do the same for object pronouns and possessive pronouns.
13. How is the possessive different from other inflectional morphemes?
14. Indicate whether the following are rules of grammar, and why or why not:
    a. To indicate plurality in English, regular nouns have a contrast in form, manifested in an affix that is pronounced "iz" as in *churches*, "s" as in *hats*, and "z" as in *shoes*, depending on the sound at the end of the stem.
    b. The following cannot take the place of noun phrases: *my*, *your*, *their*.
    c. You should not say *Everyone has their own opinion* because *everyone* is singular and *their* is plural.

FURTHER STUDY AND DISCUSSION

1. Review all the criteria for morpheme-hood; think about *-er*, *-en*, *-ing*, and *-ed*, each of which represents two or more morphemes because its function or meaning is not the same in all environments. Look at Discovery Activities 3-7 and 3-8 and the discussion following them. Then ask yourself these questions: Is the possessive inflection a mor-

pheme? Is the plural affix a morpheme? In a well-developed paragraph, suggest reasons for saying no as well as yes to both questions.

2. Notice that by the various criteria established thus far, *other* can be a noun (*Where are the others?*), a pronoun (*Others* [= "other people"] *came to pray*), or a determiner (*Other scholars expressed different views*). Does the fact that a word can belong to so many classes affect the usefulness of the classification system? Do these examples suggest that something other than class membership would be more useful in understanding English grammar?

4 | The English Verb System

The heart of every sentence is its verb. The verb takes language beyond merely naming things, for the verb carries assertive or predicating power; that is, along with their complements, verbs make up the predicates that enable us to make statements about the things we name. Without verbs, we'd be limited to making lists of persons, places, and things, and we wouldn't be able to say much of anything about them. As a native speaker of English, you regularly use verbs, as well as all other "parts of speech," in conformity to complex rules you probably didn't even know you were following. The purpose of this chapter and the next is to make you consciously aware of the intricate system of rules governing your use of English verbs.

THE VERB PARADIGM REVISITED

Chapter 2 introduced the concept of the inflectional paradigm as a way of identifying the words of English that belong to one class or another. We saw in Chapter 3 that some changes had to be made in the paradigmatic test for nouns, and it should come as no surprise that we will have to revise the requirements for membership in the verb class as well.

Our first approximation of the verb paradigm consisted of four forms: the uninflected stem, the -s form, the -ing form, and the -ed form. We noted that some verbs (e.g., *cut*) do not have an -ed form, and that some verbs have a fifth form that wasn't illustrated at all in the paradigm as presented at that point—for example, verbs like *take*, *write*, and *hide*. These verbs not only exhibit an internal vowel change instead of an -ed affix for past tense, but also accept an affix not listed at all in Chapter 2, the -en affix. Let's have a closer look at verb forms.

DISCOVERY ACTIVITY 4-1

Following the procedure illustrated by the models, complete the paradigm for the verbs listed. For each verb, make an entry in a column only if the form is actually different from those in all other columns.

Stem	Third Person Singular Present	Past	*-ing*	*-en*
walk	walks	walked	walking	—
cut	cuts	—	cutting	—
take	takes	took	taking	taken
try	_____	_____	_____	_____
go	_____	_____	_____	_____
eat	_____	_____	_____	_____
have	_____	_____	_____	_____
save	_____	_____	_____	_____
bring	_____	_____	_____	_____
fly	_____	_____	_____	_____
hit	_____	_____	_____	_____
create	_____	_____	_____	_____

1. What is the maximum number of forms for any one verb?
2. What is the lowest number?
3. In which columns do *all* the verbs have entries?
4. Think of any ten verbs other than *be*. Which two contrasts do all of them display?
5. Write a paradigmatic test for verbs.
6. For the verbs that have an entry in the *past* column but not in the *-en* column, to which column must you go for a form that fits this blank?

   I've _____ an XYZ.

7. For the verbs that have entries in neither the *past* nor the *-en* column, to which one must you go?
8. Along with new inventions we get new verbs. When we started fastening our clothes with slide fasteners, the verb *zip* (*up*) became part of our common vocabulary. How many different forms does it have altogether?

9. Write a definition of *regular verb*.
10. Why do you think children use forms like **bringed*, **buyed*, and **teached*?
11. If a new verb, say *sneach*, came into the language, would you expect *snaught* (like *taught*) or *sneached* (like *reached*)? Why?
12. Underline any of the following words that pass the paradigmatic test for verbs:

    member, always, desperate, specify, clarify, testify, verify, beautify, realize, stabilize, penalize, finalize, visualize

13. Can you think of any *-ify* words or any *-ize* words that are not verbs?
14. What class would you expect the words *bowdlerize* and *fructify* to belong to? Now check your dictionary. What class do they belong to?
15. What kind of affixes are *-ize* and *-ify*, and what can you use them for?

DEFINING THE VERB

Paradigms provide definitions. For example, we defined a noun as any word exhibiting at least one of the contrasts in a particular series. Later we added to the definition by defining nouns in terms of the specific structure class words that go with them. We can do the same for verbs. We can define a **verb** as any word that displays at least two of the contrasts, that is, has three of the five forms we have identified: stem, third person singular present, past, *-ing*, and *-en*. Specifically, we can stipulate that a word is a verb if it has a third person singular present (*-s*) inflection and an *-ing* inflection in contrast to a stem form, and that regular verbs have a past tense affix as well. To put it another way, *-s* and *-ing* are the formal contrasts that define the verb class, but some verbs may have other forms in addition to the criterial ones.

You saw in Chapter 3 that the names given to noun forms are not reliable guides to the meanings of those forms. A plural form doesn't always refer to more than one, and a singular doesn't necessarily signify only one. In short, we can use form as a criterion for deciding that a word belongs to the noun class, but we must be careful not to confuse the grammatical names of the forms, *singular* and *plural*, with number in the real world. Similarly, we can use form as a criterion for membership in the verb class, but we must be careful not to confuse the names *past* and *present* with time in the real world. As you will see, the familiar words *past* and *present*, when used to refer to grammatical devices, cannot be taken literally as equivalent to "past time" and "present time."

DISCOVERY ACTIVITY 4-2

If you have studied a Romance language, you may be aware of the relative poverty of verb inflections in English. You can see from the following chart, for example, that the Spanish verb *hablar* has six different forms for the present tense alone. There are different present tense forms for use with other verbs, but we will content ourselves with the six inflections displayed by one Spanish "regular -ar verb" to make some interesting discoveries about English. Study the chart; then answer the questions. The Spanish infinitive, *hablar*=English "(to) speak, talk." Note an important feature: Spanish *habla* (simple present tense) can be translated into English as "he/she/someone *talks*" or "he/she/someone *is talking*."

Spanish *Present* =	English *Present*	and/or *Pres. of be+talking*
hablo=	I talk	and/or I am talking
(familiar) hablas=	you talk	and/or you are talking
(formal) habla=	you talk	and/or you are talking
habla=	he/she/it talks	and/or he/she/it is talking
alguien habla=	A person talks	and/or a person is talking
hablamos=	we talk	and/or we are talking
(familiar) habláis=	you (plural) talk	and/or you (plural) are talking
(formal) hablan=	you (plural) talk	and/or you (plural) are talking
hablan=	they talk	and/or they are talking
La gente hablan=	People talk	and/or people are talking

1. How many different forms does the Spanish verb *hablar* display for present tense?
2. How many of these forms are different from the infinitive, *hablar*, the form glossed as "(to) speak, talk"?
3. How many different forms does the English verb *talk* display in the present tense? How many are different from the stem?
4. Does English have a present tense inflection for first or second person singular or for first, second, or third person plural of *talk*?
5. What is the only present tense inflection in English?
6. To say either "I talk" or "I am talking" in Spanish, you need only the verb form *hablo*; to say either "They talk" or "They are talking" you need only the verb form *hablan*. Why do you not need to specify the subject of the verb in Spanish?

7. If you say *She talks/speaks English*, does it mean or imply that she is actually talking at the present time?
8. Consider expressions like *He talks fast* or *He talks too much* or *He talks in a monotone*. Are you necessarily referring to current activity?
9. If I ask when your mother is leaving for Chicago and you answer, *Her plane leaves at eight*, what tense form are you using? Are you talking about something going on in the present time?
10. Write some brief sentences using third person singular present verb forms. Do not use auxiliaries or *be*. Can you put the word *now* or the phrase *at this moment* in any of them and still sound natural? (Compare: *He talks fast at this moment.*) Does the meaning change?
11. Does the English present tense form usually refer to or mean present time?
12. What are the meanings/uses of the simple present tense? Consider, in addition to the examples in (7), (8), and (9) sayings like *Time flies*, and *A stitch in time saves nine*. What other conventional uses do you know of?
13. Write a brief description of what you're engaged in at present. What forms did you use for reference to current (present) activity, that is, activity in progress right at the moment of discussion?

TIME AND TENSE

You can see from Discovery Activity 4-2 that **tense** is a concept of form, not of meaning. When we speak of **present tense**, we are referring to a grammatical feature, the form of a verb or auxiliary, not to time in the real world. In English, tense and real-world time are very poorly correlated, as this activity shows. You saw, for example, that English usually uses the simple present tense form to talk about habitual action or about future action, but usually not about what is taking place in the present. In Spanish, the simple present tense in *habla rapido* can be used to mean "he is talking," but in English, the simple present tense in *he talks fast* is unlikely to mean "he is talking." Similarly, *The plane leaves at eight* has a present tense form, but can refer to future time, as you saw in Discovery Activity 4-2, or to habitual behavior: *It leaves at eight every night*. Because present tense can also imply timelessness, it is used for eternal truths like *A stitch in time saves nine* and in discussions of literary works (*Hamlet tells Ophelia that he . . .*).

Just about the only use of the present tense that literally refers to present time is in play-by-play accounts like *Jones passes to Zywalevski*. To talk about present (current) activity, we almost always use forms of *be* plus an *-ing* form: *What are you doing (right now)? I am (in the process of) changing the baby*, or *I'm studying*.

Nor is there a one-to-one correspondence between **past tense** forms and past time. The sentence *If I had a dollar I would treat you* has two past tense forms, *had* and *would*, but it expresses the meaning "I *do not now, at this present time*, have a dollar and *cannot treat* you *now*." No doubt you agree that *I wish you were here* also means "now." Yet it uses *were*, a past tense form, to say so. To use the present tense form would result in ungrammatical sentences: **I wish you are here*; **I wish he is here*; **I wish I am there*.

So although English can talk about any and all the time periods that other languages can discuss, it has only two tense forms with which to do so: present and past, whose names, as you saw, are rather misleading in that they don't always correlate with real time. And although we can talk all we like about future time, English does not have a future tense to indicate future time. If you check the verb paradigm, you will see only five forms, none of which is labeled *future*. To see that there are only two tenses, make up a sentence with only a main verb (no auxiliary). Since there are only two forms, past and present, for showing tense (*John eats/ate*; *John cries/cried*) if you want to discuss the future you must add something to the sentence.

Although you may have been taught that *will* is "future tense," it is actually a present tense form, and in addition to its use to refer to the future, it can also be used to mean the present. For example, if the doorbell rings and someone says "That'll be Jane!," you understand it to mean "now." But the choice of form for reference to the future will depend on a variety of situational rather than linguistic circumstances. Of course it might be *will*, but it could also be a form of *be* followed by *going to* or *about to*, although these are not necessarily interchangeable or equally appropriate in all situations. For example, you can use either *John is going to jump* or *John is about to jump* if the event is near at hand, but if the jumping is to take place tomorrow, *is about to* seems an unlikely choice; and *John will jump* might be an appropriate answer to *What will happen if the door slams?* but probably not to *What's John doing on the window sill?*—which, of course, would elicit *he's going to . . .* or *he's about to . . . .*

DISCOVERY ACTIVITY 4-3

1. Look at the forms of *be* in the translation of *hablar* in Discovery Activity 4-2; then answer the following questions.
   a. What's the first person singular present form of *be*?
   b. What's the second person singular present form of *be*?
   c. What's the third person singular present form of *be*?
   d. What form is used for the plural for all persons in the present tense?
   e. How many different forms does *be* display in the present tense?

2. Look at the following data, then answer the questions that follow:

I spoke to her	I was speaking to her
You spoke to her	You were speaking to her
She/he/it spoke to her	She/he/it was speaking to her
We spoke to her	We were speaking to her
You two spoke to her	You two were speaking to her
They spoke to her	They were speaking to her

   a. How many different past tense forms does the verb *speak* have?
   b. Think of as many verbs as you can, other than *be*. How many past tense forms does each one have?
   c. How many past forms does *be* display? Name them.
   d. List all the forms of *be* that are marked for person, number, and tense.
   e. What two inflected forms of *be* are not included in your list?
   f. How many different forms does *be* have altogether?

IS *BE* A VERB?

As you saw in Discovery Activity 4-3, *be* is like a verb in that it exhibits contrasts for person, number, and tense, but the forms of *be* inflected for tense don't look anything like the stem: we say (at least in the standard varieties of the language) *she is*, not *she bees*, *we were*, not *we beed*. Moreover, *be* has altogether too many forms: there's no place in the paradigm for three distinct present tense forms and two distinct past tense forms. Having defined verbs in terms of a five-form paradigm, you might think that we would have to exclude *be*. But despite its uniqueness, *be* so often assumes the syntactic position and function of headword in a verb phrase that it makes sense to include it in the verb class, albeit as a one-item subset. In Chapter 5, you will see that *be* is not only a morphological oddity, but a syntactic eccentric as well.

DISCOVERY ACTIVITY 4-4

1. Consider the following constructions, which are marked with asterisks because although they may be grammatical in some varieties of English, they are ungrammatical in the standard varieties:

   *He strolling down the street   *I baking a cake
   *She talking to her mother   *You talking nonsense
   *We watching a movie   *They fighting

   a. In each non-sentence above, insert an appropriate form of *be*, then its contrasting tense form and observe the difference in time frame implied.
   b. Without the tense-carrying form of *be*, do the word strings above fall into any specific time period?
   c. Does the -*ing* inflection refer to any specific time period when not preceded by a tense-marked form of *be*?
   d. Considering your responses to (b) and (c), and the meaning of verb phrases like *was/were X-ing*, does it make sense to you to refer to the -*ing* form as a *present* participle?
   e. What sort of notion or meaning does -*ing* convey to you in general?
   f. Does *progressive form* or *durative form* seem to be an appropriate name for the -*ing* form? Why or why not?

2. Consider the following constructions, which are marked with asterisks because they are not grammatical for standard varieties of English although they are grammatical in some dialects:

   *Mary seldom spoken the truth.   *Mary never ridden on a train.

   a. Provide two different time frames for each of these word strings by inserting only a form of *have*.
   b. Does the -*en* inflection refer to a particular time period?

3. Consider the following sentence, then answer the questions that follow:

   She's been driving this car for fifteen years.

   a. Does the sentence imply that she still drives the car? Considering your response to this and to (1b) does it make sense to you to refer to *been* and other forms with -*en* as *past* participles?
   b. Doesn't the sentence also imply that she drove the car last year and the year before, and so on back fifteen years? Considering

your response to this and to (1c-d) does it make sense to you to refer to *driving* as a *present* participle?

4. Consider the following sentence, then answer the questions that follow:

Sally tells lies.

   a. What time frame do you think is implied by the sentence?
   b. Can you think of some ways to change the implication without making any change in the verb form?

5. Consider this sentence:

I've lived in Zilchville.

   a. Do you infer that I now live in Zilchville?
   b. Consider *I've lived in Zilchville for four years.* Do you now infer that I currently live in Zilchville?
   c. Is there any difference in the form of the verb phrase in the two sentences? What actually accounts for the difference in meaning or interpretation?

6. What does *used* mean in the following?
   a. This is the knife I *used* to cut the salami.
   b. I *used* to work in a Deli.

TIME AND ASPECT

Words like *past*, *present*, and *future* tend to obscure the immense complexity of time, real-world events, language, and the variety of ways they are related. Events don't happen in discrete blocks of time. Sometimes they are instantaneous, but they often begin and end at different times, they recur, endure, get interrupted, overlap. And some things we talk about are timeless. Many languages reflect such temporal features in their verbs, and some languages not only have dozens of tense forms to deal with specific time periods (past, present, and future) but also have many **aspect** forms to deal with temporal features or aspects like inception, completion, duration, repetition, frequency, and others.

If English is "deficient" in tense forms for time periods, it is equally deficient in aspect forms for temporal features. English has in the grammar of its verb phrase only two aspect forms, traditionally called the *present participle* and the *past participle*. A **present participle** always has the *-ing* inflection, and is therefore frequently called the **-ing form**, but the **past participle** takes a variety of forms, depending on the morphology of the individual verb, as you saw in Discovery Activity 4-1, questions 6 and 7. The verb form that fits the diagnostic "'*ve* frame" used in those questions is frequently called the **-en form**, even if it is not literally bearing an *-en* inflection. That is, *gone, done, had, hit,* and even *walked* are said to be *-en* forms when they are in the syntactic spot after *have* or its contracted forms, '*ve, 's,* and '*d,* as in *you've done it, she's hit it, he'd had it,* and *I've walked my feet off.*

Despite the deficiency of aspectual inflections for our verbs, we can and do discuss all of the temporal aspects that speakers of any other language can discuss, including inception, duration, completion, interruption, intermittence, and a host of others. But we use a variety of other devices besides inflection of the main verb. For example, instead of having a special aspect inflection to attach to the main verb to show "beginning" as an aspect of an event, as some languages do, we refer to its inception with verb phrases like *I began to cough* or *I started to cough.* It is common in English to use **supplementary verbs** (sometimes called **semi-auxiliaries**), like *begin, finish, keep (He kept [on] talking)* and *use (He used to work in the mines).* This *use,* of course, is a structure word, or grammatical morpheme, very much like an inflection, quite different from the lexical morpheme *use,* meaning "employ," as in *This is the knife I used to cut the salami.* If you say the two aloud, you will even hear a difference in pronunciation. The grammatical *used to* is pronounced "usta."

Perhaps the device we use most frequently in English for discussing temporal matters is the **adverbial.** *Sally tells lies* implies chronic or habitual mendacity. Without changing the verb form, however, we can change the implications by inserting appropriate adverbials: *Sally never tells lies; Sally sometimes tells lies; Sally frequently tells lies.* You can see that English does not rely on the verb alone to carry the burden of time reference. In short, despite the imbalance between time reference and tense and aspect forms, and notwithstanding the misleading names, native speakers automatically find the words to say what they mean about time, without even giving it a thought.

AUXILIARIES

Major form class words are often accompanied by structure class signals. Nouns are signaled by determiners and other structure words, including, for example, **quantifiers** (*all, a lot of*). Together, the structure class and form class words make working units or phrases, named for the form class word that is the headword of the phrase. The structure words that signal verb phrases are the **auxiliaries.** You may have learned to call them *helping verbs*, but a more accurate name might be *verb helpers*, since they themselves are always subservient to the verb. Although there can be a verb phrase without an auxiliary, there cannot be a verb phrase without a verb. In short, an auxiliary cannot be the headword of a verb phrase. Some auxiliaries are like verbs in their morphology; that is, some inflect exactly as verbs do. But they are sufficiently different from verbs in their syntactic behavior, as you will see in the following Discovery Activity, to justify their being placed if not outside the verb class altogether, then at least into a special subclass.

DISCOVERY ACTIVITY 4-5

Look at the following data; then answer the questions below.

She goes	*She shalls	She runs
She is going	*She is shalling	*She musts
She can go	*She cans go	She must run
She will go	*She is willing go	*She is musting run

1. How is the morphology of *shall, can,* and *will* different from the morphology of full verbs like *go*?
2. Are *may* and *must* like *shall* or like *go*?
3. How do you know that the *can* of *She cans beans* is not the same morpheme as the one in *She can go*?
4. Although we have the word *willing* that follows *is* in *She is willing to go*, this *willing* is not a verb and its *-ing* is not an inflection. What kind of affix is the *-ing* of *willing* and to what class does this *willing* probably belong? What syntactic evidence can you give in support?
5. Explain the difference between the two *willings* of *she is willing to go* and *she is willing her money to me*.

The Modals

One of the defining characteristics of the modal auxiliaries—*can, shall, will, may,* and *must*—is that they accept neither the third singular present tense nor the *-ing* inflection. When *can* is inflected, it is clearly a different morpheme, the full verb meaning "to put something into containers for future use." You might think that *will*, the base morpheme of *willing*, is the same morpheme as the *will* of *She will go*, and you could be right. But the "*seems very test*" will show that one of the *willings* is a derived adjective: *She seems very willing to go* (compare *She seems very eager/reluctant to go*). By changing the headword, however, we can show that the other *willing* is also not a modal, but a verb: *She is willing her money to me* is syntactically (and, by coincidence, semantically) equivalent to *She is leaving her money to me*. The verb *will* can be inflected with *-ing*, but the modal *will* cannot.

This inability to accept the definitive verb inflections requires us to exclude the modals from the verb class. The forms *could, should, would,* and *might* are in fact past tense forms of *can, shall, will,* and *may,* but the single contrast between the stem and the past form does not meet the paradigmatic requirement we established for verbs (that is, third singular present and *-ing* forms). *Must* is peculiar in that it has no past tense form, but the modals *need, dare,* and *ought* are even more peculiar than *must* in their behavior. It is beyond the scope of this book to provide detailed descriptions of idiosyncratic or eccentric forms, but you can see the difference for yourself by using these modals in some sentences, including negatives and questions.

DISCOVERY ACTIVITY 4-6

1. What meanings do you think are expressed or implied by the following modals?

We can go to the lake tomorrow.	We could go to the lake tomorrow.
What shall I do?	What should I do?
That will result in lost time.	That would result in lost time.
You may go.	You might go.
You must try much harder.	You must be very tired.

2. How would you characterize the difference in meaning between the members of each pair of sentences?
3. Why isn't it possible to interpret the two instances of *must* in the examples above as equivalent in meaning?
4. Does it make sense to you to treat *would, could, should* and *might* as forms of *will, can, shall,* and *may,* or do you perceive them as separate words?

5. Which of the sentences in question 1 are open to more than one interpretation?
6. Gather a dozen or so different sentences you have actually heard or read or used that illustrate a wide range of meanings and uses for modals. Can you and your classmates come to any consensus about what any of the modals mean or refer to? Does your dictionary help?
7. From the data you and your classmates collected, how many different senses or uses do you ascribe to each modal?
8. Have you any idea why these forms are called modals? Does your dictionary provide any useful information that would shed light on this matter?

Partly because of their history, *could*, *would*, *should*, and *might* can be considered past tense forms of *can*, *will*, *shall*, and *may*. But unlike inflected verbs and the **primary auxiliaries**, *have* and *be* (which have at least a loose relationship with time), and with the possible exception of *will* and *shall* when used to predict and/or promise future events, modals seem less obviously connected to temporal matters than to other considerations, as you have just seen. Discovery Activity 4-6 was designed to suggest the complexity of the grammatical device known as **modality**, a thorough treatment of which would encompass a whole book.

The remaining auxiliaries, *have*, *be*, and *do*, are morphologically like the main verbs, *have*, *be*, and *do*, in that they accept the full range of inflections. As auxiliaries, however, they are not headwords; hence, they do not predicate, as verbs do. You can see that the *have* in *He has washed the dog* and the *be* in *He is informing the boss* don't make statements about what he has or is, as would be the case with *He has the dog* and *He is the boss*. Auxiliaries can, however, "stand in" for verbs under certain conditions. That is, it is possible to assert something by saying *I will*, *I was*, or *I have* if a predicate has already been established: *Who will help me bake the bread?*; *Who was going to St. Ives?*; *Who has eaten my porridge?* And we use *do* as a substitute or **pro form** for a previously used or already mentioned verb, in somewhat the way we use a pronoun to substitute for an antecedent noun phrase. The second sentence in this paragraph, for example, says that auxiliaries "do not predicate, as verbs *do*," that is, "as verbs *predicate*." *Do* is also a pro form in sentences like *Harry had a ball and so did I*, and Sally *liked it, and I did too*.

DISCOVERY ACTIVITY 4-7

1. Consider the following data; then complete the activity.

He can go.	Can he go?	He can't go.
He should go.	Should he go?	He shouldn't go.
He has gone.	Has he gone?	He hasn't gone.
He is going.	Is he going?	He isn't going.

   a. What syntactic change was made in order to turn the statements above into questions answerable by yes or no?
   b. Make a yes/no question out of *he goes.*
      Make a yes/no question out of *he went.*
   c. What did you have to add to *he goes* and *he went* to make the yes/no questions?
   d. What other change did you have to make in the verb phrase?
   e. What was done to make the statements negative? Be specific.
   f. What do you have to do to make *he goes* negative?
   g. Make a hypothesis about when it is necessary to add a form of the auxiliary *do.*
   h. Test your hypothesis by writing some sentences of your own.
   i. Write a descriptive generalization (grammatical rule) covering yes/no questions and negatives in English.

2. Now look at the following data; then respond to the questions that follow.

She is a professor.	Is she a professor?	She isn't a professor.
	*Does she be a professor?	*She doesn't be a professor.

   a. In these sentences, is *be* an auxiliary?
   b. If necessary, revise your grammatical rule for when it is necessary to use *do* to make yes/no questions and negatives.

3. Now look at the following data; then discuss what is unique about *have.*

You have the time.	Do you have the time?	You don't have the time.
	Have you the time?	You haven't the time.

What *Do* Can Do

You have seen that there are two *haves* and two *bes*—the *have* and *be* that fill the verb function (*She has my car; He is my friend*) and the *have* and *be* that serve as primary auxiliaries (*have/has/had gone; is/was going*). There is yet another word with this kind of double identity. The question *Do you have the time?* illustrates one use of auxiliary *do*, the third type of auxiliary, called the **periphrastic auxiliary** because it adds an extra word that contributes no meaning of its own. That is, the American *Do you have the time?* is a periphrastic equivalent of the British *Have you the time?*

As Discovery Activity 4-7 shows, all speakers of English— British or American—need this periphrastic *do* to make certain yes/ no questions and negatives because verbs do not invert with subjects nor attract the negative particle. English no longer has structures like *He goes not,* *Goes he?* and *Goes he not?* Nor do we have *He goesn't/*Goesn't he?* Instead, we have *Does/doesn't he go?* and *He doesn't go.* In short, with the exception of those with *be*—and for British English, *have*—in the main verb function, all yes/no questions and negative sentences must contain an auxiliary form. *Be* is syntactically very odd: it acts like an auxiliary even when it's the main verb. If a modal or primary auxiliary is present, there is no need for *do*, hence *She can't go,* but not *She doesn't can go; She*

TABLE 4-1   A Structural View of the English Verb

STEM	THIRD SING. PRESENT	PAST	-ING	-EN	NUMBER OF CONTRASTS	NUMBER OF FORMS
talk	talks	talked	talking	—	3 (regular)	4
cut	cuts	—	cutting	—	2 (minimum)	3
take	takes	took	taking	taken	4 (maximum)	5

Like the noun paradigm, which does not specify a particular plural form, the verb paradigm does not guarantee, predict, or specify the actual form or particular nature of the contrast—only that some contrast is possible; hence:

STEM	THIRD SING. PRESENT	PAST	-ING	-EN
go	goes	went *goed	going	gone
have	has *haves	had *haved	having	—
do	/dəz/[a] */duz/	did */dud/	doing	/dən/ */dun/
dive	dives	dived dove	diving	—

[a]Slant lines indicate pronunciation. See Chapter 9.

TABLE 4-2   Summary: Inventory of Auxiliaries

1. Modals: *can/could, shall/should, will/would, may/might, must*
   a. Do not inflect for third singular present: **musts go.*
   b. Do not take *-ing* inflection: **musting.*
   c. Invert with subject for yes/no questions and attract negative particle: *You can do it. Can you do it? You can't do it.*
   d. Cannot assume headword position and function in verb phrase.

2. Primary Auxiliaries: *have* and *be*
   a. Inflect just as main verbs *have* and *be* inflect.
   b. Despite important "grammatical meaning" or function, do not have the same lexical content as the verbs *have* and *be*; hence, do not predicate.
   c. Invert with subject and attract negative particle: *He has gone. Has he gone? He hasn't gone.*

3. Periphrastic Auxiliary: *do*
   a. Inflects just as main verb *do* inflects.
   b. Is used as the auxiliary in yes/no questions and negatives, except where a modal, *have,* or *be* (as auxiliary or main verb) is present. Is also used for emphatic statements (*He does love you*) and as a pro form or substitute for a previously mentioned verb (*He passed the test and so did I*).
   c. Does not have the lexical content of main verb *do*; hence, does not predicate alone.

hasn't gone, but not **She doesn't has gone; She isn't going,* but not **She doesn't is going.* We also use forms of *do* to make emphatic statements. Sentences like *I did do what you asked, But it does do some good,* and *I do do the housework* exemplify the use of both emphatic *do* and main verb *do.*

THE SYNTAX OF THE VERB SYSTEM

You may be wondering why we need so many structure words for verb phrases, and in particular why the double identity of *have, be,* and *do.* Part of the answer is that the morphological rule limiting us to one inflection per stem makes it necessary to commandeer stems to inflect when we have complex or multiple meanings to convey. Since we cannot say **eatsening,* we must find something to carry the *-s,* the *-en,* and the *-ing;* hence, has been eating.

That being the case, it should be clear that the verb system in English is more than a matter of morphology. Thus far, we've been looking only at the forms and formal contrasts that define the verb and auxiliary classes but very little has been said about the syntactic arrangement of those items. Such a narrow treatment ignores the complex interaction of the items, the intricate set of relationships among the forms, and the effect of one form on another within the system. The summaries of this chapter in Tables 4-1 and 4-2 merely present a static list that fails to show that such phenomena as modality and aspect are not merely facts about form, but dynamic and interacting syntactic processes. In the next chapter, we'll look more closely at the syntactic facts about verb phrases.

STUDY QUESTIONS

1. What is the meaning of the verb *predicate*?
2. What is the maximum number of forms a verb can have? Name them.
3. What specific formal features are used for classifying a word as a verb?
4. What is anomalous about *be*?
5. What formal characteristics distinguish modals from other auxiliaries and from verbs?
6. In what ways besides form do auxiliaries differ from verbs?
7. What devices besides tense and aspect inflections does English use to imply or express features of time such as inception, duration, repetition, and the like? Give examples of your own.
8. What is the rationale for saying that the terms *past participle* and *present participle* are misleading?
9. How many tense forms are there in English? What are they?
10. How many aspect inflections are there in English? What are they?
11. Name the three classes of auxiliaries and the members of each class.
12. What do *periphrasis* and *periphrastic* mean in general? In reference to verb phrases? Refer to your dictionary, but answer in your own words.
13. What are the functions of periphrastic *do*? Exemplify each one.
14. In what sense does the verb paradigm constitute a grammatical rule?

FURTHER STUDY AND DISCUSSION

1. In a well-constructed paragraph, explain to someone who has not taken this course the distinction between time and the grammatical devices of tense and aspect. Support your discussion with examples of your own.
2. The modal auxiliaries are just a part of the complex concept of modality. Nevertheless, for the sake of discussion, assume that modals represent one of the grammatical devices for expressing modality. That being the case, how would you define *modality*? What notions would you have to include?

5 | The Syntax of the Verb System

In the previous chapter we looked at the morphology of the basic parts of the English verb phrase, but by now it should be obvious that the picture presented there leaves a great many questions unanswered. This chapter presents the grammatical facts in a slightly different light, which should provide more insight into the complexity of the verb system than a mere inventory of its members could possibly convey. In this chapter we will look at the various parts of the verb phrase not as individual forms, but as participants in phrases, syntactic arrangements or structures. This chapter introduces a "phrase structure" model of our verb system that stresses, as the name implies, the structure of the phrase rather than the word.

WHAT'S IN A VERB PHRASE?

You have already seen that in the case of noun phrases, a phrase can be realized as a single word, and the same thing is true of the verb phrase. A sentence like *The birds sang* has a one-word ("head-only") verb phrase, consisting of the tense-marked verb and nothing else. As its name implies, a verb phrase has a verb as its headword (commonly called the **main verb**) and may or may not include a variety of other things, including the semi-auxiliaries like *keep/keeps/kept*, mentioned in Chapter 4, adverbial modifiers like *seldom*, negative particles like *not*, and so on. It is beyond the scope of this book to discuss all of these potential participants; instead, we will just take **verb phrase** to refer to the verb headword plus accompanying modal and primary auxiliaries, and will take a closer look at their interaction. Like all grammatical structures, the verb phrase is governed by very strict rules, which you follow without even knowing you're doing so.

DISCOVERY ACTIVITY 5-1

Consider this sentence: *Mary goes crazy.*

1. Add a modal auxiliary to the sentence, but nothing else. What change must you make to the form of the headword (main verb)?
2. Instead of the modal, add the perfective (*-en*) aspect inflection to the verb. What other changes or adjustments did you make in the verb phrase?
3. What happens to the auxiliary *has* if you add a modal to the sentence now?
4. Instead of a modal or the perfective, add the progressive (*-ing*) aspect inflection to the verb. What adjustments did you make in the phrase?
5. What form does the auxiliary *be* assume?
6. Write your sentence with a modal and both the *-en* and the *-ing* aspects. What form of *have* does it contain?
7. In general, then, what effect does a modal auxiliary have on the auxiliary or verb stem that follows it?
8. Were you consciously aware of knowing the grammatical rule you just articulated?

The AUX Rule

The preceding activity was designed to make you aware of something called the **AUX rule** (or one formulation of it). Note that it is not called the *auxiliary rule*, because AUX is not exactly equivalent to the familiar term *auxiliary*. AUX, always expressed in capital letters, is a conventional cover symbol, which actually stands for whatever you do in the verb phrase to show tense, modality, and aspect. In order to make the "whatever" explicit, there is a formula that spells out exactly what configurations are possible in a verb phrase in an English sentence. The AUX rule looks like this:

$$AUX \rightarrow T \ (M) \ (PERF) \ (PROG)$$

The arrow is equivalent to "can be analyzed as" or "can be rewritten as." Compare $24 \rightarrow 3 \times 8$. Just as we can rewrite 24 as a multiplication operation of three times eight, we can rewrite AUX as a series of operations that result in a verb phrase—that is, a syntactic structure instead of a mathematical one. And just as we can analyze 8 as 4 + 4, we can analyze the parts of the AUX formula. For example, we can analyze T (for tense):

$$T \rightarrow \left\{ \begin{matrix} \text{Past} \\ \text{Present} \end{matrix} \right\}$$

That simply means that the T must be analyzed as a choice between past and present, the only tense forms we have in English. The analysis on the right side of the arrow is a kind of definition of the term on the left side; thus, you can say that the AUX rule defines tense as a choice between two contrasting forms, specifically, present and past.

Before going any further, let's look at the AUX rule again, and complete its analysis, or rewriting of all its parts:

$$\text{AUX} \rightarrow \text{T (M) (PERF) (PROG)}$$
$$T \rightarrow \left\{ \begin{matrix} \text{pres} \\ \text{past} \end{matrix} \right\}$$
$$\text{M} \rightarrow \text{can, will, shall, may,}$$
$$\text{must} \ldots$$
$$\text{PERF} \rightarrow \text{have + -en}$$
$$\text{PROG} \rightarrow \text{be + -ing}$$

You will note that in the AUX rule the T is the only element that is not surrounded by parentheses. That means that tense is the only feature of AUX that is absolutely required in a predicating verb phrase. The parentheses around the M (modal), are the conventional symbol for something that is optional. In other words, whereas all predicating verb phrases must have a tense, they are not required to have a modal. Modal is "defined" by a list of modals. (There are actually more modals, but for the sake of simplicity we'll look only at the prototypical members of the class.) We don't have to list *could, would, should,* or *might,* because they are the past tense forms of *can, will, shall,* and *may,* and in projecting a sentence, *past + can* will result in *could, past + will* will result in *would, past + shall* will yield *should,* and *past + may* will emerge as *might.* You have seen that tense form is not always an indicator of time, especially in the case of modals. Instead, modals generally reflect a speaker's perceptions about degrees of capability, possibility, probability, obligation, feasibility, certainty, doubt, and the like, and a change in the tense form of a modal is more likely to reflect a difference in that sort of meaning than a shift in temporal

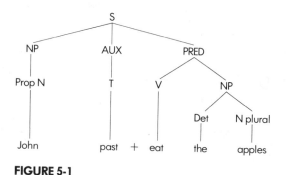

FIGURE 5-1

reference. For example, many speakers judge that *we might get there by tomorrow* implies less certainty than *we may get there by tomorrow*, but both sentences refer to the same future possibility, rather than to past and present time.

Now look at the next two items in the AUX rule formula, PERF and PROG, the aspects. Like the modals, grammatical aspects are optional, as their enclosure in parentheses indicates. That means that not all verb phrases are required to have aspect indicators. The AUX rule names and defines each aspect, independently of tense, as a two-part structure consisting of a primary auxiliary plus an inflection. It defines the **perfect aspect** (PERF) as a form of auxiliary *have* plus an inflection to attach to the following stem and the **progressive aspect** (PROG) as a form of auxiliary *be* plus an inflection to attach to the main verb.

Although this chapter deals only with AUX and its effect on the structure of verb phrase, let's look at a simplified phrase structure analysis, or "tree diagram" of a sentence, *John ate the apples.*

The tree diagram in Figure 5–1 shows that a sentence (S) is factored into a noun phrase (NP), the AUX, and a predicate (PRED) consisting of the verb headword and any complements, in this sentence a determiner (Det) and a plural noun. Each of these items is further analyzed until no further analysis can occur below it, at which point the lexical items of the sentence are inserted. The final string consists of *John past + eat the apples.* When we add *past* to *eat* we get *ate*, a "head-only" verb phrase. If we had wanted to project *John eats the apples* we would have put *pres* instead of *past* under the T in the diagram.

Examine the following tree diagrams and read the accompanying exposition; then use these as models as you work out some verb phrases of your own in Discovery Activity 5-2.

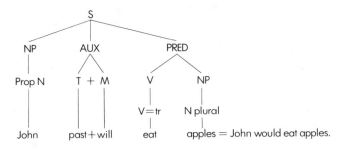

FIGURE 5-2

You can see from Figure 5-2 and Figure 5-3 that whatever comes after a modal—whether auxiliary or verb—will appear in its stem form. V-tr means "transitive verb," that is, one followed by an NP, the grammatical object.

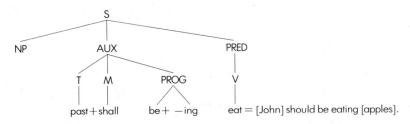

FIGURE 5-3

Figure 5-3 demonstrates that after the modal, the stem form of *be* remains, and the stranded *-ing* is added to the next stem in line. (Note that here and in the following examples, irrelevant parts are left out.)

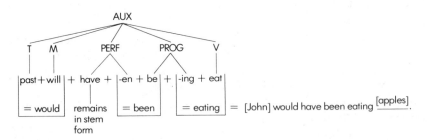

FIGURE 5-4

Figure 5-4 shows that after a modal, the next stem will not be inflected. The stranded *-en* attaches itself to *be* and the stranded *-ing* must move to the headword, the main verb.

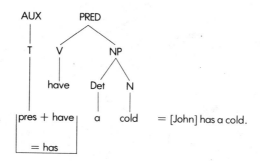

FIGURE 5-5

In Figure 5-5, *have* is not an auxiliary; that is, it is not part of aspectual *have + -en*. In this example, *have* is the headword, hence, the predicating verb.

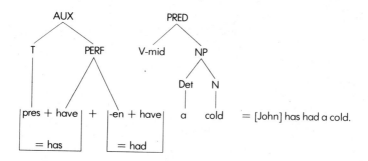

FIGURE 5-6

In Figure 5-6, *have* is part of PERF and *have* is also the predicating verb, which emerges as *had* when *-en* is added to the stem.

Figure 5-6 clearly illustrates the difference between tense and time: even though John's cold was in the past and is now gone, the auxiliary *have* is in the present tense form.

In the examples in Figure 5-7, *be* is part of PROG and is also in the headword function.

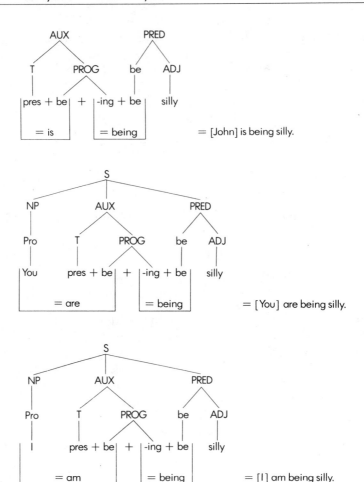

FIGURE 5-7

DISCOVERY ACTIVITY 5-2

1. Draw a tree diagram like that in Figure 5-7, with *I* as subject, but substitute *past* for *pres*. What will be the resulting sentence?

2. Draw two new diagrams based on the diagram from question 1, but leave out PROG. Put only T under AUX. Put *pres* under T in one diagram and *past* in the other. Put a third-person singular subject pronoun under the NP instead of *I*. What sentences will result?

3. For each of the following diagrams, figure out what the resulting sentence will be. It may help to draw boxes around the elements that must be added together. Remember: Any item after the modal

will be in stem form because a modal "absorbs" the tense inflection and leaves nothing stranded. (V-int means "intransitive verb," one that can predicate without a complement.)

a.

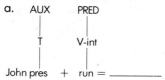

John pres + run = _____

b.

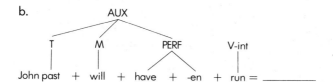

John past + will + have + -en + run = _____

c.

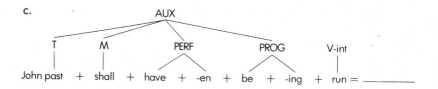

John past + shall + have + -en + be + -ing + run = _____

d.

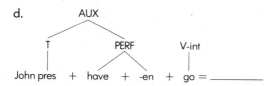

John pres + have + -en + go = _____

e.

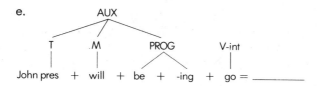

John pres + will + be + -ing + go = _____

f.

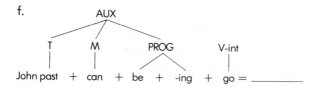

John past + can + be + -ing + go = _____

4. In the following diagrams, supply any missing parts; then write out the resulting sentences. Note that the items you put into the diagram

will determine what the resulting sentence will be. Remember to always select items in exactly the same order as they appear in the AUX rule. Otherwise, you will get ungrammatical strings of items. Here is the AUX rule and its analysis for your reference:

$$\text{AUX} \rightarrow \text{T (M) (PERF) (PROG)}$$

$$\text{T} \rightarrow \left\{ \begin{array}{c} \text{pres} \\ \text{past} \end{array} \right\}$$

$$\text{M} \rightarrow \text{ can, will, shall, may, must . . .}$$

$$\text{PERF} \rightarrow \text{have +-en}$$

$$\text{PROG} \rightarrow \text{be +-ing}$$

a.
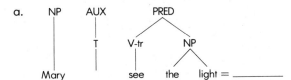

b.
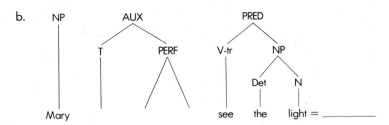

c. Change the tense of the sentence in (b), but nothing else:

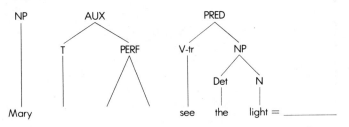

d. Change the aspect of the sentence in (b), but nothing else:

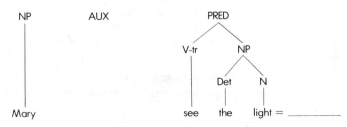

e. Change the tense and the aspect of the sentence in (b):

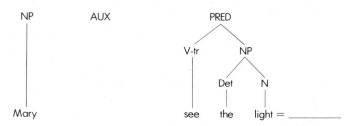

NP   AUX   PRED

                                V-tr   NP

                                            Det   N

Mary   see   the   light = _____

5. On separate sheets of paper, draw tree diagrams projecting ten sentences of your own. *Do not* think up the sentences first. Instead, put eligible items into the diagram and let your choices determine what sentences will result. If you change only one item of the AUX rule each time, you could get at least sixteen different sentences with the same subject and verb. Try it and see.

    Note that there is a subset of verbs which ordinarily do not take the progressive aspect. For example, we are unlikely to say **I am knowing the answer.* If you use a verb of that kind you will get unacceptable sentences because the AUX rule, in the simplified form we are using here, does not distinguish between the sub-categories of verb types. If you get an unacceptable sentence by using PROG on an inappropriate verb, try again with a new verb choice.

What the AUX Rule Tells Us

Discovery 5-2 shows how useful the AUX rule really is. A formula with only five terms, the AUX rule specifies in brief but explicit terms what native speakers unconsciously know about the basic structure of a predicating verb phrase in English. The AUX rule makes it clear that:

1. A verb phrase must have tense, but it is not required to have a modal or indicators of aspect.
2. Tense will always be reflected in the first item in the verb phrase, whether it's a modal, one of the aspect auxiliaries (the primaries, *have* and *be*), or the predicating verb.
3. The headword (main verb) will always come last, and will have a tense inflection only if there are no auxiliary forms, that is, if it's the only verbal item in the verb phrase.
4. The tenses are mutually exclusive, but the aspects are not; that is, only one tense is possible, but two aspects (or one or none) can appear in a verb phrase.
5. The items listed can appear only in the specified order.

Working with the AUX rule, you can see that each item in the verb phrase has a kind of "domino effect" on what follows. If there is nothing but T (tense) in the AUX, there will be no auxiliaries in the verb phrase, and the job of carrying the tense will fall to the headword. A modal (M) will force the next item to appear in stem form because the modal "uses up" the tense inflection, leaving nothing to apply to the next item in line. If the sentence has PERF or PROG, the verb phrase will have to have primary auxiliaries so that there will be enough stems to carry both the tense and the aspect inflections. Finally, PERF and PROG are not merely "aspect inflections," as the previous chapter implied, but phrases, two-part syntactic structures consisting of an auxiliary plus another stem to carry the aspect inflection itself.

In Discovery Activity 5-2, you saw that we can create sixteen *different* sentences with a single subject and predicating verb. As a matter of fact, the illustrative list below could be made even longer by using all the modals in turn.

    1 & 2: T only: X eats/ate.

    3 & 4: T and M: X may/might eat.

    5 & 6: T and PERF: X has/had eaten.

    7 & 8: T and PROG: X is/was eating.

    9 & 10: T, PERF, and PROG: X has/had been eating.

  11 & 12: T, M, and PERF: X may/might have eaten.

  13 & 14: T, M, and PROG: X may/might be eating.

  15 & 16: T, M, PERF, and PROG: X may/might have been eating.

DISCOVERY ACTIVITY 5-3

    1. For each of the following sentences, specify the tense and name all the other AUX elements. Underline or spell out the stem of the headword (e.g., the stem of *told* is *tell*). Ignore any modifiers (e.g., *always*).

Examples
Mary is my friend. Present tense only. (Be is functioning as the headword, not as part of PROG, hence, not part of AUX.)

Mary has always <u>worked</u> in the mines. *Present tense and PERF; main verb is work.*

    a. I've lost everything. _____
    b. Sam's seeing Esmerelda on a steady basis. _____
    c. Sam's been hitting the books. _____
    d. Esmerelda must have been dancing. _____
    e. John has repeatedly told lies. _____
    f. Sam's had his last exam. _____
    g. Everybody tells white lies. _____
    h. Esmerelda was dancing up a storm. _____
    i. John's been telling white lies about Esmerelda. _____
    j. John could do better. _____
    k. Mary is doing her homework. _____
    l. John will be home by tomorrow. _____
    m. You would look good in that outfit. _____
    n. The medium was holding a seance. _____
    o. She's gone to heaven. _____
    p. By Friday we will have been studying grammar for six weeks.
2. In the following sentences, change only the tense:
    a. Sam's been seeing Esmerelda. _____
    b. Sam's doing the dishes. _____
    c. You'll like Mary. _____
    d. You lose everything. _____
    e. I'm going home. _____
3. In the following sentences, change only the aspect. If more than one change is possible, you need give only one. Do not add or delete modals.

Example
I'm going mad. <u>I go/have been going/have gone mad.</u>

    a. She's had very bad luck. _____
    b. The weather is nice. _____
    c. I'll be seeing you again. _____
    d. You should be ashamed of yourself. _____
    e. I planned the party carefully. _____
4. With the AUX rule as formulated in this chapter, you could get (a) but not (b) of the following pairs. Why?
    a. He finished the book.   b. He finished reading the book.
    a. He started the book.   b. He started writing the book.
    a. He talks.   b. He keeps talking.
    a. He is slim.   b. He used to be slim.
5. Why couldn't the following sentence be included in question 2? <u>You must be dreaming!</u>

If question 5 in Discovery Activity 5-3 stumped you, don't feel bad. The answer is simply that *must* doesn't have a past tense form. If you want to use *must* for events in the past, you have to do it by adding perfective aspect, because there is no contrasting tense form. That is, we say *You must have been dreaming*, not *You musted be dreaming*, and surely not *You must were dreaming*, since the latter changes the tense of the second item in the phrase instead of the first. And note that *must* cannot be used in the sense of "required to" for something in the past. For example, you can say, concerning some time in the future, *I must see the dentist*, but if you were obliged to see your dentist yesterday, you have to paraphrase it as *I had to see my dentist*, not *I musted see*. And you can't use *I must have seen*, because that means you probably did.

DISCOVERY ACTIVITY 5-4

1. Analyze the verb phrases in the sentences below; then specify what items are in each verb phrase.

   Example
   Charlie was mending fences. past + be + -ing + mend

   a. That advertisement is seen everywhere. _____
   b. That advertisement was seen everywhere. _____
   a. He has been seen with some famous people. _____
   b. He had been seen with some famous people. _____
   a. The letters are being written. _____
   b. The letters were being written. _____

2. Does the AUX rule allow for *be* to be followed by an *-en* form?
3. What form does the AUX rule require after *be*?
4. Does the AUX rule let *be* have two auxiliary functions in one verb phrase?
5. Of the sentences below, the (a) sentences conform to the AUX rule but the (b) sentences, like the ones in (1), above, do not. For each sentence, analyze the verb phrase. Then complete the activity.

   a. Pam took the cat to the vet. _____
   b. The cat was taken to the vet by Pam. _____
   a. Pam is taking the cat to the vet. _____
   b. The cat is being taken to the vet by Pam. _____
   a. The waiter pours the coffee. _____
   b. The coffee is poured by the waiter. _____
   a. The waiter poured the coffee. _____
   b. The coffee was poured by the waiter.

6. What is added to each verb phrase in the change from the (a) sentences to the (b) sentences in (5)?
7. Does the change from the (a) to the (b) sentences in (5) constitute a tense change?
8. Besides a change in the verb phrase, what else was done to change the (a) sentences into the (b) sentences in (5)?
9. In going from the (a) to the (b) sentences, what remains *unchanged*?

BEYOND AUX

In Discovery Activity 5-4, all the sentences in (1) and the (b) sentneces in (5) are in the **passive voice**, whose verb phrases cannot be accounted for by the AUX rule alone. Their verb phrases do not conform to the possible combinations permitted by the AUX rule. To begin with, the AUX rule says that *be* will always be followed by a form inflected with *-ing*, yet in the sentences of (1) and the (b) sentences of (5), *be* is followed by a form inflected with *-en*. Moreover, the AUX rule predicts only one instance of *be* as an auxiliary, but *are being written* appears in (1) and *is being taken* in (5), both of which have two instances of *be* in auxiliary functions.

It is typical of many passive voice sentences to have an active voice counterpart, an obviously different syntactic structure, that is a near paraphrase; that is, *The coffee is poured by the waiter* and *The waiter pours the coffee* are alike in meaning despite differences in form. Not only is there a radical difference in the verb phrase, where *be* is followed by a perfective form, but unlike the active counterpart, whose subject NP names an active agent, *the waiter*, the passive has as its subject an NP referring to a passive entity, *coffee*, which is affected by the action, not performing it.

The Passive Construction

Given that passive sentences occur in both the present and the past tense (*is/was poured*) it is obvious that passive voice is independent of tense but always requires perfective aspect. We could write the AUX rule to project this structure:

AUX → T (M) (PERF) (PROG) (PASS)

This revised rule predicts that verb phrases can occur with another feature, passive (PASS), in addition to the items enumerated in the original AUX rule. Then, as PERF and PROG are rewritten as *have + -en* and *be + -ing*, PASS would be rewritten as *be + -en*. But such a revision of the AUX rule would not adequately describe passive constructions. In failing to mention subject and object functions, the rule not only overlooks the special relationship between transitive verbs and their objects, but also ignores the connection between certain passive voice sentences and their active counterparts. We need a rule that will recognize that relationship and reveal a connection between the two kinds of sentence. A **passive voice rule** might look like this:

$$\text{NP}_1 + \text{AUX} + \text{V-tr} + \text{NP}_2 \Rightarrow \text{NP}_2 + \text{AUX} + \text{be} + \text{-en} + \text{V-tr} + (\text{by NP}_1)$$

This rule specifies that a passive sentence is related to a possible or hypothetical active version, whose subject NP (NP_1) refers to an active agent, whose verb is transitive, and whose object NP (NP_2) names an entity that is affected by the action. Addition of *be* and the perfective aspect inflection forces a change in the grammatical relationships such that the object of the verb in the hypothetical active sentence must move out of the predicate and become the subject of a passive version. The rule further stipulates that the agent of the action, now marked by an overt signal, *by*, will move into the predicate of the passive sentence. And finally, it says that the "*by* phrase," which incorporates the active agent, may sometimes be dropped, as in *The coffee was poured*. In short, an entire passive voice sentence can often be made from the active version's predicate alone.

In Table 5-1 the passive voice rule is applied to three basic sentences. As you look at the sentences, notice that all these changes are accomplished in the maneuver that the rule summarizes. Then use this maneuver as you work through Discovery Activity 5-5.

DISCOVERY ACTIVITY 5-5

1. Write the passive voice rule across the top of a sheet of paper. Following the models given in Table 5-1, copy out each sentence below with its verb phrase fully analyzed as shown in the examples. (Don't try to do this in your head.) Then complete the passivization as shown in Table 5-1.

Example
John is mending fences $= \text{NP}_1$ pres $+$ be $+$ -ing $+$ mend NP_2
John has mended fences $= \text{NP}_1$ pres $+$ have $+$ -en $+$ mend NP_2

TABLE 5-1 Passive Sentences

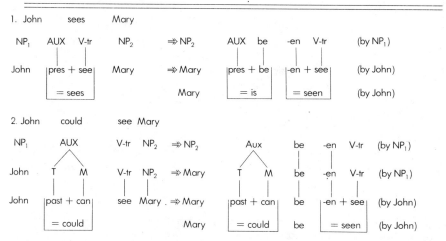

1. John   sees   Mary

NP₁	AUX	V-tr	NP₂	⟹ NP₂	AUX	be	-en	V-tr	(by NP₁)

John   ⌐pres + see⌐   Mary   ⟹ Mary   ⌐pres + be⌐   ⌐-en + see⌐   (by John)
        ⌊ = sees ⌋   Mary   ⌊ = is ⌋   ⌊ = seen ⌋   (by John)

2. John   could   see Mary

NP₁   AUX   V-tr   NP₂   ⟹ NP₂   Aux   be   -en   V-tr   (by NP₁)

John   T   M   V-tr   NP₂   ⟹ Mary   T   M   be   -en   V-tr   (by NP₁)

John   ⌐past + can⌐   see   Mary   ⟹ Mary   ⌐past + can⌐   be   ⌐-en + see⌐   (by John)
        ⌊ = could ⌋   Mary   ⌊ = could ⌋   be   ⌊ = seen ⌋   (by John)

Notice that whatever follows a modal takes the stem form, hence *could be seen*. Notice, too, that the passive voice *does not* affect tense. The tense in the active sentence will surface unchanged in the passive version. In (2), if the active sentence had been *pres + can + see = can see*, the passive sentence would have become *pres + can + be + -en + see*, hence, *can be seen*.

3. John has seen Mary

NP₁   AUX   V-tr   NP₂   ⟹ NP₂   Aux   be   -en   V-tr   (by NP₁)

John   T   PERF   see   Mary   ⟹ Mary   T   PERF   be   -en   V-tr   (by NP₁)

John   ⌐pres + have⌐   ⌐-en + see⌐   Mary   ⟹ Mary   ⌐pres + have⌐   ⌐-en + be⌐   ⌐-en + see⌐   (by John)
        ⌊ = has ⌋   ⌊ = seen ⌋   Mary   ⌊ = has ⌋   ⌊ = been ⌋   ⌊ = seen ⌋   (by John)

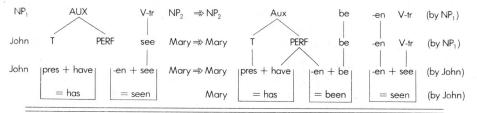

   a. Susan carries the ball.
   b. Susan is carrying the ball.
   c. Someone has sent those men to the moon.
   d. The administration promoted Fosnick.
   e. Television fosters violence in children.
   f. Everybody there saw the fight.
   g. Fosnick had taken the dog to the vet.
   h. Somebody paints that building every year.
   i. Somebody is washing the dishes.
2. In addition to the insertion of *be + -en*, passivization requires you to make another adjustment in some of the verb phrases. In which ones and why? (Look at sentence 1c, for example.)

3. Turn the following into passive voice sentences without writing out the analysis.
   a. The assistants do all the work.
   b. The assistants have done all the work.
   c. The assistants are doing all the work.
   d. The assistants did all the work.
   e. The assistants had done all the work.
   f. The assistants were doing all the work.
   g. The assistants can do all the work.
   h. The assistants could do all the work.
4. Convert the following passive sentences to active voice. You will have to supply subject NPs for those sentences where agents have been deleted.

Example
Smoking is prohibited.=Somebody prohibits smoking. (In this case, smoking=an NP, not a verb. Compare "It is prohibited" and "Somebody prohibits it.")

   a. The floor has been swept.
   b. We were met at the airport by a cheering crowd.
   c. We were clobbered!
   d. The children are being put to bed.
   e. Their meetings are held on Tuesdays.
   f. Fosnick is being held by the authorities.
   g. Everybody in the office is blamed for his mistakes.
   h. The Coast Guard has restricted swimming in this area.
5. Study the following sentences; then answer the questions.

Into each life some rain must   Some rain must fall into each
    fall.   life.

   a. Are the verb phrases different in any way?
   b. What is the subject of *must fall* in both sentences?
   c. Why can't *Some rain must fall into each life* be passivized?
6. Look at the following sentences. Then answer the questions.

By morning, the revelers had been drunk for hours.
By morning, all the wine had been drunk.

   a. In one sentence, *drunk* is not a verb. To what class does it belong, and how can you prove it?
   b. To which sentence can you add another "by phrase"?
   c. Which of the two sentences is not in the passive voice?
7. In the following sentences, convert active to passive and passive to active. Supply missing agents and/or delete agents if the result sounds strange with a "by phrase."

a. The lights have been turned out.
b. Mary and Sue are giving a party for the contest winner.
c. Mary and Sue were unceremoniously ushered out of the room.
d. Mary and Sue are always scolding John and Sam.

Postscript on Passive

The passive is useful when a speaker or writer wants the emphasis on the affected thing or person, or when the action is more important than the identity of the actor. It's handy, too, when the identity of the agent is unknown. It would sound strange if someone ran in and exclaimed "Some person or persons unknown have stolen my car!" instead of "My car's been stolen!" The passive can also help writers avoid "top heavy" sentences that result from heavily modified noun phrases in the subject position. Instead of *The woman who used to live next door to us many years ago when we lived in New York painted it,* which is difficult to interpret because the predication is suspended for so long, the passive puts the predicate right up front: *It was painted by the woman who lived . . .*

Discovery Activity 5-5 shows that the passive construction is not merely a stylistic rearrangement, as is the case in *Into each life some rain must fall* versus *Some rain must fall into each life,* where the subject remains *some rain.* Rather, it changes the grammatical relationship between the NPs and the verb, making the subject an inert, passive entity, affected by a completed action or process but not participating in it. The passive voice thus depicts stasis rather than process. Moreover, because it allows us to delete the agent of the action, the passive voice depersonalizes the message, and is therefore appropriate, for example, for laboratory reports, a genre where the observer's identity must not intrude on the observations themselves.

SUMMARY

I. The AUX rule covers tense, modals, and aspect.
  A. Tense
    1. Form/Structure
      a. Two only, present and past.
      b. Usually, but not invariably, manifested in affixes (note

past tense forms of irregular verbs and of modal auxiliaries).

c. Affects only the first item in the verb phrase.

2. Function/Meaning/Semantics: Despite their names, only very loosely correlated with specific time periods.

B. Modals

1. Form/Structure

a. Inflect for past only; do not take third singular present or progressive.

b. The form following a modal is never inflected because the modal absorbs the tense marker.

2. Function/Meaning/Semantics: Express perceptions of the degree of certainty, possibility, probability, likelihood, obligation, permissibility, ability, and others.

C. Aspect

1. Form/Structure

a. Two only, perfective and progressive.

b. Manifested in two-part syntactic structures, an auxiliary followed by an inflected stem.

2. Function/Meaning/Semantics: Contribute to the expression of perceived temporal features like duration, beginning, ending, and others.

II.   The distinction between tense and aspect rests partly on:

A. Structure

1. a. Tense is a one-item fact of morphology, affecting only the first item in a verb phrase.

b. The aspects are two-item syntactic structures consisting of an auxiliary form (*have* or *be*) plus an affix that attaches to the next stem in the phrase.

2. a. A verb phrase must have tense, but cannot have both tenses.

b. A verb phrase is not required to have aspect, but can have both aspects in the same phrase, or one, or none at all.

3. a. The item after a modal is never inflected.

b. The item after auxiliary *have* or auxiliary *be* is *always* inflected because aspects are two-part structures and the affix has to appear somewhere.

B. Meaning and Reference

1. a. Even though the tenses do not show one-to-one cor-

respondence with time, they are named for specific time periods.

    b. The aspects are not named for specific time periods, but for other temporal features that can best be characterized as inception, duration, and the like.

2. a. In English, real-world temporal reference is seldom expressed exclusively in the verb phrase alone.

    b. A wide variety of lexical and grammatical structures, including (but not limited to) adverbs and adverbial phrases and clauses, can be used to make temporal references.

III. Voice

  A. The AUX rule accounts for active voice only: T (M) (PERF) (PROG).

  B. The passive voice rule adds (PASS) rewritten as *be* + *-en*.

    1. Form/Structure: Must have *be* plus *-en/-ed* in addition to items predicted by AUX.

    2. Function/Meaning/Semantics

      a. NP that names the item affected by the action, not the NP that names an agent, is the grammatical subject.

      b. Is impersonal, because it permits deletion of agents.

STUDY QUESTIONS

1. How many tense forms does the English verb have? Name them.
2. How many aspect forms can an English verb phrase have?
3. How does the AUX rule define tense?
4. How does the AUX rule define the aspects?
5. What is the only obligatory element in AUX?
6. Why isn't it necessary to list *could*, *would*, *should*, and *might* with the modals in the AUX rule?
7. What form does the item after the modal always assume, and why?
8. What is peculiar about the modal *must*?
9. Describe the structure of the hypothetical active voice counterpart of any passive voice sentence.
10. What can be deleted from a passive voice sentence?
11. Describe the verb phrase of a passive voice sentence and specify how it differs from a verb phrase predicted by AUX.
12. Is the AUX rule a rule of English grammar? Why or why not? Is the passive voice rule? Why or why not?

FURTHER STUDY AND DISCUSSION

Some people used to say that passive sentences are simply stylistic varia-tions of active counterparts. Citing a perceived or putative equivalence in meaning between some pairs, they suggested that such pairs might be two different surface manifestations of one underlying structure. Do you think the following pairs are equivalent in meaning? Provide some examples of your own. Then, in a well-developed paragraph, comment on the issue in any way you like.

a. Beavers build dams.   b. Dams are built by beavers.
a. I write books.   b. Books are written by me.
a. Elephants eat peanuts.   b. Peanuts are eaten by elephants.

6 | Adjectives, Adverbs, and Qualifiers

Traditional grammars of English usually define nouns and verbs in semantic or notional terms: nouns name persons and things; verbs refer to actions and states of being. Adjectives and adverbs, on the other hand, are usually defined in terms of what they do grammatically rather than what they refer to or mean: adjectives modify nouns; adverbs modify adjectives, verbs, and other adverbs. These observations are not false, but they can be misleading, because they do not specify defining criteria. Because of their vagueness, they are not helpful to the beginning student of grammar, and contemporary linguists have tried to establish more precise criteria for classifying and defining groups of words. This task is not difficult for nouns and verbs because a high percentage of nouns and 100 percent of verbs can pass the paradigmatic tests. Moreover, nouns and verbs combine with different sets of structure words to form the noun and verb phrases they head.

The task of identifying adjectives and separating them from adverbs, however, is a bit more complicated, because many adjectives do not inflect for degree, while some adverbs do. Therefore, the ability or failure to inflect with -er and -est does not provide sufficient basis for exclusion from or inclusion in either class. Furthermore, -ly, the derivational ending most commonly associated with adverbs, characterizes only a subset of the adverbs and is commonly used to derive adjectives as well, as you saw in Chapter 2. In addition, some of the structure words that accompany adjectives can also accompany some adverbs. And if all this didn't provide headache enough, some of the structure words themselves (including *very* and *too*) have traditionally, but mistakenly, been called adverbs. This chapter will try to establish some objective criteria for sorting out these various classes.

CAUSES OF CONFUSION

The line between adjectives and adverbs is not clear, and there is a history of constant drift between the two classes. Normally, speakers of standard varieties of English add -ly to adjectives to make them available for use in adverbial jobs: *happy, happily*. But in some varieties of English, speakers ignore this distinction and use one form for both functions. To the consternation of purists, others "overcorrect" and use the adverbial form where most standard speakers would choose adjectives, and we get expressions like the much maligned *I feel badly*. Moreover, even speakers of standard English use. words like *funny* (clearly an adjective on formal grounds) in positions they otherwise "reserve" for adverbs. For example, although they say *He talks constantly*, not *constant*, they don't say that someone talks *funnily*, but *funny*. The words *fast* and *straight* are but two of many others that behave like *funny*: we stand *straight*, not *straightly, and we walk *fast*, not *fastly.

There is further confusion in the case of words like *deep* and *late*, which not only belong to both classes but are used adverbially without -ly in some environments but require the -ly in others. Compare *He came late* and *He hasn't been here lately*, where both *late* and *lately* are adverbial; or *drink deep* and *feel deeply*, where *deep* and *deeply* are both adverbial.

DIAGNOSTIC TEST FRAMES FOR ADJECTIVES AND ADVERBS

In order to sharpen the functional definitions of adjectives and adverbs of traditional grammars, linguists devised the **diagnostic test frame** and **substitution tests** to supplement formal criteria and function word signals as means for distinguishing one form class from another. In standard English, certain verbs cannot predicate alone but will accept complements only from the adjective class. A second group also requires complements, but will accept only adverbs and prepositional phrases. A third set does not require a complement at all, but will accept adverbial modifiers. The behavior of these verbs enables us to separate adjectives from adverbs. Moreover, the test frames reveal that some of the words traditionally thrown in with the adverbs actually belong in a set of structure words.

DISCOVERY ACTIVITY 6-1

1. To find out the distribution of the members of these three classes, try inserting them in the frames. Words that work in any of the frames in (A) are adjectives. Those that work in the frames in (B) are adverbs.

    A. The <u>course</u> seems <u>easy</u>.
       The <u>sweet</u> (noun) seems very <u>sweet</u>.
       The _____ (noun) seems more _____ than I expected.

       The _____ (noun) seems as _____ as . . .
    B. It/she/he sneaks/sneaked <u>homeward</u>_____.

       It/she/he resides/resided _____.

       It/she/he behaves/behaved _____.

       It/she/he vanishes/vanished _____.

       It happens/happened _____.

2. Test the words listed below. If a word works with *seem*, label it *Adj.*; if a word works with any of the verbs in (1B), label it *Adv.*; if it works with both, it belongs to both classes.

sweet ___	there ___	well ___	elsewhere ___
good ___	bad ___	sad ___	sadly ___
straight ___	narrow ___	soon ___	sometime ___
fast ___	now ___	clockwise ___	somewhere ___
homeward ___	strong ___	upward ___	somehow ___
forever ___	then ___	quickly ___	friendly ___

3. Do(es) any of the following work alone in any of the test frames? very, somewhat, rather, extremely, quite.

Discovery Activity 6-1 shows that "linking" verbs like *seem*, *taste*, *sound*, and *feel* always take as complements prototypical **adjectives** like *sweet*, which inflect for degree (*sweeter*, *sweetest*) and occur as heads in adjective phrases like *too sweet*, *as sweet as*, *sweeter than*, and *very sweet*. These linking verbs consistently reject prototypical **adverbs** like *there* and derived adverbs like *sweetly*: *it tastes there, **it tastes sweetly*. In contrast, intransitive verbs like *reside* just as consistently take as complements those words and phrases that are excluded by *seem*: *he resides there*, but *he resides sweet. Verbs like *vanish*, which require no complement, will nevertheless accept a whole host of adverbial modifiers. The choosy

behavior of these verbs enables us to separate the adjectives from the
adverbs. The words and phrases that complement the *seem* kind of
verb are adjectival; those that complement (or modify) the others in
the activity are adverbial. The "*sneak* or *vanish* test" gives us model
adverbs like *somehow, somewhere,* and *sometime* to use as a yard-
stick of "adverb-ness." If you want to know whether a word or
phrase is functioning adverbially, try substituting one of those
words. If your substitute works, the word or phrase is almost certainly adverbial.

QUALIFIERS

Notice some interesting fallout from Discovery Activity 6-1.
Neither the verbs that accept adjectives nor those that accept adverbs will take *very, quite, rather, somewhat,* or *extremely* as complements or modifiers: *It tastes somewhat,* but *It tastes somewhat
bitter;* *She behaves rather,* but *She behaves rather well;* *He vanished very,* but *He vanished very soon.* Obviously, the words like
very do not belong to either the adjective or adverb class. Rather,
they are **qualifiers,** a class of structure words that modify adjectives
and adverbs, but can neither complement nor modify verbs.

We now have these guidelines: for adjectives, complementation
of *seems;* for adverbs, substitution of *somewhere, somehow,* or
sometime, complementation of *sneaks, resides,* or *behaves,* or mod-
ification of *vanishes;* and for qualifiers, insertion in the spot reserved for them in front of adjectives and adverbs. Notice that the
tests merely enable us to separate the classes of words from one
another; they do not imply that those words appear only in those
positions and functions.

DISCOVERY ACTIVITY 6-2

1. The italicized words in the following sentences are considered
   qualifiers, although they have been borrowed from a variety of
   form classes. Using morphological tests, identify the form class of
   each one; then answer the questions that follow.

Example
A *great* big bear came along. Adjective; passes the inflectional test
great/greater/greatest and is a member of a diagnostic derivational
series: great/greatly/greatness.

It was *bone* dry.
A *steaming* hot plate was set before me.

His face, a *pretty* awful sight, would require plastic surgery.
She had gone *completely* mad over the incident.

  a. On what grounds did you decide the class of *bone*?
  b. On what grounds did you decide the class of *steaming*?
  c. On what grounds did you decide the class of *pretty*?
  d. In the first sentence above, could you inflect the word *bone*?
  e. In the second sentence above, could you replace *steaming* with *steams* or *steamed*?
  f. In the third sentence above, could you inflect the word *pretty*?
  g. In the example sentence, could you inflect the word *great*?

2. Why do you think the italicized words are called *qualifiers* in these sentences instead of noun, verb, adjective, and adverb? If you cannot infer the reasons, review the discussion of structure class words as presented in Chapter 2.
3. Define *qualifier* without reference to meaning or to grammatical function.
4. In the sentences in (1), would you do any damage to the grammatical structure if you crossed out the italicized words?

Discovery Activity 6-2 shows that words temporarily lose their identity as form class words, that is, their ability to accept the series of inflections that characterize their form class, when they usurp the position belonging to qualifiers. This simply confirms the general criteria for structure words: they "own" certain positions but with rare exceptions do not participate in inflectional morphology.

DISCOVERY ACTIVITY 6-3

1. Underline all the qualifiers in the following sentences. Some sentences have more than one.

  a. A pretty awful scene ensued.
  b. It looks rather badly damaged.
  c. It worked somewhat too easily.
  d. Are you quite sure of that?
  e. It's fairly clean.
  f. She's a terribly fast runner.
  g. It seems awfully pretty.
  h. I'm almost ready.
  i. He sounds plumb crazy.
  j. Stark naked, he stood his ground.
  k. He spoke much too quickly.
  l. It wasn't that good.

2. If you cross out the qualifiers, do you damage the grammatical integrity of these sentences?

As the name implies, a qualifier like *somewhat* or *rather* limits the meaning of any word it modifies. Words like *very* and *extremely*, on the other hand, intensify the meaning; some grammarians therefore subdivide the qualifier class to include a subclass called **intensifiers**, and that makes sense on semantic grounds. Generally, however, all the qualifiers behave alike syntactically or grammatically, often being interchangeable in a given sentence. That is, although there's a big difference in meaning between *It's rather dirty* and *It's very dirty*, there's no difference in the structure because the words *rather* and *very* are grammatically equivalent. What this implies is that it is the grammatical position just ahead of adjectives and adverbs, not the word that occupies it, that is being named *qualifier*.

Unlike adjectives and adverbs, which are often essential to the grammatical structure, qualifiers are seldom essential to the structure and can almost always be deleted without any damage. *Are you sure of that?* is just as grammatical as *Are you quite sure of that?* but **Are you quite of that?* is not. We find occasional exceptions in adjective phrases like *too hot to handle,* which would become ungrammatical if the qualifier were deleted: **it's hot to handle.* But in general, qualifiers are structurally unessential.

TEST FRAMES REVISITED

Although certain syntactic positions are reserved for particular structure class words, you must not assume that form class words can also "own" certain positions. For example, you may be tempted to assume that a word appearing in front of a noun is an adjective just because adjectives so often appear there. But despite their frequent use as noun modifiers, adjectives do not own the modifier spot immediately preceding a noun, a functional position that is in fact open to all classes. Many pre-nominal modifiers can't pass the "*seems very*" test, strong evidence that they are not adjectives. You cannot say, for example, **the crying baby seems very crying,* nor **the upstairs maid seems very upstairs,* and for that reason *crying* and *upstairs* do not count as adjectives.

The position after *be* is equally useless as an adjective test frame for the same reason, namely, that it admits any class, as these examples show: *I'm outside* (adverb); *Mice are pests* (noun); *Sugar is sweet* (adjective); *They are swimming* (verb); *It is hidden* (verb). A space that can be filled by all classes is not exclusive enough to be a test. In choosing a diagnostic frame, we do not use just any syntactic position that accommodates the word; rather, we find those frames that force one specific kind of word or phrase to the virtual exclusion of others, insofar as that's possible in English.

Of course, if a word doesn't fit the "*seems* frame," it might still be an adjective by formal criteria, such as derivational affixes like *-al, -ous, -ar, -ible/-able,* or *-less* or membership in a derivational series, as pointed out in Chapter 2. Most people would agree that the word *unanimous,* for example, can't be compared because unanimity doesn't come in degrees; that is, a vote is either unanimous or it isn't: **The decision seemed more/less unanimous than I had expected.* But because of the derivational *-ous,* it counts as an adjective on the basis of form, to which we now return.

PARADIGMS REVISITED

In general, most people will agree that one-syllable adjectives like *tall* can be inflected for degree and that longer words like *beautiful* cannot. Moreover, words from specific groups, like those ending in *-ous,* seem to resist inflection. For such words, we use the **periphrastic comparative/superlative,** the addition of structure words that are equivalent to the inflections: *more beautiful, most famous, most adorable.* On the other hand, some adverbs (particularly those that belong to the adjective as well as the adverb class) do inflect for degree: *late/later/latest, early/earlier/earliest.* Obviously, inflection with *-er* and *-est* does not by itself provide a reliable means of distinguishing adjectives from adverbs, and grammarians have devised a formal test that combines both inflectional paradigms and derivational series as one way of establishing membership in the adjective class. If a stem takes the comparative and superlative inflections and can accept *-ly* to make an adverb or *-ness* to make a noun, it's an adjective. For example, *soon* inflects but cannot be considered an adjective because we cannot derive **soonly* or **soonness.*

DISCOVERY ACTIVITY 6-4

1. Apply the combination of tests and label *Adj.* any adjectives in the following list:

sticky ___	sweet ___	seldom ___	big ___
sad ___	fast ___	late ___	holey ___
high ___	gentle ___	gloomy ___	icy ___

stony ___   funny ___   tasty ___   greedy ___
sleepy ___   oily ___   short ___   lacy ___

2. Analyze the words in (1) ending in -y.
   a. What is their morphological structure? To what classes do the base morphemes belong?
   b. Write at least six more words of the greedy type.
   c. Test your words as you did in question 1. Are they adjectives?
   d. Do you think that noun+-y is a good predictor of "adjective-hood"? What about verb+-y?
3. The function words more and most function just like -er and -est: more beautiful rather than *beautifuller. The following words, to which you may be reluctant to attach -er and -est, will work with more and most. If these words can also accept -ly and/or -ness, label them Adj.

sensible   famous   economical
childish   picturesque   prosperous
glorious   pompous   vicious

4. Write out at least ten words ending in -ous/-ious/-eous.
   a. To what class do all these words belong?
   b. To what class does supercalifragilisticexpialidocious belong?
5. Write out at least six -ible/-able words.
   a. To what class do the -ible/-able words belong?
   b. Can you think of any -ible/-able words that aren't adjectives?
6. What about the derivational -ive?
7. Most words ending in -ful will test out as adjectives: seems hopeful, seems careful, and so on. Provide morphological as well as syntactic evidence that words like spoonful, cupful, and earful are not adjectives.
8. Give a summary of all the criteria for identifying adjectives.

DIFFICULT CASES

As you've worked on the Discovery Activities throughout this chapter, you may have thought of some words that you know to be adjectives that simply do not conform to the requirements established for the class. For example, even the combined inflectional and derivational test found in Discovery Activity 6-4, if applied rigidly, would fail to catch long and young, because their morphology does not conform to the specific pattern established. These words are among the group of adjectives from which we derive nouns not by addition of -ness, but -th, which (as you may recall from Chapter 2) "deforms" the base morphemes so that we end up with *youth*, not *youngth, and *length*, not *longth. Nevertheless, the tests provide means of identifying most of the prototypical or central members, and most words that fail the formal tests will pass the syntactic tests with *seems very* or with *more* and *most*. Some, however, are so recalcitrant as to resist all group norms.

DISCOVERY ACTIVITY 6-5

1. Submit each of the following words to all the adjective tests (inflection; participation in derivational series; occurring with *as . . . as, very,* or *more*; complementation of *seems*). Then answer the questions that follow.

main	daily	edible
lunar	alone	due
principal	mere	extinct
dental	unable	defunct

   a. List the words above that fail the syntactic tests.
   b. Do any of them have endings that are characteristic of adjectives?
   c. Submit all the words in this exercise to the tests for nouns, verbs, adverbs, and qualifiers. How do they fare?
   d. Can you suggest some reasons why these words have traditionally been included in the adjective class even though they fail to meet the requirements for membership set forth thus far?

2. What is the grammatical, not semantic, rationale for saying that *moving* in a *moving van* is not an adjective? What is the grammatical, not semantic, rationale for saying that *moving* in a *moving experience* is an adjective?

3. In Discovery Activity 6-1, you checked words like *homeward*. Did you call them adjectives, adverbs, or both? Does *backward* have the same meaning in its adjectival use as it does in its adverbial?

4. You also tested some words like *clockwise, slantwise,* and *sidewise* in Discovery Activity 6-1. Does *-wise* seem to you to be reserved for adverbs? Now consider the word *otherwise*. Do you think it's an adjective, an adverb, a qualifier, all, none? What's the rationale for your answer?

Although *principal* and *dental, edible* and *unable,* and *lunar* all have derivational affixes that you may have recognized as typically adjectival, some of the words in Discovery Activity 6-5 bear no such

morphological clues. Moreover, for most people the words in question do not inflect for degree or work with qualifiers or intensifiers
like *very*. Yet despite atypical morphology and restrictions on syntax, those words are indeed adjectives, and not merely by default,
as question 1d might imply. These words are classed as adjectives for
the very reason you might have wanted to put other words into the
adjective class that *don't* belong there; namely, they perform the
most common grammatical tasks that central members of the class
perform, modifying and complementing nouns.

What, then, is the difference between the words that we admit
to the class and others to which we deny membership? Generally,
the ones we exclude are central members of other classes whose
primary functions are not those that are performed by the words
under discussion here. That is to say, *weep*, for example, is first and
foremost a verb. When *weeping* modifies a noun, it is still a member
of the verb class. On the other hand, *moving* is both a verb and an
adjective; it appears as the head in verb phrases (*has been moving*)
and as head in adjective phrases as well (*very moving*). But although *due* has an identity as a noun, as you see in *paid my dues*,
most of the words in question 1 of Discovery Activity 6-5, including
alone, defunct, and *main*, do not owe first allegiance to some other
class, as *weep* does. And given that their primary work is the kind
that is also the major work of central members of the adjective class,
membership is extended to those under discussion. Such reasoning
has the practical advantage of limiting the proliferation of many
classes, each having very few members, and has the weight of
tradition in its favor.

DISCOVERY ACTIVITY 6-6

1. Using morphemic analysis, the adjective test frame, substitution, or
   your dictionary, identify each of the following as *Adj.* or *Adv.*; then
   answer the questions.

   friendly_____ worldly_____ quickly_____ sisterly_____
   manly_____ beastly_____ bravely_____ quietly_____

   a. If you take the -*ly* off the adverbs, what's left?
   b. If you take the -*ly* off the adjectives, what's left?
   c. Complete this generalization: You can tell an -*ly* word is an
      adverb if _____, but an adjective if
      _____.

2. Write several sentences using the words *partly* and *mainly*. Are

these words adjectives, adverbs, qualifiers, all, none? What is your rationale?

3. What is anomalous about *deadly, sickly,* and *kindly?*
4. What is peculiar about words like *basically, specifically,* and *drastically?* (Hint: Identify their adjective forms, or compare their morphology with that of words like *logically* or *accidentally.*)

FORM vs. FUNCTION

You have seen that we can identify most of the words in the form classes on the basis of formal characteristics and function word signals. Even without a larger syntactic context, if we hear or read the expression *those zarbers,* we can immediately assign *zarber* to the noun class on the basis of its derivational *-er,* its inflectional *-s,* and its occurrence with the structure word, *those,* which we know to be a noun signal. Actually, we have recognized a noun phrase, a small syntactic structure. But we cannot know the grammatical function of the noun phrase, *those zarbers,* without a syntactic context, since words and phrases have no function at all in isolation from one another. You will need to guard against confusing categories, which have taken up most of our time thus far, with functions, which will be the focus of our attention in Chapter 7.

Perhaps an analogy will help. A person is classed as female because of physical characteristics and will be female regardless of the work she does. Her professional function, however, does not require her to be a member of the female class; a person doesn't have to be female to be a college professor, for example. Nor can her professional role be established without reference to a particular discipline. She can't just be a professor, period. She must be a professor of chemistry, history, English, or whatever. And finally, a person has different functions in different contexts. At home, the professor may be "head of the household," but not "professor of the family."

A phrase, analogously, is classed as a noun phrase (NP) on the basis of its form (or structure) and will remain an NP regardless of the work it does. Just as the job of professor doesn't have to be filled by a female, the grammatical job of subject doesn't have to be filled by an NP. Moreover, the function of a word or phrase, like the professor's, can be established only in reference to a specific context. It can't just be an object. It must be an object of this or that verb, or of this or that preposition. And finally, a word or phrase, like a person, has different functions in different contexts. In one sentence a noun or NP might be the object of a verb: *He sells furniture*; in another, a subject: *Furniture is expensive*; in another, a modifier: *He works in a furniture store*.

In general, we can't assume a one-to-one correspondence be tween membership in a form class and grammatical function or functions. Because of the peculiar nature of English syntax, where phrases, not words, perform major functions, and the order of the phrases, not word class, usually determines what's functioning as what, a word belonging to any major form class can assume the function customarily performed by another class, and frequently does. (This is not true of structure class words; as you have seen, most of them are more rigidly fixed in their positions and functions.)

In the sentence *The poor are always with us,* we have an adjective, *poor,* serving as the headword of the subject noun phrase, a function typically served by nouns. In the sentence *He likes downhill skiing,* we have a verb, *skiing,* acting as the headword of the object, another function normally associated with nouns and noun phrases. In both cases, you can see by formal tests that the words are *not* nouns; they do not take plural inflections, for example. But you can see that they're doing jobs usually done by noun phrases, because in either instance we could substitute a pronoun for the phrase: *They are always with us* and *He likes it* (or *that* or *something*). And as you saw in the section on qualifiers, just about any part of speech can be a modifier. In summary: for defining a form class or phrase type we can use two kinds of information— typical form and typical structure word "partner"—but we cannot predict with certainty what grammatical function the word or phrase will perform in the larger syntactic framework of a sentence.

In the next chapters we will take a look at the major syntactic functions, namely, subject, predicator, complement, and modifier. In Chapter 7, we will look mainly at subjects, predicators, and complements which constitute the nuclei of English sentences. In Chapter 8, we'll examine some modifying structures.

SUMMARY

1. Adjectives (a form class)
   a. Typically complement linking verbs like *seem* and *feel*.
   b. Have recognizable derivational affixes like *-ous* and *-able*, and *-ly*.

c. May be able to accept comparative and superlative degree inflections.
2. Adverbs (a form class)
   a. Typically complement intransitive verbs like *sneak, reside, behave.*
   b. Have recognizable derivational affixes like *-ward, -wise,* and *-ly.*
   c. May be able to accept comparative and superlative degree inflections.
3. Qualifiers (a structure class)
   a. Typically precede (and modify) adjectives and adverbs.
   b. Cannot complement or modify verbs.
   c. Typically do not accept inflections.
   d. Are rarely essential to the grammatical structure.

STUDY QUESTIONS

1. Give at least one test frame for adjectives.
2. State the combined formal test for defining adjectives.
3. List at least five derivational affixes that are exclusive to the adjective class.
4. Give a test frame for adverbs.
5. What are the model adverbs you can use as substitutes to test for "adverb-ness"?
6. What position do qualifiers occupy?
7. Traditional grammars included words like *very* in the class of adverbs. For what reasons have we excluded them?
8. What criteria are used to establish membership in the major form classes?
9. When and why are form class words reclassified as qualifiers?
10. In English, what generally determines grammatical function?
11. What is the grammatical rationale for saying that *weeping* is not an adjective in *the weeping child*?
12. Do paradigmatic tests constitute rules of English grammar? Why or why not?
13. "Don't say *I felt badly*, because *badly* is an adverb, and adverbs can't complement verbs like *feel*." Is this statement a rule of grammar? Why or why not? If not, what is it?

FURTHER STUDY AND DISCUSSION

1. Some people argue that the word *unique* can be applied only to an entity that is the only one of its kind. They maintain that *the most*

unique and *rather unique* should not be tolerated because they are "logically impossible." Similar arguments have been made for "absolute" terms like *round, square, legal, perfect* (despite *more perfect union*), *dead* (despite *deader than a doornail*), *married, pregnant,* and others. Can you think of other qualities that don't come in degrees? Do you agree that "we can't say *more unanimous*"? In a well-developed paragraph, comment on this issue in any way you like.

2. With the help of your dictionary, write a usage rule or set of guidelines for the use of the adjective/adverb *well* in standard edited English, and give appropriate examples of your own. Read the appropriate entry for *good* in addition to the one(s) for *well*, so that you distinguish not only between *well* as adverb and *well* as adjective, but between *good* and *well* as adjectives.

3. Most scholarly traditional grammars are quite thorough and usually very insightful, yet some contemporary grammarians criticize them for classing *very* and other qualifiers with the adverbs. Contemporary linguists have called the adverb class, as traditionally understood, "a dumping ground" and "a grammatical garbage can." One explanation might be that traditionalists couldn't bring themselves to tamper with the number of word classes handed down from the ancients. Can you suggest any reasons for the traditional classification?

7 | Syntax: Basic Sentence Patterns

Language activity goes on, not in individual words, but in sentences. The study of syntax, or sentence and phrase structure, is therefore the heart and soul of grammar. While we were discussing the morphology of English we were also dealing with phrases, syntactic structures larger than words but smaller than sentences. Now you will see that **syntax**, the structure and order of phrasal units, is usually more important than morphology in determining what an English sentence means. Grammarians have shown that the vast number of sentences we actually use can be subdivided into a small number of syntactic patterns. In this chapter, we'll work with those basic sentence structures.

SENTENCE vs. BASIC SENTENCE

One obstacle to an intelligent introductory discussion of syntax is the problem of definition. A sentence is a syntactic structure that can be defined only in terms of grammatical functions and relations. Since everything about a sentence must be defined relationally, there is no "logical" place to begin. No single function that participates in the structure can be defined without reference to some other. Thus, almost all definitions turn out to be circular. Suppose, for example, we define a sentence as a grammatical structure consisting of a subject and a predicate, and a subject as "what comes first in a 'normal order' sentence." The shortcoming of such a "definition" should be obvious: if you are to understand it, you must first know what a "normal order sentence" is, but "normal order sentence" can be defined only as one that has the subject before the predicate.

Because of such difficulties, it's better not to attempt a definition. Instead, we will simply stipulate what configuration of phrasal structures constitutes a basic sentence and emphasize that the definition of *basic sentence* is not to be taken as a definition of *sentence* in general. The inventory of basic sentence types is very limited and should not be taken as an inventory of sentence types in general. You will notice, for example, that there are no questions, commands, or passive voice sentences in the set of basic sentence types. Nor are there any compound or complex sentences. **Basic sentences** are all simple, declarative statements with tense-carrying verbs in the active voice. The constituents are limited to **subject**, prototypically realized by an NP; **predicating verb phrase**, realized by AUX + verb headword; and **complement**, which completes the structure and which can be realized by a variety of phrase types. Technically, these skeletal structures contain no modifiers, but you will find modifiers in some of the Discovery Activity sentences throughout this chapter.

DISCOVERY ACTIVITY 7-1

To each of the following word strings, add words only if the string absolutely requires a complement.

a. Mary is sleeping _____

b. You sound _____

c. I'm sweating _____

d. He puts _____

e. We're _____

f. Sidney has _____

g. Everyone wants _____

h. Mary feels _____

i. Pam sneezed _____

j. My dog died _____

k. Time flies _____

l. The British are coming _____

m. You're getting _____

n. Everyone considers _____

Assuming, despite their brevity, that the now complete structures in Discovery Activity 7-1 are representative of typical English sentences, you can see that although there are some verbs (*sleep, sneeze,* and *sweat,* for instance) that can predicate single-handedly, many sentences in English really consist of three major parts. Because of this general tendency, we assume a three-part structure, **SVX**, as the prototypical basic sentence: S for subject function, V for the predicating verb function, and X for the complement function.

Why X instead of C? Because complements are variable. You saw in Chapter 6, for example, that intransitive verbs take only adverbial complements and linking verbs of the *seems* type take only adjectival complements, and it should come as no surprise that some verbs take only nominal complements. Thus, we can divide basic sentences into groups on the basis of the type of grammatical structure in the variable X and on the nature of the verb + complement relationship. In other words, the combination of a specific verb and the particular type of structure it requires for its completion (i.e., the combined V + X or complete predicate) provides the basis for subdividing sentences into four subsets, as shown in Tables 7-1 and 7-2.

DISCOVERY ACTIVITY 7-2

1. Identify the structure in the X slot in each of the following sentences, and say whether the headword in the V function is *be* or some other verb.

   a. She's just being facetious.
   b. He seems terribly quiet
   c. People sometimes become sick.
   d. Linus appears terribly insecure.
   e. It must be somewhere!
   f. Harry became a topnotch bowler.
   g. They are becoming terrible enemies.
   h. The doctor is outside.
   i. I am a camera.
   j. The sky is looking ominous.
   k. She must be there.
   l. He feels very bad.
   m. Lucy is a fussbudget.
   n. Charlie is feeling blue.
   o. The honeysuckle smells strong.
   p. You are my best friend.
   q. Mother is downstairs.
   r. The gravy tastes good.
   s. That sentence sounds funny.
   t. All the children are here.

2. How many different verbs are represented in sentences a–t?
3. What classes are used for complement structures in the sentences a–t?
4. Which sentences above have adverbial complements?
5. Can any of the verbs other than *be* accept adverbial complements?
6. Can you use an *-ly* adverbial as complement to any of the verbs above?

PATTERNS WITH *BE*

If you look at the summary of basic sentence patterns in Table 7-2, you should notice that *be* is syntactically unique. You have already seen that it differs from other verbs morphologically, in that

TABLE 7-1   Basic Sentence Types: Structural Formulas

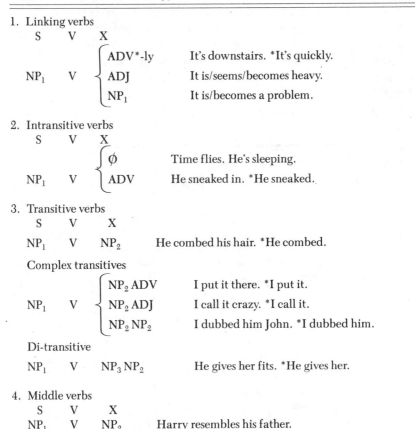

1. Linking verbs

S	V	X	
NP₁	V	⎧ ADV*-ly	It's downstairs. *It's quickly.
		⎨ ADJ	It is/seems/becomes heavy.
		⎩ NP₁	It is/becomes a problem.

2. Intransitive verbs

S	V	X	
NP₁	V	⎰ ∅	Time flies. He's sleeping.
		⎱ ADV	He sneaked in. *He sneaked.

3. Transitive verbs

S	V	X	
NP₁	V	NP₂	He combed his hair. *He combed.

Complex transitives

NP₁	V	⎧ NP₂ ADV	I put it there. *I put it.
		⎨ NP₂ ADJ	I call it crazy. *I call it.
		⎩ NP₂ NP₂	I dubbed him John. *I dubbed him.

Di-transitive

NP₁	V	NP₃ NP₂	He gives her fits. *He gives her.

4. Middle verbs

S	V	X	
NP₁	V	NP₂	Harry resembles his father.
			*His father is resembled.

it has eight forms instead of five. You have also seen that it differs from other verbs syntactically, in that it does not require periphrastic *do* for question and negative formation, behaving like an auxiliary even when it is the headword. Now you see that *be* is also unlike the other verbs in the linking verb group in that it not only takes nominal and adjectival complements, but adverbial complements as well, with no apparent change in meaning. Compare *appear*, for example, which is a linking verb like *seem* when its complement is adjectival (*Linus appears insecure*) but which becomes an intransitive verb meaning "come into view" when it is followed by an adverbial: *Linus appears somewhere.* (As an auxiliary with any kind of verb, of course, *be* is completed by a verb inflected with *-ing*

TABLE 7-2   Basic Sentence Types: Complement Functions Specified

1. Linking verbs
   Temporal or locative Adverbial Complement   It's downstairs.
   (only with *be*); no manner adverbials: *-ly*   *It's quickly.
   Predicative Adjective   It is/seems/becomes heavy.
   Predicative Nominal   It is/becomes a problem.

2. Intransitives
   elapse type: No complement required   Time flies.
   sneak type + Adverbial Complement   He sneaked upstairs.
        *He sneaked.

3. Transitives
   comb type + Object   He is combing his hair.
        *He is combing.

   Complex Transitives
   put type + Object + Adverbial Obj Comp   I put flowers there.
        *I put flowers.
   consider type + Object + Adjectival Obj Comp   I consider him silly.
        *I consider him.
   dub type + Object + Nominal Obj Comp   We dubbed him FDR.
        *We dubbed him.

   Di-transitive
   give type + Indirect Object + Direct Object   He gives me fits.
        *He gives me.

4. Middle verb + nominal complement (not an   I have a dog.
   object because it can't be passivized; not a   *A dog is had.
   predicative nominal or subject complement   Harry resembles you.
   because it doesn't always predicate about the   *You are resembled.
   subject)

or -*en*: *is/was eating, is/was eaten*.) In any case, you can now see that we need at least three variables for X—ADV, ADJ, and NP—because *be* can have adverbial (ADV), adjectival (ADJ), or nominal complements; hence the structural formulas NP V ADV, NP V ADJ, and NP V NP.

Some grammarians exclude *be* from the verb class because of its idiosyncracies. They argue that despite its inflectional morphology, *be* is a nearly meaningless structure word used only to fill a syntactic slot and to provide a form for tense inflection. In a sentence like *He's my best friend*, they point out, *be* is needed only because English syntax, at least in standard varieties, demands a tense-carrier in every sentence. In some languages (Russian, for example) and even in some American dialects, *be* is left out of such sentences. It is in fact not *be*, but the noun phrase, *best friend*, that predicates something about the *he* named by the subject NP.

The very fact that *be* must always take a complement implies that by itself the word has little meaning, and except in very rare instances ("*I think; therefore I am*" and *God is*) *be* alone cannot predicate. Thus it makes sense to call the complements of *be* and the other linking verbs **predicative nominals** and **predicative adjectives**. Note that these are complements, not modifiers. Without them, there would be no predication. We cannot say *She's just being* and stop. We need a complement, like *facetious*. In *She made a facetious remark*, where *facetious* is not grammatically essential to the NP it occurs in, it is a modifier. In *She's just being facetious*, it is essential and is therefore a complement. Because these nominal and adjectival phrases predicate about the subject, they are also known as **subject complements**.

DISCOVERY ACTIVITY 7-3

1. Provide a subject complement for each of the following:

   a. Harry is feeling _____   e. The honeysuckle smells _____
   b. The soup tastes _____   f. The house looks _____
   c. This piano sounds _____   g. This course seems _____
   d. Mary appears very _____   h. Susan is becoming _____

2. What class of word or type of phrase generally completes sentences a–g?

3. What two classes can serve as complements in sentence h? Write two or three more sentences with the verb *become*, all with nominal (NP) complements. What do you notice about the subject and complement NPs of a *become* sentence? What does the complement refer to?

4. Can you use adverbials to complete any of the sentences above?

OTHER LINKING VERBS

Assuming that *seem*, *feel*, *taste*, *sound*, and *become* are representative, it's obvious that linking verbs other than *be* can take only adjectival and nominal complements; unlike *be*, they cannot take adverbials. You may have noticed that these verbs, together with their subject complements, ascribe some quality, characteristic, condition, or state to their subjects. In other words, predicates with linking verbs usually do not refer to what we do, but to what we are. For that reason, many grammarians consider *be* the par excellence member of the set, despite the peculiarities pointed out above.

Notice in the outline of sentence pattern types in Table 7-1, that complement NPs in linking verb sentences, like the subject NPs, are marked NP_1. That means that both NPs refer to the same person or thing. To be more precise, the subject and complement NPs in linking verb sentences either have exactly the same referent (*You are my best friend*) or one NP refers to a member of a larger class named by the other (*Harry became a topnotch bowler*). The NPs *you* and *my best friend* refer to the same person, and *Harry* names a member of the larger set, *topnotch bowlers*.

Before leaving the subject of linking verbs, we need to look at some more complex complement structures than those presented in the Discovery Activities 7-1 to 7-3.

DISCOVERY ACTIVITY 7-4

1. In each of the following sentences, identify the phrase in the X slot as a noun phrase (NP), adjective phrase (AP), or prepositional phrase (PP). Then, perhaps by substituting a pronoun, an adjective, or an adverb *for the entire complement*, decide whether the complement is a predicative nominal or a predicative adjective or is functioning as an adverbial complement.

Examples

Mary is *above reproach*: PP used adjectivally (compare *irreproachable*), i.e., predicative adjective or adjectival subject complement.

Linus is *extremely insecure*: AP, predicative adjective or adjectival subject complement.

Linus has been *on the scene*: PP, used adverbially (compare *there*).

a. Mary must be at my house. _____
b. It happened in the morning. _____
c. Potatoes are the principal crop. _____
d. The principal crop is potatoes. _____
e. She was feeling under the weather. _____
f. She seems as happy as a clam at high tide. _____
g. Sam and Eric are the inseparable twins in the story. _____
h. Those are my best shoes. _____
i. Those are the wrong size. _____

     j. You sound like Frank Sinatra. _____

     k. My chocolate chip cookies taste like nothing you've ever had. __

     l. Some of my best friends are dyed-in-the-wool grammarians. ____

Discovery Activity 7-4 shows that a phrase—a syntactic structure—acts as a unit; the long AP, *as happy as a clam at high tide*, is, syntactically speaking, the equivalent of *happy*. Similarly, the PP, *like nothing you've ever had*, which incorporates a whole clause, functions just as if it were a one-word AP, like *great*, and is thus its syntactic equivalent. *The inseparable twins in the story* is just an expansion of *the twins*, and in this case the PP, *in the story*, is a modifier of the headword, *twins*.

Notice that we don't have a one-to-one correspondence between a particular type of phrase and a specific function. PPs, for example, can function adverbially when complementing *be* or an intransitive verb: *She must be at my house; It happened in the morning*. But when complementing linking verbs, including *be*, they can also function adjectivally, as exemplified by the complements of *taste* and *sound*, *like nothing you've ever had*, and *like Frank Sinatra*, as well as by *above reproach*.

Even NPs are as changeable as chameleons. You can see that *Those are my best shoes* would work with the NPs reversed: *My best shoes are those*. Moreover, we could substitute a pronoun like *mine* for the complement: *Those are mine*. But an NP like *the wrong size* is peculiar. Inversion with its subject would result in something odd, if not outright ungrammatical: *?The wrong size is those*; and pronoun substitution seems unlikely. But if we replace *the wrong size* with an adjective phrase, like *too big*, the sentence works as the original one does: *Those shoes are too big*. In sum, this NP is not being used to identify or "rename" the subject, as NP_1s usually do, but to ascribe some quality to the subject, as predicative adjectives do.

DISCOVERY ACTIVITY 7-5

1. In the following structures, use any kind of word or phrase that works, but supply a complement only where one is grammatically required to complete the structure.

  a. Susan is singing _____   d. Tom has vanished _____

  b. The race car was heading ___   e. My insurance coverage

  c. Everyone was coughing ____   lapsed _____

f. We had trudged _____

g. Her temperature was rising _____

h. They were sneaking _____

i. Time flies _____

j. Susan is lurking _____

k. It's falling _____

l. She is standing _____

m. Mary used to live _____

n. The stuff was oozing _____

o. I am residing _____

p. The earth revolves _____

q. He's sweating _____

r. He was sleeping _____

2. Would any of the complements you provided (whether one word or phrase) work in the "seems frame"; that is, are any of them adjectival?

3. Can you substitute *somewhere* or *sometime* or *there* or *then* for any of the complements you provided?

4. Were you able to use any -*ly* adverbs as complements?

5. Can you use -*ly* adverbs to modify any verbs that don't require complements?

6. Do any of the verbs that *require* a complement take NPs? If so, can you substitute an adverbial, rather than a pronoun, for the NP?

INTRANSITIVE VERBS

Intransitive verbs are frequently defined as verbs that can predicate without complements, but the sentences above confirm what you learned in Chapter 6—namely, that some intransitive verbs do require complements. Most people will agree, for example, that *We had trudged* is an incomplete structure that requires an adverb or a prepositional phrase like *around* or *up the hill*. These words and phrases are usually adverbial, and serve to locate the action in space or time. Even if we complete *trudge* with *home* we can substitute an adverbial phrase, but not a pronoun, for the complement: *we trudged toward home*, but not **we trudged it*. Therefore, we will call all words and phrases that complement intransitive verbs **adverbial complements** even when they aren't literally adverbs or adverbial phrases, and write the formula for any sentence with an intransitive verb that requires a complement as NP V ADV.

Notice that if the adverbial after an intransitive verb can be deleted, it's not a complement, but a modifier. If, for example, we add *in the bathtub* or *soundly* to *He is sleeping*, what we add is not grammatically essential to the structure, no matter how essential it might be to our meaning. **Manner adverbs** (in general, those with -*ly*) are almost always modifiers rather than complements because they can usually be deleted. But whatever you added to the *sneak* sentence in Discovery Activity 7-5 is a complement because *sneak*, most people will agree, does not constitute a predicate by itself.

Nevertheless, judgments vary, and we can't expect unanimity about which verbs require complements. Some people consider *the stuff was oozing* a complete structure; others do not. A handful of intransitive verbs, including *tamper*, for example, specifically require a *"with* phrase." The word *cope* used to belong to this group, but many people today say *He just can't cope*, without specifying what it is he can't cope with. During the transition period, some people insisted that *he can't cope* was not a complete structure.

So the common definition of an intransitive verb as one that requires no complement is true of only a subset of intransitive verbs. Nevertheless, we can sometimes confirm that a verb is being used intransitively by deleting whatever follows it to see if what remains is structurally sound and retains the original sense of the verb. Regardless of where, when, or how Susan was singing, *Susan was singing* is structurally complete; so in the sentence *She was singing at La Scala, sing* is intransitive. In that respect, the subset of sentences with these intransitives is unique, and has a separate formula, NP V Ø. No other kind of verb can appear without a complement.

Let's sum up what we've found thus far:

1. Linking verbs all require complements.
2. All linking verbs can have predicative adjectives or predicative nominals (both of which are also called subject complements) but of the linking verbs, only *be* can have an adverbial complement.
3. Some intransitive verbs do not require complements.
4. Those intransitives that do require complements do not take adjectival or nominal complements; they take adverbial complements only.
5. Only intransitives can predicate without complements.
6. Only *be* and intransitives can take adverbial complements.

DISCOVERY ACTIVITY 7-6

1. Identify the verb in each of the following sentences as linking or intransitive, and identify the structure and function of the phrases following the verbs, some of which may not be complements, but modifiers. With some intransitive verbs, you and your classmates

may not agree on whether a particular item is a modifier or a complement.

a. Reagan retired to his ranch.
b. Sally is turning green.
c. Sally was turning into the driveway.
d. Sally and John remained friendly.
e. Sally and John remained at home.
f. Mary left sometime around noon.
g. The incident occurred on Sunday.

h. The smoke rose up the chimney.
i. A child fell into the river!
j. He fell silent.
k. The doctor got awfully sick.
l. The doctor got into the car.
m. He was walking on the dock.
n. The patient died last night.
o. Mice become awful pests.
p. Mice become awfully pesty.

2. Identify the NP complements that are not NP_1s.

a. Little acorns become great oaks.
b. Loggers harvest great oaks.
c. Susan is just a baby.
d. Susan just delivered a baby.
e. Harold broke his arm.
f. Harold broke the window.
g. I heard a noise.

h. This class is a circus!
i. Everyone enjoys a circus.
j. Mice are vermin.
k. Mice eat vermin.
l. Susan cut the cake.
m. Susan cut herself.
n. I saw some birds.

PATTERNS WITH TRANSITIVE VERBS

Unlike intransitive verbs, some of which can predicate without complements, a transitive verb requires a complement, and as you might expect, it must be of a specific kind. Just as intransitive *lurk* requires an adverbial complement, transitive *cut* requires a nominal. Transitive verb complements, called **objects**, will be NPs, pronouns, or structures for which pronouns can substitute.

But unlike a linking verb, whose nominal complement is an NP_1, the prototypical transitive verb has an NP_2 in the X. That simply means that the subject and object NPs usually refer to different entities. In *Susan is just a baby*, the words *Susan* and *a baby* are simply two different labels for the same person, hence both are indexed NP_1. In *Susan just delivered a baby*, the words

Susan and *a baby* identify two different persons; hence NP$_1$ and NP$_2$. Nevertheless, it is not the identity of the object NP, but rather the meaning of the verb that establishes membership in the transitive subset. In general, transitive verbs specify not just what the subject does, but what the subject can do *to* something or somebody.

An NP complement of an intransitive verb is not something that is affected by the verb; that is, we're not doing anything to *home* in *We trudged home.* Nor is an NP complement of a linking verb affected by the action; rather, it comments on the subject: *Those shoes are the wrong size.* But the object of a transitive verb is often, though not invariably, affected in some way. Hence, *Susan cut herself* belongs in this set, alongside *Susan cut the cake*, and not with the linking verbs, even though the object NP, *herself*, has the same referent as the subject NP and it thus deviates from the general formula for transitives, NP$_1$ V NP$_2$. On the other hand, even though the referents of the object NPs *a noise* and *some birds* are not affected in sentences like *I heard a noise* and *I saw some birds*, *hear* and *see* are transitive not only because they conform to the formula but also because they pass other tests of transitivity, as you will soon see.

DISCOVERY ACTIVITY 7-7

Identify the complements by structure and function and the verb type in each of the following sentences.

Examples
Mice eat cheese. NP$_1$ V-tr NP$_2$ (object)
Mice become pests. NP$_1$ V-link NP$_1$ (predicative nominal)
Mice scamper around. NP$_1$ V-int ADV (adverbial complement)
Mice can run. NP$_1$ V-int (no complement)
Mice sound squeaky. NP$_1$ V-link ADJ (predicative adjective)

Mary felt bad.	The guru sounded the gong.
Mary felt the wind in her hair.	The gong sounded loud.
Susan stayed indoors.	The chef tasted the soup.
Susan stayed very quiet.	The soup tasted salty.
The caller left a message.	I was choking.
The caller left early.	The collar is choking me.
She's doing the dishes.	She's doing very well.

VERBS: CLASS vs. USE

You may have noticed while doing Discovery Activities 7-6 and 7-7 that despite references to intransitive verbs, transitive verbs, and linking verbs, some verbs seem to jump from one category to another, freely taking complements from a variety of classes; *fall* is intransitive in *fall into the river*, but linking in *fall silent*. In fact, English doesn't have a specific or particular group of verbs that are intransitive, and a different set that are linking, and yet another that are transitive. We cannot say that this or that verb irrevocably belongs to a particular subclass.

To be more precise, we should refer to transitive, intransitive, and linking use of a verb. For example, *remain* is used as a linking verb with adjectival or nominal complements (*remain friendly* and *remain friends*) and intransitively with no complement or with an adverbial complement or modifier: *only one remains; he remained at home.* Most people will generally agree that *sleep, sneeze, cough, sweat, itch, rise, fall*, and scores of other verbs do not need complements in their most common use—that is, that they are basically intransitive. Yet you know that you can metaphorically "sweat *blood*" or "cough *yourself* silly," in which case the verbs, now with nominal rather than adverbial complements, are behaving like transitives. In English, we can use almost all verbs in a wide variety of sentence patterns. Even *seem*, which so often chooses a predicative adjective as its complement that we use it as a "sure fire" diagnostic for adjectives, occasionally transcends its own character and takes a nominal complement: *it seems a shame.* Discovery Activity 7-8 is designed to illustrate the phenomenon of the protean English verb.

DISCOVERY ACTIVITY 7-8

1. The following groups of sentences are designed to show that verbs can be used in various patterns, often transcending their central or typical behavior. In each sentence, identify the complement structure, name its function, and specify how the verb is being used.

Examples

He got *sick*. predicative adjective, linking verb (or adjectival subject complement)

She got *a raise*. grammatical object, transitive verb

She got *into the cab*. PP used as adverbial complement, intransitive verb

She was playing *a game*. grammatical object, transitive verb

She was playing *dead*. predicative adjective, linking verb (or adjectival subject complement)

She was becoming *a great actress*. predicative nominal, linking verb

a. The milk was turning sour.
She was turning toward me.
She was turning the pages.

b. Farmer Brown grows corn.
You certainly have grown!
Father grew very pensive.

c. She was looking pretty good.
She was looking everywhere.

d. He left.
He left the best part.

e. She was doing crossword puzzles.
She was doing very well.

2. In which sentences can you substitute a pronoun for the complement?

3. Which sentences can be passivized?

Questions 2 and 3 in Discovery Activity 7-8 actually provide two tests for transitivity. The first is that the NP complement of a transitive verb can be replaced by an object pronoun (*me, you, him, her, it, us, them, whom*). Intransitive verbs, on the other hand, are followed by adverbials, for which a pronoun cannot be substituted: *The man died at home, the man died there*, but not **the man died it*. Secondly, if a verb is used transitively, the predicate can usually undergo passive conversion; those with intransitive or linking verbs cannot. In *Mary runs the factory, run* is transitive and the NP, *the factory*, is its object; you could paraphrase it as *Mary runs it* and/or *The factory is run by Mary*. In *Mary runs/ran home, run* is intransitive; you can't paraphrase the sentence as **home is/was run* or **Mary runs/ran it*.

DISCOVERY ACTIVITY 7-9

Identify the following sentences that have intransitive verbs (I) and those that pass the transitivity tests (T). Put a (?) by any that fit neither set.

The creature stole away. ___
You stole my heart. ___
Charlie kept in touch. ___
Charlie kept the cash. ___
Harry weighed the baby. ___
Harry weighs a ton. ___

The university lacks the funds. ___
Susan has two sisters. ___
Harry resembles you. ___
It lasted five weeks. ___
Harry totaled the car. ___
The bill totaled five dollars. ___

MIDDLE VERBS

The sentences that earned a question mark in Discovery Activity 7-9 illustrate the use of **middle verbs**. They look like transitive verbs in that they are followed by an NP$_2$, but they act like intransitive or linking verbs in that they do not appear in the passive voice. The predicate *resembles you* cannot be paraphrased as **you are resembled.* The word *have* usually functions as a middle verb, as you can see from the unacceptability of **two sisters are had,* and is often cited as the central or prototypical middle verb. But the expression *a good time was had by all* has become so familiar that it no longer sounds odd, and *have* may ultimately become transitive in other contexts.

So we can't subclassify verbs without considering the context. Instead, we must refer to how the verb is used in a particular instance rather than classify the verb itself. Moreover, it's difficult to decide what to call the complement of a middle verb. Although it's an NP$_2$, it doesn't behave like an object in that it doesn't passivize. Sometimes, despite its NP structure, it seems more like a predicative adjective than a nominal: *Harry weighs a ton = Harry is/seems very heavy.* The best move is just to call it a **nominal complement** (but certainly not a subject complement or predicative nominal, since it doesn't always predicate about the subject, as is obvious from sentences like *Harry has a dog*). If the V as well as X were a variable, the formulas for sentences with nominal complements could then reflect a difference in the V rather than in the X, and might look something like this: NP$_1$ V-link NP$_1$; NP$_1$ V-tr NP$_2$; and NP$_1$ V-mid NP$_2$.

Once again, native speakers do not always agree that a particular verb can or cannot be used in passives, and you and your classmates may have responded differently to some of the sentences in Discovery Activity 7-9. For example, *cost, lack, undergo,* and *last* are all middle verbs for some people but not for all speakers. What are your judgments on these verbs?

DISCOVERY ACTIVITY 7-10

1. Examine the following basic sentences; then answer the questions.

The eggs are in one basket.   The president is in the White House.

The walls are bright blue.   Mary is reliable.
Mary and John are my emis-   Joan is chairwoman.
  saries.

a. What is the name of the function performed by *in the White House* and *in one basket* in these basic sentences?
b. What name besides predicative adjective can we apply to the function of *reliable* and *bright blue* in these sentences?
c. What name besides predicative nominal can we apply to the function of *chairwoman* and *my emissaries* in these sentences?

2. Now look at the following sentences:

You placed the eggs in one   I consider Mary reliable.
  basket.   We elected Joan chairwoman.
We put the president in the   I made Mary and John my emis-
  White House.   saries.
He painted the walls bright
  blue.

a. In these sentences, is the relationship between *the president* and *in the White House* the same as their relationship was in (1)? What about *the eggs* and *in one basket*?
b. Is the relationship between *the walls* and *bright blue* and between *Mary* and *reliable* the same in (1) and in (2)?
c. Is the relationship between *Joan* and *chairwoman* and between *my emissaries* and *Mary and John* the same in (1) and in (2)?
d. Substitute pronouns for the NPs in (2) that were the subject NPs in the sentences in (1).
e. What does pronoun choice tell you about the grammatical function of *the president, the eggs, the walls, Mary, Joan,* and *John and Mary* in the sentences of (2)?
f. Can you suggest a name for the function performed by *in the White House* and *in one basket* in the sentences in (2)?
g. Suggest a name for the function of *bright blue* and *reliable* in (2).
h. Suggest a name for the function of *chairwoman* and *my emissaries* in (2).

COMPLEX TRANSITIVES

The sentences in question 2 of Discovery Activity 7-10 illustrate the kind of verbs that are called **complex transitives** because the objects that enter into their complements require complements of their own. For example, it is not possible just to "put something."

Rather, we must put some*thing* some*where*. Verbs like *put* not only require an object, but also an adverbial complement like *in the White House*. Verbs like *consider*, on the other hand, typically have objects that require adjectival or nominal complements: *We consider him foolish, We consider him a fool*. In every case, the relationship between the object and its complement is like the relationship between the subject of a linking verb and its complement. Hence, both NPs in predicates like *consider him a fool* or *made them my emissaries* are indexed NP_2 (for the same reason that they were both indexed NP_1 in the linking verb sentences) and the formulas for this pattern are $NP_1 \; V \; NP_2 \; ADV$, $NP_1 \; V \; NP_2 \; ADJ$, and $NP_1 \; V \; NP_2 \; NP_2$.

DISCOVERY ACTIVITY 7-11

1. Some of the following sentences have complex transitives like those just discussed, but others are simple transitives with compound objects—that is, objects composed of NPs conjoined by *and*. In each sentence, identify the items in the X slot by structure and function.

Examples

He made the coffee strong. *The coffee*, an NP_2, is the object; *strong* is an adjectival object complement.

He made the book his bible. *The book*, an NP_2, is the object; *his bible*, another NP_2, is a nominal object complement.

He read the Bible and the Koran. *The Bible and the Koran* (which could be replaced by *them*) is an object.

a. He considers her a friend.
b. He considers her beautiful.
c. We applauded Frick and Frack.
d. He ushered me into the room.
e. She summoned me to her office.
f. Birds lay their eggs in nests.
g. She called her dad her buddy.
h. I baked a cake and some cookies.
i. The audience judged her talents.
j. The jury judged her innocent.
k. I like ice cream and candy.
l. He escorted her to the dance.
m. They certified him insane.
n. They tied the knot tight.
o. I called Mary and John.
p. I call my car the grey goose.

2. The following sentences all have two NPs in the X, yet they are neither compound objects like *a cake and some cookies*, which constitutes just one NP_2, nor complex complements like *my car the grey goose*, exemplifying $NP_2 \; NP_2$. Look at the sentences carefully; then answer the questions.

a. John threw Mary the ball.
b. I'll order you a salad.
c. The IRS sent me a check.
d. He was offering me a loan.
e. I've given the dog some bones.
f. He bought his son a car.
g. I'll bring the class a treat.
h. She willed her niece a fortune.

3. Assume all the subject NPs in (2) are indexed as NP_1. In each sentence, label the NP referring to the object that is thrown, ordered, sent, offered, and so forth (that is, the last NP in the sentence) as NP_2.
4. Should the NP between the verb and the NP_2 be indexed NP_2, or something else? Why?

DI-TRANSITIVE VERBS

It should be clear that the NPs labeled NP_2 are the same kind of object found in a simple transitive sentence, but that the NP between a di-transitive verb and the NP_2 is a beneficiary or intended recipient of the item named by the NP_2. This intervening NP must be indexed some other way than NP_1 or NP_2 since its referent is not the same as either of theirs. We call this NP, indexed NP_3, the **indirect object** and the NP_2 the **direct object**. The formula is thus NP_1 V NP_3 NP_2. In general, these double complements can be paraphrased by changing the order of the NPs and turning the indirect object into a prepositional phrase, usually beginning with *to* or *for*: *John threw the ball to Mary, I ordered a salad for you.*

Sometimes it is impossible to tell whether the NPs should carry the same index because they are coreferential (and therefore complementary) as in *we called him our friend* (i.e., "considered him or referred to him as our friend") or whether they refer to different entities or persons and thus have one of the indirect object/direct object relationships, as in *We called him a cab* (= "we called a cab *for* him"). This ambiguity, which results from the multiple meanings of some English verbs, is the basis for many of our puns ("Call me a taxi." "OK, you're a taxi.").

In general, we can separate sentences with direct and indirect objects from those with objects and object complements not only by identifying the referent(s) of the two NPs, but also by syntactic tests. Sentences with indirect objects can be reworded with prepositional phrases; those with object complements cannot. On the other hand, sentences with object complements can frequently be paraphrased with *be*; those with direct and indirect objects cannot:

I sent her some flowers   = I sent flowers to her.
                            ≠ *I sent her to be flowers.
I consider her my friend   = I consider her to be my friend.
                            ≠ *I consider my friend to her.

DISCOVERY ACTIVITY 7-12

1. For each of the following sentences, identify the structure and function of all the items in the X slot.

Example
He found her a good conversationalist. (Both *her* and *a good conversationalist* could be NP$_2$s, complements of one another: *He found her to be a good conversationalist*; or *her* could be an NP$_3$, indirect object: *He found a good conversationalist for her*.)

   a. The baker made him a cake.
   b. A magician made him a prince.
   c. We consider them unhappy.
   d. Her accountant made her mad.
   e. He was telling her his life history.
   f. Susan's father calls her his best friend.
   g. He called her into his presence.
   h. I find your remarks insulting.
   i. He wished her luck.
   j. They designated me their leader.
   k. I put my dime into the vending machine.
   l. Some of the people in Pittsburgh consider the climate healthy.
   m. Owls consider us unhappy victims of too much sun.
   n. Dinosaurs laid their eggs in the desert.
   o. They voted me the most likely to go out and eat worms.
   p. He made his brother a mud pie.
   q. The invention made him millions.
   r. The invention made him a millionaire.

2. The following basic sentences have been expanded with many modifiers, auxiliaries, and other elements (e.g., negative particles). Nevertheless, you should still be able to pick out the NP$_1$ and the V; classify the verb type; and identify the items in the X slot and specify their functions.

Example

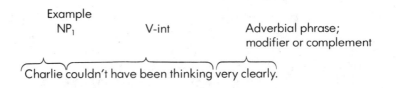

| NP₁ | V-int | Adverbial phrase; modifier or complement |

Charlie couldn't have been thinking very clearly.

The NP₁, *Charlie*, is the subject; *think* is an intransitive verb; *very clearly* is an adverbial phrase, more likely to be a modifier than a complement for two reasons: *-ly* adverbs are seldom essential to the structure, and *couldn't have been thinking* seems to be a complete predicate. However, if you believe that the predicate is not complete, you would have to say that *very clearly* is a complement.

a. Those nice young people living in the upstairs apartment above me have become as quarrelsome as a nest of hornets.
b. Esmerelda has never seemed happier.
c. Esmerelda and Fosnick have never seemed happier than they do now.
d. A long line of cars was slowly crawling up the road to Zanzibar.
e. Fosnick has bought his sweet old Aunt Tillie a great big stone mansion in the country.
f. The senior class of Weybelo Normal voted me the least likely person to succeed at frisbee.
g. The speeding car was heading right into the crowd.
h. All the millionaires in our town own big fancy American made cars.
i. Some of my best friends were at the conference.
j. The best things in life may be awfully expensive.
k. Some of those guys at the Pentagon are terribly industrious.
l. My mother uses sugar in her salad dressing.
m. Charlie had never seen anyone so beautiful.
n. Shakespeare may not really be dead.
o. Somebody with a lousy sense of humor has sent Esmerelda a comic valentine in very poor taste.
p. The foundation has given the Society for Preservation of Good Humor an enormous endowment.
q. Susan was running on empty.
r. Some people in the United States consider the Russian people happy benefactors of the revolution.
s. Everyone who saw the accident considered it the speeding driver's fault.
t. Everybody I know likes ice cream and cookies.
u. The team named Charlie their representative.

  v. I don't know anything about black holes in the sky.
  w. I know why the caged bird sings.
  x. The Smiths of Jones Street named their dog the Baron of Wimpole Street.
  y. A bird in the hand is an unlikely prospect.
  z. A bird in the hand is worthy of great respect.
3. Specify how each of the following items deviates from the basic sentence pattern formula. Be specific. "It's a question" does not specify the deviation.
  a. Is John your friend?
  b. Sit down!
  c. There's a fly in my soup.
  d. the reason being that her parents never liked her boyfriend
  e. I like cottage cheese but I hate yogurt.
  f. I like this course although it makes me work.
  g. The outraged citizen impatiently awaited the decision that was to come.

THE LIMITATIONS OF BASIC SENTENCES

The sentences in question 3 of Discovery Activity 7-12 illustrate only a few of the multitude of structures not represented by the notion *basic sentence* and suggests how lightly we have scratched the surface of English syntax. Because a yes/no question has an auxiliary in first position and a command has no subject, (a) and (b) are not classed as basic structures. Most grammar books used to identify *a fly* as the subject of sentence c, and according to that analysis the sentence deviates from basic in that *a fly* is not in subject position. Recent writers argue, on the basis of syntactic evidence like *isn't there?* (a tag question, which always "copies" the subject) and *there* is the subject; in that case the deviation is merely that *there*, not being an NP, is an atypical form for subject function. The long phrase, *the reason being that . . .* fails a crucial test: it lacks tense and therefore doesn't meet the AUX + Verb requirement that was stipulated for all basic sentences. We can't include sentences e and f because each of them consists of two conjoined SVXs, the first with a coordinating and the second with a subordinating conjunction, which we will discuss in Chapter 8. And finally, (g) isn't included because it has been expanded with modifiers, some of which we are about to explore in Chapter 8.

GRAMMATICAL FUNCTION AND STRUCTURAL MEANING

You may recall that Chapter 1 refers to the "devices" in the language that convey certain kinds of information or have structural meaning or grammatical meaning. For example, the characteristic derivational affix of a particular word (e.g., -*ness*) can convey information like "membership in the noun class." Inflectional affixes convey information like "plurality," "tense," or "degree"—again, "membership in a particular form class." The intonation and word order of an utterance can convey information like "this is a statement" or "this is a question." Syntactic function is also part of structural or grammatical meaning. The position of a word or phrase conveys information like "subject of the sentence," "object of the verb," or "noun modifier." All the information that we get without knowing the meanings of the words themselves counts as structural or grammatical meaning because it is built into the system and works even when nonsense words are used, as *A granflon is nemiously zobbling your fonical smarchivity* illustrates.

In this chapter, we saw that each position in the basic sentence is the "home slot" of a particular syntactic function: S houses the subject function, V houses the predicating verb function consisting of AUX + Verb, and X houses complements of various kinds. Using the basic sentence as our point of departure, we can now safely define *subject* as the element that can be eliminated in commands or as that which, in standard English, controls number in the predicating verb. We can define it as the sentence constituent between the auxiliary and predicating verb in a yes/no question. Similarly, we can define *grammatical object* as the word or phrase in the predicate of an active sentence that can become the subject of a passive counterpart. All such definitions are based on objective observation of syntactic properties.

We must be cautious, however, not to confuse statements like those just made about subjects and objects, which constitute defining criteria, and observations about the usual meaning of particular grammatical structures or functions. If we accept, for example, the statement that (in general) the subject of a transitive verb in the active voice will be an agent or a performer of an action, we need to bear in mind that the observation is not criterial, hence not part of the definition of *subject*. It would be hard to argue that trees and counterpanes perform some kind of action in sentences like *Trees surround the house* or *A lace counterpane covers the bed*. Yet *trees* and *counterpane* are the subjects and these are unquestionably active voice sentences with transitive verbs.

Similarly, if we observe that "linking verbs refer to what the subject *is*," that "transitive verbs refer to what the subject can do *to* something," or that "the object of a transitive verb is somehow affected," we are not defining linking verbs, transitive verbs, or objects. Rather, having already identified and defined those structures by their syntactic properties, we are merely observing their general tendencies to suggest this or that concept. Consider an analogous situation: even if it's true that monkeys are cute and generally make good pets, we do not include "it makes a good pet" in the definition of *monkey*, because being a pet is not part of what the word *monkey* must mean; no matter how many people keep monkeys as pets, being a pet is not a criterion of "monkey-hood." We must not only remember the many exceptions to the broad generalizations but even more importantly, we must insist that all definitions be based on specific grammatical properties.

SUMMARY

I. Subclassification of basic sentences is based on the type of structure in the complement (X) position and on the nature of the verb-complement relationship. Tables 7-1 and 7-2 show the subdivisions, which are grouped, in the traditional way, according to whether:

A. The verb "links" the subject to a nominal or adjectival complement that predicates a "state of being" about the subject, or (in the case of *be*) permits adverbials that locate the subject in time or space.

B. The verb predicates without a complement or with adverbial complements only.

C. The verb requires a grammatical object, prototypically an NP_2, as complement.

D. The verb has an NP_2 complement that is neither an object nor a predicative nominal.

II. Complements are subdivided into various types:

A. Complements of linking verbs (including *be*) are called predicative complements or subject complements; prepositional phrases in this pattern may be adjectival with all linking verbs but adverbial only with *be*.

B. Complements of intransitive verbs are referred to by the structural/functional name, adverbial complement, without further specification or particularization; prepositional phrases count as adverbial.

C. Complements of transitive verbs are referred to by more specific names, according to the particular verb-complement relationship:

1. If just one NP_2 follows the verb, it's called an object.

2. Some objects themselves require complements; these can be adverbial, adjectival, or nominal object complements.

3. If an NP_3 and an NP_2 follow the verb, they are called the indirect and direct object, respectively.

D. Complements of middle verbs are called simply nominal complements, not objects (because they don't passivize), nor predicative nouns, or subject complements (because they do not always predicate about the subject).

III. Four types of structures fill the X slot:

A. Adverbs and adverbial phrases (e.g., *somewhere, somehow, sometime*).

B. Adjectives and adjectival phrases (e.g., *too hot, as hot as*).

C. Nominals (nouns, noun phrases, pronouns). Nouns and NPs, but usually not pronouns, can perform the functions of the other types of structures. (*I walked home; They are the wrong size.*)

D. Prepositional phrases. These usually perform adjectival or adverbial functions; very rarely do they perform nominal functions (i.e., can rarely be used as grammatical objects).

IV. The basic patterns include: (See diagrams in Table 7-3.)

A. *Linking* verbs.

1. Only *be* takes adverbial complements, which "locate" the subject.

> S V ADV: He is here; *He is quietly; *He seems/ becomes here.

2. Adjectival complements predicate some quality of the subject.

> S V ADJ: He is/seems/became/remained sick/ friendly.

3. Nominal complements predicate some kind of "equivalence" between the complement and subject.

> S V NP_1: They are/became/remained friends.

B. *Intransitive* verbs: This is the only form with the option of

TABLE 7-3   Diagrams of Basic Sentence Patterns

A. *Linking*: Only *be* takes adverbials; all can take ADJ or NP₁.

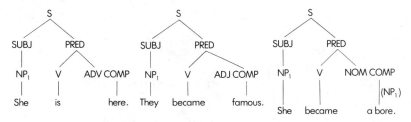

B. *Intransitive*: If a complement appears, it is considered adverbial.

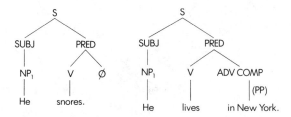

C. *Transitive*: NP₂ = object.

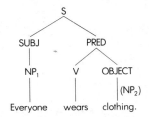

Complex transitive: Objects have complements.

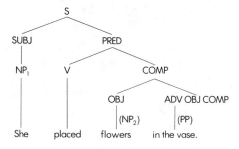

TABLE 7-3   Continued

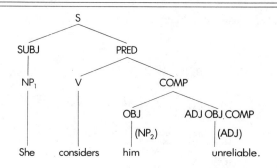

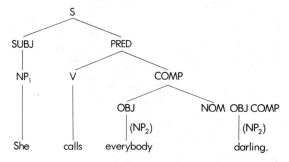

Di-transitive: Include indirect and direct objects.

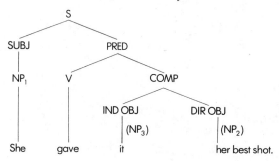

D. *Middle*: Complement is NP$_2$, but not an object or subject complement.

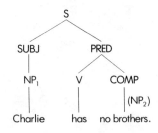

no complement. If a complement appears, it will be adverbial by definition.

S V Ø: He sneezed.

S V ADV: He resides there.

Verbs used intransitively generally do not affect their complements. If we trudge up a hill, we're not doing anything to it. Manner adverbials (typically, those ending in -*ly*) are usually modifiers, not complements, because they are seldom essential to the grammatical structure.

C. *Transitive* verbs: The NP_2 can typically be replaced by an object pronoun and is called the object; typically, the form can undergo passivization.

S V NP_2: He eats/ate the cake/it⇒The cake/it is/was eaten.

Complex transitive with adverbial object complement: The adverbial complement locates the object.

S V NP_2 ADV: I put the flowers there.

Complex transitive with adjectival object complement: The adjectival complement predicates some quality or characteristic of the object:

S V NP_2 ADJ: I consider him foolish.

Complex transitive with nominal object complement: The two NPs are coreferential:

S V NP_2 NP_2: I consider him a fool.

Di-transitive: The two nominal complements are called the indirect and direct object:

S V NP_3 NP_2: I gave her everything.

D. *Middle* verbs: The predicate typically cannot be passivized:

S V NP_2: He resembles a monkey * ⇒ *a monkey is resembled.

STUDY QUESTIONS

1. How are the following sets of terms different? That is, what do the terms in (a) name? What do the terms in (b) name? What do the terms in (c) name?
   a. noun, verb, adjective, adverb
   b. NP, VP, AP, PP
   c. subject, verb, object, complement, modifier
2. What does syntax deal with?
3. What is a basic sentence?

4. Summarize the morphological and syntactic differences between *be* and all other verbs.
5. What syntactic property sets a subset of intransitive verbs apart from all other verbs?
6. Describe two syntactic properties that distinguish intransitive verbs from transitive verbs.
7. What is a middle verb and/or what syntactic property distinguishes middle verbs from transitive verbs?
8. How is the syntax of intransitive verbs different from that of linking verbs?
9. Give syntactic evidence that *swimming* is the grammatical object of the verb, and not part of the verb itself, in *Everybody likes swimming.*
10. "A middle verb cannot undergo passivization." Is this statement a grammatical rule? Why or why not?
11. Give syntactic evidence that the two prepositional phrases, *out of his mind* and *out of his way,* are not grammatically equivalent in the following: *He must have been out of his mind to do that* and *He went out of his way to do that.*
12. What syntactic properties define *subject of the sentence*?

FURTHER STUDY AND DISCUSSION

Write a thoughtful paragraph discussing the structural difference, and its semantic implications, of *He died happily* vs. *He died happy.* Be sure you make an explicit connection between grammar/grammatical devices and meaning.

8 | Beyond the Basic Sentence

By now you are probably aware that the inventory of basic sentences constitutes a very limited repertory of structures. If you were required to use nothing but basic sentences, you would become very frustrated. You wouldn't be able to ask questions or give commands in the usual way, and you would sound repetitious, since no provision is made for conjoining or for subordinating one item to another or for deleting excess repetition. People do not speak or write in basic sentences. Instead, we all use modifiers to expand the various phrases, we conjoin phrases and delete redundancies, we rearrange phrases for emphasis, and so on. We will not be able to review all the possible syntactic variations on the basic sentence, but we will look at the structure of relative and subordinate clauses, as well as some structures that serve as NP substitutes, which will serve as examples of syntactic variation. This chapter should help you understand the structural relationships between and among clauses, as well as the punctuation conventions that are used to signal clause relationships in standard edited English.

DISCOVERY ACTIVITY 8-1

Examine the following sentence; then answer the questions.

The girl that delivers the paper lives next door.

1. How many tense-marked verb phrases are there in the sentence?
2. Is the sentence a basic sentence?
3. By making a yes/no question out of the sentence, isolate its subject NP.
4. If you delete *that delivers the paper* from the original sentence, does the remainder constitute an SVX?
5. Which of the two tense-marked verbs did you have to alter when you made the yes/no question?

6. Which of the two tense-marked verbs is the predicating verb of the original sentence?
7. What do you think is the grammatical function of *that delivers the paper*?
8. What is the grammatical function of the NP *the paper*? That is, what is its relationship to *delivers*?
9. Since *delivers* is marked for tense and number, we can assume that it must be governed by a subject. What do you think is the subject of *delivers*?

THE RELATIVE CLAUSE: AN NP MODIFIER

The sentence in Discovery Activity 8-1 is obviously not a basic sentence, the headword of its NP_1, *the girl*, having been expanded by insertion of a modifier, *that delivers the paper.* The modifier is a fairly typical **relative clause**, consisting of a subject, *that*; a tense-marked verb, *delivers*; and an object, *the paper.* Because it contains the three major syntactic functions, and because it has its own tensed verb, it is called a **clause** rather than a phrase. You will soon see, however, that a relative clause differs from a basic sentence in that the subject is not always in first position. Moreover, under specific conditions its "signal"—prototypically *who, which,* or *that*—can sometimes be deleted.

Before presenting a description of the structure of relative clauses, a disclaimer is in order: No one suggests that people actually think through a process or consciously construct relative clauses. The description of relative clauses given here is not intended to be a model of anything anyone does. It should be seen, rather, as a way of explicitly showing the underlying relationship between one structure—a noun phrase—and an embedded clause used to modify its headword.

The relative clause is usually incorporated as a modifier right after the head noun in an NP; hence, it is often called an **NP expander.** Because it lets us "telescope" two or more ideas into one expanded NP, effective use of the relative clause cuts down repetition, and "expansion" thus turns out to be compression. To discover how ideas can be consolidated through the use of relative clauses, look at the following basic sentences.

NP_1 V NP_2
The boy obviously has an allergy.

NP₁   V   X
The boy (or He) sneezes all day.

NP₁   V   NP₂
The allergy (or It) needs treatment.

Notice that the noun phrase *the boy*, whether actually repeated or replaced by *he*, has the same referent in both the first and the second sentence. That is a necessary precondition for the relative clause construction, which we accomplish by putting *who, which*, or *that* (a **relative pronoun**, abbreviated as R) in place of some repetitious NP:

NP₁   V   X   R   V   X
The boy (or He) sneezes all day⇒who/that sneezes all day

Now we can embed the relative clause as an NP modifier in the original sentence, resulting in:

$$\text{NP}_1 \left\{ \begin{array}{ccc} \text{Relative Clause} \\ \text{R} \quad \text{V} \quad \text{X} \end{array} \right\} \qquad \text{V} \quad \text{NP}_2$$
The boy [who sneezes all day] obviously has an allergy.

Here's another example. A relative pronoun is once again the subject of the relative clause, but this time we will use the relative clause to modify an object NP instead of a subject NP:

NP₁   V   NP₂   R   V   NP₂
The allergy (or It) needs treatment⇒which/that needs treatment

We embed the new relative clause to modify *an allergy*, the object NP of the original sentence:

$$\text{NP}_1 \qquad \text{V} \quad \text{NP}_2 \left\{ \begin{array}{ccc} \text{Relative Clause} \\ \text{R} \quad \text{V} \quad \text{NP}_2 \end{array} \right\}$$
The boy obviously has an allergy [that needs treatment].

This process of adding relative clauses can go on indefinitely. With these examples, we could embed both of the relative clauses into the original sentence, one to modify the subject NP, *the boy*, and one to modify the object NP, *an allergy*:

$$NP_1 + RelativeClause \qquad NP_2 + RelativeClause$$
$$= ExpandedNP_1 \quad V \qquad = ExpandedNP_2$$

Theboy[whosneezesallday]hasanallergy[thatneedstreatment].

"The House That Jack Built" provides a perfect example of the recursiveness (repeatability) of the relative clause:

Here is the farmer all shaven and shorn
Who married the maiden all forlorn
Who milked the cow with the crumpled horn
That tossed the dog
That worried the cat
That chased the rat
That ate the malt
That lay in the house
That Jack built.

Like the story of the house that Jack built, our example about the sneezing boy could have gone on as long as we could think of NPs to modify:

The boy who sneezes all day has *an allergy* that needs *treatment* that can be obtained at *any clinic* that is staffed with *doctors* who/that know about *substances* that cause *reactions* that are symptomatic of . . .

A Different Kind of R

We have seen that a relative clause is made by putting an R in place of an NP, but that is not the only way. There is one R, *whose*, that takes the place of a determiner, not an NP. The result, however, is still a relative clause:

$$NP_1 \qquad\qquad V$$
The boy has no doubt been crying.

Det   N be ADJ   R   N be ADJ
The boy's (= his) eyes are so red. ⇒whose eyes are so red

When we embed the relative clause, we get:

NP_1 Relative Clause   V
The boy [whose eyes are so red] has no doubt been crying.

An Extra Step with Object NPs

To make a relative clause by replacing an NP from the X slot (that is, a grammatical object), there's an extra step. We have to move the R out of its place and put it at the front of the relative clause, as illustrated in the following example:

NP_1 V NP_2
The bicycle had a bent frame.

NP_1 V NP_2 R   R
I   sold the bicycle.⇒I sold which/that⇒which/that I sold

The result:

NP_1 Relative Clause   V NP_2
The bicycle [which/that I sold] had a bent frame.

If a relative pronoun substitutes for the object of a preposition, it is once again necessary to move the relative pronoun to the beginning of the clause, but the choice of whether to carry the preposition along or leave it behind is usually open. When the preposition is carried along, however, constraints are placed on the choice of relative pronoun.

NP_1 V NP_2
She raised a large card.

NP_1 V NP_2 Prep   Obj. of Prep
Someone had written a little verse   on   the large card (it).⇒

R NP_1 V NP_2 Prep
that/which someone had written a little verse   on

Prep   R NP_1 V NP_2
on   which/*that someone had written a little verse

She raised a large card that/which someone had written a little verse on.

She raised a large card on which/*that someone had written a little verse.

The constraint on the relative pronoun applies in the case of *that* vs. *who* and *whom* as well. Even though it's the object of a preposition, *who* rather than *whom* is often used, particularly in speech, when the preposition is left behind. Thus, we have *the bank officer that you told me about, the bank officer who you told me about,* and *the bank officer about whom you told me,* but not **the bank officer about that/who you told me.*

DISCOVERY ACTIVITY 8-2

Convert sentence b in each of the following pairs into a relative clause. First write out the relative clause; then write the result of embedding it in the first sentence.

Example
People should not throw stones.
People (they) live in glass houses. _____who live in glass houses_____
People who live in glass houses should not throw stones._____

1. a. A car is worth keeping.
   b. A car/it runs perfectly. _____

   _____

2. a. Ye draw near with faith.
   b. Ye do truly and earnestly repent of your sins. _____

   _____

3. a. The driver hollered at the rowdy boys.
   b. The boys (they) were pushing their way onto the bus. _____

   _____

4. a. The woman needs your attention.
   b. The woman's (her) hair is standing on end. _____

   _____

5. a. I live next door to the man.
   b. The man's (his) dog rescued the baby. _____

   _____

6. a. These are problems.
   b. We can't solve them. _____

_____

7. a. I learned a whole poem.
   b. John Milton wrote it. _____

_____

8. a. The school produced a bunch of zombies.
   b. He praised the school so highly. _____

_____

9. a. He praised the school.
   b. The school had produced a bunch of zombies. _____

_____

10. a. I like the snazzy car.
    b. They gave her a snazzy car for her birthday. _____

_____

11. a. A restrictive clause is a modifier.
    b. It is embedded in an NP. _____

_____

DISCOVERY ACTIVITY 8-3

Read the following sentences aloud, and listen carefully for differences in the way you intone them—in other words, pay attention to the pitch of your voice and how it's related to the pauses you take.

Freshmen who live in dorms never catch cold.
Freshmen, who live in dorms, never catch cold.

1. Of the two sentences, which one seems more appropriate as an answer to the question "Which freshmen are immune to colds?"
2. What is implied by a question like "Which freshmen . . ."?

Restrictive vs. Nonrestrictive Clauses

Discovery Activity 8-3 was designed to call attention to another function of the relative clause. You can see that although the two sentences consist of exactly the same words, they do not mean exactly the same thing. In the first sentence, the entire expanded NP, *Freshmen who live in dorms*, is the subject, and would be a reasonable answer to a question like "Which (specific) freshmen are immune?"—a question that implies that not all of them are. The embedded clause picks out a subset of freshmen, the dorm-dwellers, and restricts the predicate, *never catch cold*, so that it applies only to them; hence, it is called **restrictive**. The subject of the second sentence, however, is just *freshmen*. Without the embedded modifier, the use of *freshmen* implies "all of them." The commas show that the relative clause is not embedded as part of the subject NP; rather, it comes between the subject and predicate, interrupting the sentence to give merely incidental information. The predicate, *never catch cold*, is not restricted to a subset of freshmen, but applies to the whole group named by the subject NP, (all) *freshmen*; hence this modifier is called **nonrestrictive**.

The difference between restrictive and nonrestrictive modifiers is proof that the changes we make in pitch, the pauses we take, and the way we vary the stress of what we say can make a difference in meaning. In writing, punctuation marks indicate these differences in intonation patterns. Notice, incidentally, that in addition to the commas, standard edited English prescribes *who* or *which* (never *that*) in all nonrestrictive clauses. In addition, some people frown on the use of *that* in reference to persons. Chapter 13 provides instruction in these usage conventions.

DISCOVERY ACTIVITY 8-4

1. For each pair of sentences that follow, decide from the circumstances described whether the information in the second sentence is essential for identifying a subset or is merely incidental information about the whole group. Then construct a relative clause from (b), embed it in (a) if it's restrictive, adjoin it if it's nonrestrictive, and punctuate according to your decision.

Example
Circumstances: About ten boys and ten girls were in a classroom.
a. Some of the boys weren't paying attention.
b. They were sitting by the window.
   The boys who/that were sitting by the window weren't paying attention.

Of the ten in the room, we are restricting the predication, *weren't paying attention*, to a subset—those by the window.

Circumstances: Only two boys were in the classroom.
a. The boys weren't paying attention.
b. They were sitting by the window.
   The boys, who were sitting by the window, weren't paying attention.
Circumstances: All the referees saw what happened.
a. The referees didn't take action.
b. They saw the low blows.
Circumstances: Some referees did not see what happened.
a. The referees didn't take action.
b. They saw the low blows.
Circumstances: I have only one brother.
a. My brother works at the library.
b. He has a degree in tiddlywinks engineering.

2. Explain the different implications of the relative clauses in the following pair of sentences:
   a. The book that Ms. Jones wrote in 1980 is still in print.
   b. The book, which Ms. Jones wrote in 1980, is still in print.
3. Which of the following sentences implies that the speaker knows
   more than one Smith family? Specify how this implication is
   made.
   a. The Smiths that live across the street are from England.
   b. The Smiths, who live across the street, are from England.
4. Write three or four sentences using relative clauses to modify non-
   plural proper nouns. Are the relative clauses restrictive or nonrestrictive? Why are restrictive clauses less likely to be used with a proper
   noun than with a common noun?
5. Write two sentences on unrelated topics that clearly show that you
   understand the difference between restrictive and nonrestrictive
   clauses.

Discovery Activity 8-4 was designed to emphasize the important
distinction between two structures whose audible difference can be
made visible in print only by punctuation. It is not the punctuation,
however, that makes a clause restrictive or nonrestrictive (for the
commas are merely an aid to reading) but the logical relationship,
expressed intonationally in speech, between the clause and the rest
of the sentence. Question 4 illustrates that point. Because the restrictive clause so often specifies a subset, it is unusual, though not
impossible, to use one to modify a proper noun, whose most likely
referent will be a unique entity—something that can hardly be
divided into subsets.

DISCOVERY ACTIVITY 8-5

1. Look at the following expanded noun phrase:
   the/a beautiful pit bull terrier kept by those people living in the luxurious condo on the beachfront

In five original sentences, use this NP (or one modeled on it) in the following functions: as subject; as object of verb; as an object complement; as predicative complement of *be* or a linking verb; as object of a preposition.

EXPANDED NOUN PHRASES

So far, we've discussed the fundamental grammatical functions—subject, predicating verb, complement, and modifier—but for the sake of simplicity, all those functions have been illustrated by prototypical structures. For example, most subjects and objects (including objects of prepositions) have been filled by NPs—short, skeletal ones at that. In most speech and writing, such phrases are the exception rather than the rule.

Activity 8-5 was designed to emphasize that NPs come in a variety of sizes, and to remind you of some typical NP functions before introducing you to some of the structures other than NPs that can perform those functions. But there's still one fairly common NP function to be mentioned in passing: the **appositive**, a (usually) nonrestrictive modifier that renames something just mentioned. The expanded NP in the following example is used as an appositive:

San Tan O'Lazy Lan, that beautiful pit bull terrier kept by the people living in the luxurious condo on the beachfront, has entertained the entire neighborhood.

Note that an appositive, *a (usually) nonrestrictive modifier that renames something just mentioned,* defined the word *appositive* in the sentence just before the example.

DISCOVERY ACTIVITY 8-6

1. In some of the following sentences, the *-ing* forms are predicating verbs; in others, they are in NP functions. Specify the function of each of the *-ing* forms.

a. He is becoming a pest.
b. He was speaking about working.
c. Working is disheartening.
d. Do you call that working?
e. He was working really hard.
f. He hates working.

2. How were you able to tell which -*ing* forms were predicating verbs?

NP SUBSTITUTES: VERBAL PHRASES

You may not have realized that verbal structures can perform many of the grammatical functions we associate with NPs, although the notion is implicit in earlier chapters. In Chapter 5, for example, *smoking* was used instead of an NP as the object of *prohibit* in an active sentence and as the subject in its passive counterpart, *Smoking is prohibited.* One of the study questions following Chapter 7 showed that by substituting *it* for *swimming* you could prove that the -*ing* form was not the headword of the verb phrase, but rather the headword of an NP substitute, functioning as the grammatical object of *like.* The verb-object relationship between *like* and *swimming* would hold even if *swimming* were expanded with complements and modifiers of its own: *I like swimming in a backyard pool rather than in the ocean; I like competitive swimming.*

This tenseless -*ing* structure, with or without modifiers and complements, is called a **gerund, gerundive,** or **gerundive phrase.** Gerunds can be used in all the functional positions that NPs can fill, as illustrated in Discovery Activity 8-6, where *working* is used as a subject in (c); an object in (f); an object complement in (d); and the object of a preposition in (b), where the entire prepositional phrase itself is either a complement or modifier of the intransitive verb, *speak.* Like the examples with *swimming,* these head-only gerundive phrases could be expanded: *Working for a grumpy boss is disheartening, He hates working under stressful conditions,* or *He was speaking about working the colors into the clay.* In form and function, the complements of gerunds are just like the complements of predicating verbs, and you can see that gerundive phrases look a lot like the predicates of hypothetical sentences, except that they lack the tense-carrying auxiliary. Compare, for example, *I work/am working for a grumpy boss, Everybody works/is working under stressful conditions,* and *She worked/was working the colors into the* _clay_. The grammatical relationships between the gerundive form and its complements are the same as those between predicating verbs and their complements, but the gerundive phrase itself has an NP function.

DISCOVERY ACTIVITY 8-7

1. In each of the following sentences, underline the non-NPs that are in functions typically filled by NPs, and specify what the functions are.
   a. To win the scholarship would be a real achievement.
   b. The worst thing you can do is to sneak around.
   c. Nobody wants to become a statistic.
   d. I don't want to seem unfair.
   e. He needs someone to love.
2. Besides _to_, what do the structures you underlined have in common?
3. How are the NP substitutes above different from the following "_to_ phrases":
   to Rainy Mountain, to the lighthouse, to school, to hell and back

---

Discovery Activity 8-7 introduces another NP substitute, the **infinitive phrase**, which is often (though not invariably) signaled by _to_ and always contains an uninflected verb stem as its headword. An infinitive phrase can even have a subject, as you can see from the following examples:

I _don't_ want _you to become a statistic_.

I heard _him sneeze_.

Because their structure so closely resembles an SVX, some grammar books refer to infinitive phrases (and even to gerundives) as clauses; but because they lack tense, others call them phrases. Infinitives, like gerunds, can include complements of their own: in _to win the scholarship, win_ has an object; in _to sneak around_, intransitive _sneak_ has an adverbial complement; in _to become a statistic_ and _to seem unfair_, the linking verbs have nominal and adjectival complements.

The infinitive phrase itself usually has an NP function, as you saw in Discovery Activity 8-7, where the "_to_ phrase" is a subject in (a); a subject complement in (b); and objects of _want_ in (c) and (d). You might not have recognized the complement function of _to love_ in (e), however, because it has not previously been made explicit that nouns may take complements, although it is implicit in the notion of subject complements and object complements. In the case of *someone to love,* the headword, *someone,* would hardly express the intended meaning without the infinitive phrase to complete it. Nevertheless, there is not always unanimous agreement about whether a particular phrase should be considered a complement or a modifier, as you saw in the case of intransitive verbs.

One final note about infinitive phrases: there is one NP function that an infinitive cannot perform. In contrast to a gerundive, an infinitive cannot be the object of a preposition. We can say, for example, *I plan to tell him* and *I plan on telling him,* but not **I plan on to tell him.*

DISCOVERY ACTIVITY 8-8

1. Examine the following clauses; then complete the activity.

   (i) that you gave me
   (ii) that you were going to New York University

       a. What is the grammatical function of *that* in clause (i)?
       b. Does *that* have a function in clause (ii)?
2. Incorporate each of the clauses above into a different sentence.
       a. What function does clause (i) perform in your sentence?
       b. What function does clause (ii) perform in your sentence?
3. Study the following sentences; then answer the questions.

   (i) I learned the poem *that/which was written by Milton.*
   (ii) I learned it from the person *that/who taught you.*
   (iii) I learned it from the person *that/who(m) you taught.*
   (iv) I know professors *that/who work hard.*
   (v) I know *that/*who professors work hard.*
   (vi) I didn't know *that/*which you liked poetry.*

       a. What is the function of *that was written by Milton* in (i)?
       b. What is the function of *that taught you* in (ii) and *that you taught* in (iii)?
       c. What is the function of *that work hard* in (iv)?
       d. Which of the sentences above are still grammatical sentences if you substitute *something* or *it* for the italicized clause?
       e. What is the function of *that professors work hard* in (v)?
       f. What is the function of *that you liked poetry* in (vi)?
       g. What is the specific function of the relative pronoun in (ii)?
       h. What is the specific function of the relative pronoun in (iii)?

NP SUBSTITUTES: CLAUSES

Discovery Activity 8-8 illustrates two points: first, the function word *that* is a quick-change artist par excellence, playing several different grammatical roles; and second, the two kinds of "*that* clauses" generally have different grammatical jobs to do. Let's consider these matters one at a time in more detail.

We can tell that *that* is a relative pronoun rather than some other kind of function word if we can put *which* or *who/whom* in its place and maintain the same type of structure. For example, *I know professors that/who work hard* demonstrates that *that* is a relative pronoun. But if we try substitution for *that* in *I know that professors work hard*, we will get the ungrammatical **I know who professors work hard* or the grammatical but syntactically non-equivalent *I know which professors work hard*. Therefore, we can be sure that the second *that* is not a relative pronoun, but something else—namely, a function word of a different class, a **complementizer**. And finally, there is another difference between these two *thats*: we can almost always delete complementizer *that* (*I didn't know you liked poetry*) but can delete relative *that* only when it is a grammatical object: *I learned it from the person you taught* is grammatical because *that/who(m)* is the object of *taught*, but **I learned it from the person taught you* is ungrammatical because *that/who* is the subject of *taught*.

As you saw in Discovery Activity 8-8, it is not possible to substitute *something* or *it* for noun modifiers like *that work hard, that was written by Milton*, or *that taught you*: **I learned it from the person something/it*. On the other hand, pronoun substitution is evidence of NP equivalence, hence NP function, in the case of *that professors work hard* and *that you liked poetry: I know/didn't know it/something*. Both of those NP substitutes happen to be the objects of *know*, but a **nominal clause**, as this structure is called, is not limited to the object function alone. Nominal clauses are frequently used as noun complements, as in *I wasn't aware of the fact that you liked poetry* or *The fact that you liked poetry wasn't relevant*. Nominal clauses also make good subjects: *That he would succeed was a forgone conclusion*.

DISCOVERY ACTIVITY 8-9

1. In each of the following sentences a clause has been embedded as the object of the verb. In each case, specify the S, the V, and the X of the embedded clause.

Example
I could see *that he was feeling sick.* The S is *he,* the V is *was feeling,* and the X is *sick,* an adjectival complement of the subject, *he.*

   a. I don't know if John's going to join us.
   b. I didn't know whether you were mad.
   c. I can understand why you like it.
   d. I'll take whatever I can get.
   e. I'll do anything you suggest.
   f. I know whose woods these are.
   g. I know who committed the crime.
2. Using the embedded clauses above as a model, write five sentences with clauses as subjects, rather than objects, of a verb.

Note that in sentences a, b, and c, the embedded clauses consist of a function word (*if, whether, why*) added to an already complete SVX. In (d) through (g), however, the clauses in question consist only of an S, V, and X, with no added function words. In (d) and (e), *whatever* and *anything* are the objects of *get* and *suggest;* we can posit hypothetical SVXs from which to derive them: *I can get something* and *You suggest something.* In (f), *these* and *whose woods* are subject and subject complement; in (g), *who* is a subject. In short, (d) through (g) resemble the relative clause in structure: no additional function word is added to the SVX, but an indefinite pronoun has taken over the first position in the clause even when it's not the subject—just as a relative pronoun takes the first position whether or not it's the subject in a relative clause. But unlike the relative clauses you worked with earlier, whose function was to modify NPs, this **indefinite relative clause** is used the way we use the nominal clauses with the added function words—as NP substitutes to fill such major syntactic functions as subject and object. Before going on to a new topic in syntax, work through Discovery Activity 8-10 in order to consolidate and confirm what you have learned about NP expanders and NP substitutes.

DISCOVERY ACTIVITY 8-10

1. In the following sentences, various types of structures have been put into functions typical of NPs. Nevertheless, the sentences retain the general SVX framework. Locate the S, the V, and the X in each sentence and identify the S and X items by structure and function, as illustrated.

Examples

She liked *coming home.*

The gerundive phrase, *coming home,* is the object of *like.* Although it is a noun, *home* is not an object (**coming it*) but an adverbial complement of *coming* (compare *coming here*).

She liked *coming home to a warm house that smelled of bread baking.*

The expanded gerundive phrase is still the object of *like.* The prepositional phrase *to a warm house* is an adverbial modifier or complement of *coming home;* the relative clause *that smelled of bread baking* modifies *a house,* which is also modified by *warm; baking* is a verbal, but it is simply a progressive *-ing* form, not a gerund (compare *bread that is baking*).

    a. Working in the mines is what caused his illness.
    b. I didn't even know that he had been working in the mines.
    c. I don't know why he's working in the mines.
    d. Mary believed the rumor that John was spreading.
    e. Mary believed the rumor that John had been involved in the trouble.
    f. John always ate whatever his mother cooked.
    g. Any intelligent person will wonder what's going on.
    h. Telling white lies is as bad as telling any other kind.
    i. I wouldn't even think of giving in to pressure.
    j. Being unable to refuse the offer resulted in his downfall.
    k. He was always trying to be funny.
    l. He tried being funny as a defense against insecurity.
    m. He called it throwing out the baby with the bath.
    n. She wanted to tell him the truth.
    o. She wanted him to tell the truth.
    p. I was thinking about moving to Mexico.
    q. That his parents had come from Zilchville didn't bother him a bit.
    r. To have some free time would be nice for a change.

2. Write a sentence of your own for each of the following descriptions.
    a. a sentence with a restrictive relative clause
    b. a sentence with a nonrestrictive relative clause
    c. a sentence with a gerundive phrase in any NP function
    d. a sentence with an infinitive phrase in any NP function possible
    e. a sentence with an embedded nominal clause in any NP function
    f. a sentence with an indefinite relative clause in any NP function

POSTSCRIPT ON THE INFINITIVE PHRASE

You have seen that correspondence between structures and functions is not one-to-one, but one-to-many and many-to-one. In other words, an NP—one kind of structure—performs many functions, including subject, object, complement, and object of a preposition. On the other hand, many structures—including NPs, gerundive and infinitive phrases, indefinite clauses, and nominal clauses—can perform one function, the subject function, let's say. You should be aware, therefore, that although this chapter discusses infinitive phrases in connection with their ability to perform functions prototypically assigned to NPs, they have other uses, as complements and/or modifiers of nouns, verbs, and adjectives. Like prepositional phrases, they are felt to be more or less adjectival when complementing or modifying nouns, but more or less adverbial when complementing or modifying verbs or adjectives.

DISCOVERY ACTIVITY 8-11

1. For each infinitive below, give your judgment: Is it a complement or modifier? Is it like an adjectival or an adverbial phrase?
   a. I'll have a hamburger *to go.*
   b. He uses gum *to hold up his socks.*
   c. He went to college *to find himself.*
   d. It was a night *to remember.*
   e. He has a tendency *to gain weight.*
   f. He went *to get some refreshment.*
   g. The way *to show your appreciation* is not always clear.
   h. It was bound *to happen.*
   i. It was too hot *to handle.*
   j. I was too mad *to smile.*
   k. I've got a good mind *to report this.*

2. In *It caused John to sneeze,* you can see that *John* is the subject of the infinitive phrase, *to sneeze.* That being the case, what is the function of *him* in *It caused him to sneeze?*

3. Analyze the NPs beginning with *something* in the sentences below. That is, identify the class of each word following the headword and specify its relationship to the other components of the phrase.
   a. He gave me something to remember him by.
   b. It gave her something to live for.
   c. It's not exactly something to write home about.

Perhaps the sentences in (3) of Discovery Activity 8-11 gave you pause. In each case, the sentence contains a preposition without an object, a fairly common occurrence in English. We have many sentences like *They were sneaking around,* where a preposition with no object acts as an intentionally vague locative adverbial. But hypothetical sentences corresponding to the infinitive phrases in the sentences in (3) would be ungrammatical without objects for the prepositions: *I remembered him by, *She lives for, *We write home about. In order to understand what goes with what, we could posit pairs of hypothetical sentences like *He gave me something* and *I remember him by something/it*. In that way, it becomes obvious that these "something phrases" are a little like tenseless versions of indefinite relative clauses. In each case the "missing" object of the preposition can be made to reappear as *which—by which to remember him, for which to live,* and *about which to write home*—providing further evidence that although they contain infinitives instead of tensed verbs, these "*something* phrases" are relative clauses in disguise.

As for question (2), although *him* is an object pronoun, the answer is, of course, "the subject." The whole infinitive phrase, *him to sneeze,* not just the pronoun, is the object of *cause*. But because of its position directly after *cause,* the subject of the embedded verb, *sneeze,* is perceived as the object of *cause.* Thus, despite the underlying subject-verb relationship between the pronoun and *sneeze,* *It caused he to sneeze* is ungrammatical.

DISCOVERY ACTIVITY 8-12

1. Consider the structure and meaning of the following sentence; then answer the questions that follow.

He says good morning only after he's had his coffee.

   a. What do you think the sentence means? What idea(s) does it convey? Paraphrase the sentence in such a way as to express the "main idea" in entirely different words of your own and/or in a different form or structure.
   b. Which clause do you think is the main (or independent) clause and which the subordinate (or dependent) clause?
   c. Can you assign the main idea to one or the other of the clauses? Why or why not? Do you think the main clause expresses the main idea?

CONJOINING: SUBORDINATION

In writing, an SVX can start with a capital letter and end with a period, in which case it constitutes a **simple** (one-clause) **sentence**.

If two or more SVXs are joined together to make a longer sentence, each SVX is called a **clause**. If two clauses are related through a **subordinating conjunction** or **subordinator** such as *although*, the two-clause sentence is called a **complex sentence**. Consider the following sentences:

Although I like yogurt, I hate cottage cheese.

I hate cottage cheese, although I like yogurt.

The addition of the subordinating conjunction turns the SVX *I like yogurt* into a **subordinate** (or **dependent**) **clause**; the subordinator destroys the structural integrity of the SVX, making it structurally, logically, and semantically dependent on (or subordinate to) another. *I hate cottage cheese*, not having a subordinator, retains its structural independence and is therefore called the **main** or **independent clause**. Notice that regardless of the linear order, the clause with the subordinator is still subordinate to or dependent on the main clause.

Discovery Activity 8-12 was designed to make the point that these terms, *main clause* and *subordinate clause, independent clause* and *dependent clause*, refer to form or structure, not to meaning. It is unwise to equate "main clause" with "main idea." In the first place, there are no objective criteria for deciding what a main idea is. In the second place, it's often impossible to isolate the main idea and assign it to one or the other of the clauses; in most cases it spans or is tied up with both. It could be argued that in the example the main idea is not that he says good morning, but that he doesn't; yet the main clause is *he says good morning.*

Like nominal clauses, subordinate clauses are created by adding a function word to an SVX. However, unlike nominal clauses, which are embedded inside SVXs as if they were NPs or inside NPs as noun complements, subordinate clauses are adjoined to other SVXs, frequently to serve adverbial functions relating to how, when, where, and why. There is some latitude about punctuating the resulting complex sentence, but it's customary to put a comma between the two clauses when the subordinate clause comes ahead of the main clause:

Because I don't see well, I tend to have a lot of accidents.

I tend to have a lot of accidents because I don't see well.

DISCOVERY ACTIVITY 8-13

1. Make a subordinate clause out of either sentence in each of the following pairs and put the two clauses together to form a complex sentence that makes sense. Underline your main clause. Try not to use any subordinating conjunction more than once. Here is a partial list of subordinating conjunctions.

as	before	since	when
as if	because	so that	whenever
as soon as	even though	unless	whereas
after	if	until	while
although	provided that		

Example
We spend millions on road construction. Our highways are full of holes.
Although we spend millions on road construction, <u>our highways are full of holes.</u>

a. We were traveling through   We learned of an impending
   New York.   hurricane.
b. It was raining jelly beans.   Nobody bothered to look up.
c. He cheated on his exams.   He was thrown out of the
                                      academy.
d. I was coming through the door.   A baby started crying.
e. You behave yourself.   I'll give you a lollipop.
f. You can go to a show.   You're not too tired.

2. Write five complex sentences of your own with a different subordinating conjunction in each one. Use some conjunctions you didn't use in (1).

Despite the label *complex sentence*, you will probably agree that the sentences in Discovery Activity 8-13 are relatively uncomplicated. In real life language use, many simple sentences are probably far more elaborate than the complex sentences you wrote. We use the traditional term *complex sentence* not to refer to complexity of thought, but to distinguish one type of grammatical configuration from another, called *compound sentence*, to which we now turn our attention.

DISCOVERY ACTIVITY 8-14

1. Mark any sentences you consider ungrammatical.
   a. Esmerelda likes dancing because Ed likes dancing.
      Because Ed likes dancing, Esmerelda likes dancing.
      Esmerelda likes dancing because Ed likes it.
      Because Ed likes it, Esmerelda likes dancing.
      Esmerelda likes dancing and Ed likes dancing/it (too).
      And Ed likes dancing/it (too), Esmerelda likes dancing.
   b. Esmerelda likes dancing, although Ed finds it boring.
      Although Ed finds it boring, Esmerelda likes dancing.
      Esmerelda likes dancing, but Ed finds it boring.
      But Ed finds it boring, Esmerelda likes dancing.
   c. My car doesn't work when my motorcycle works.
      When my motorcycle works my car doesn't work.
      My car works or my motorcycle works.
      Or my motorcycle works my car works.
2. What can you do to the ungrammatical sentences to make them grammatical?

CONJOINING: COORDINATION

The sentences in Discovery Activity 8-14 point up a significant and striking difference in the syntactic properties of subordinating and coordinating conjunctions. If we assign a subordinating conjunction to one member of a pair of clauses, the linear order of the clauses is flexible for many speakers even when it results in "backward pronominalization," the use of a pronoun before its coreferring "antecedent," as in sentences like *Although Ed finds it boring, Esmerelda likes dancing*.

On the other hand, once we attach a **coordinating conjunction** (*and, but, or, for, nor,* and *yet*) to a clause, we no longer have the choice of putting that clause first. When the sense permits it, we can of course reassign the conjunction, and that enables us to invert the clauses. That is, we can change the ungrammatical **And Ed likes dancing Esmerelda likes dancing,* to *Ed likes dancing and Esmerelda likes dancing.* Obviously, this option is not open when the meaning of the clauses entails or even implies logical or temporal sequencing. For example, we could hardly rearrange the two clauses, *Ed/he was in Philadelphia* and *and he/Ed visited Indepen-*

dence Hall as **He/Ed visited Independence Hall and Ed/he was in Philadelphia*, not only because of the possible unacceptability of backward pronominalization here, but also because it would violate the implied order of events in time. Note, however, that no violation occurs with subordination: *While/when he was in Philadelphia, Ed visited Independence Hall* is as good as *Ed visited Independence Hall while/when he was in Philadelphia.* Such examples emphasize the distinction between complex and compound sentences: namely, if we choose subordination, ordering the clauses is relatively unconstrained, both logically and grammatically; if, on the other hand, we choose compounding, ordering the clauses is highly constrained, only sometimes by logic, but always by the grammar.

In short, we have more choices about arranging the clauses of a complex sentence than we have in ordering the parts of a **compound sentence**, the name assigned not only when two or more clauses are conjoined by the coordinating conjunctions but also when clauses are related to one another by still a third set of "connectors"—a set not classed as conjunctions. Before leaving the subject of coordinating conjunctions, however, here is a punctuation tip: a comma is optional in a compound sentence when the clauses are short. When a comma is used, it is placed at the end of the first clause, not after the conjunction:

I like yogurt, but I hate cottage cheese.

not

I like yogurt but, I hate cottage cheese.

DISCOVERY ACTIVITY 8-15

1. Observe the behavior of the word *however* in the clauses below:

however, Charles declared his complete indifference
Charles, *however,* declared his complete indifference
Charles declared his complete indifference, *however*

2. Write a basic sentence to use as a companion clause to go with the clause in (1)—for example, *Esmerelda called the law unfair.*
3. Does it matter what linear order you put those two clauses in?
4. Now look at the following list of clauses.

of course we were shocked by the vehemence of her remarks
in fact we were shocked by the vehemence of her remarks
because we were shocked by the vehemence of her remarks
although we were shocked by the vehemence of her remarks
if we were shocked by the vehemence of her remarks
nevertheless we were shocked by the vehemence of her remarks

5. Which of the italicized words and phrases in (4) can you move to one or more positions other than the first position in its clause?
6. For each clause in (4), write a different basic sentence to use as a companion clause.
7. Of your pairs of clauses, which pairs make sense regardless of the linear order and which ones don't?

COMPOUNDS WITH NON-CONJUNCTIONS

As Discovery Activity 8-15 implies, we can relate clauses to one another with a variety of structure words other than conjunctions, including those known traditionally as **conjunctive adverbs**. These words and phrases are often confused with the subordinating conjunctions, but they are not conjunctions, and the SVXs they relate are in fact not conjoined. Rather, they remain structurally independent of one another and can even be written as separate sentences: *Esmerelda called the law unfair. Charles, however, declared his complete indifference.* And since they differ in certain respects from prototypical members of the adverb class, the term *conjunctive adverb* can be very confusing; therefore, it might help to call them **logical connectors** or **logical relators**. They include *instead, therefore, in fact, then, consequently, for example,* and others. But you needn't memorize the list; instead, just remember this simple test for distinguishing them from conjunctions: logical relators are "portable." That is, they may be moved around to various positions within their clauses, as illustrated here:

But you needn't memorize the list; remember, instead, this simple test.

But you needn't memorize the list; remember this simple test instead.

The syntactic behavior of conjunctions is entirely different. A conjunction, whether subordinating or coordinating, must always appear first in its clause, as the following examples illustrate.

John was hotheaded, *but* he tried to be fair.
*John was hotheaded, he *but* tried to be fair.
*John was hotheaded, he tried to be fair *but.*

Although John was hotheaded, he tried to be fair.
*John *although* was hotheaded, he tried to be fair.
*John was hotheaded *although,* he tried to be fair.
John was hotheaded, *although* he tried to be fair.
*John was hotheaded, he *although* tried to be fair.

And unlike subordinate clauses, which can precede or follow the clauses to which they are related, clauses with logical relators are almost invariably required by the dictates of logic to follow the other.

Although he was hotheaded, John tried to be fair.
John tried to be fair, *although* he was hotheaded.
**Nevertheless* he tried to be fair; John was hotheaded.

So you have a double test: If the relating word is portable but the clause is not, the word is a logical relator and the clause is structurally independent, regardless of how dependent on the other it may be for its meaning. Given that clauses related with logical relators are structurally independent, those who follow the conventions of standard edited English do not splice them together with a comma, but use either a period or a semicolon to signal their mutual independence, as illustrated here.

John was quite volatile. In fact, he was hotheaded.
John was quite volatile; in fact, he was hotheaded.

DISCOVERY ACTIVITY 8-16

1. Relate each of the following pairs of sentences *in two different* *ways.* For example, make one complex sentence and one compound sentence, or write two different kinds of compound sentences. Remember that you may use a comma in addition to (but not instead of) a coordinating conjunction. You may use a semicolon instead of a period.

Example:
Esmerelda refused his offer. Sidney went out and ate worms.
Complex:
When Esmerelda refused his offer, Sidney went out and ate worms.

Sidney went out and ate worms because Esmerelda refused his offer.
Compound:
Esmerelda refused his advances; then Sidney went out and ate worms.
Esmerelda refused his advances(,) and then Sidney went out and ate worms.
Esmerelda refused his advances(,) and Sidney went out and ate worms.

   a. He contributed generously to the chowder society.
      He refused to join the organization.
   b. Sidney returned Esmerelda's copy of *Sonnets from Zap*.
      She knew it was all over between them.
   c. The guest was famous. The hosts were not impressed.
   d. I'll bring my guitar. Charlie promises not to sing along.
   e. He promises not to sing along. I might not bring my guitar.
   f. Esperanto is the most successful of the invented languages.
      It is spoken by about eight million people around the world.
   g. The rain had slowed the trip by about fifteen minutes.
      We reached South Point at nine o'clock.
   h. It's not a good idea to tell Sidney your secrets. He won't keep
      them to himself.
2. Write five pairs of two-clause sentences. Of each pair, make one a
   compound, one a complex sentence. Use correct punctuation.

SUMMARY

I. Relative Clause
  A. Structure
     Relative pronoun R + VX or R + SV. (An R usually fills some
     NP function in the relative clause but *whose* replaces a
     determiner.) Only *who(m)* or *which* can be used in non-
     restrictives (those incidental clauses set off by commas).
     That, which, and *who(m)* can all be used in restrictives
     (those embedded as specifiers within an NP).
  B. Functions
     1. Function as noun expanders: *who live in glass houses*
        expands *people*, the headword of the NP *people who live
        in glass houses*.
     2. Provide parenthetical information: *His father, who died
        years ago, still seems to be influencing his decisions*.
II. Verbal Phrases Used as NP Substitutes (Lacking tense, they are
    not complete SVXs; hence they are not called clauses.)
  A. Gerund/Gerundive/Gerundival Phrase

1. Structure: An *-ing* form and any complements and modifiers; the *-ing* word is the headword of the construction.
2. Function: All NP functions. Examples:

   Subject: *Flying over the mountains* (= it) is scary.

   Object of verb: I don't like *flying over the mountains* (= it).

   Object of preposition: I'm thinking about *flying over the mountains* (= it).

B. Infinitive Phrase
1. Structure: An uninflected verb stem with complements and modifiers, frequently (but not invariably) preceded by *to*, and sometimes including a subject. The verb stem is the headword.
2. Function: NP functions except object of preposition. Examples:

   Subject and complement: *To fly over the mountains* is *to know joy.*

   Complement/modifier of noun: I'd like a hamburger *to go.*

   Complement/modifier of verb: He went *to find a policeman.*

   Object of verb: I want *you to win.*

   Object of preposition: *I dreamed of *to fly over the mountains.*

III. Clauses as NP Substitutes

   A. Structure:
   1. A function word preceding an SVX: I know *why you're angry.*
   2. An SVX without any added function word but with an indefinite pronoun in first position though not necessarily in subject function: *What* (= object of *did*) *you did* was unethical.

   B. Function: All NP functions.

IV. Subordinate Clauses

   A. Structure:
   1. Subordinating conjunction plus SVX.
   2. Conjoined to another clause (unlike nominal clauses, which are usually embedded and function as NPs inside a superordinate SVX or as noun complements inside NPs).

   B. Function: Often function adverbially: *Whenever the phone rings*, the baby starts to cry.

V. Independent Clauses

A. Structure:
1. A basic sentence: *He's fun.*
2. An SVX with an added coordinating conjunction: *but he's fun.*
3. An SVX with an added logical connector: *nevertheless, he's fun.*

B. Function:
1. Main clause in a complex sentence: Although he's crazy, *he's fun.*
2. Coordinate clause in a compound sentence: *He's crazy but he's fun.*
3. Member of a compound sentence whose clauses are related through a logical connector: *He's crazy; nevertheless, he's fun.*

STUDY QUESTIONS

1. What is the necessary precondition for relative clause formation?
2. What is the usual function of a relative clause?
3. What is the function of the relative pronoun in a relative clause?
4. How does *whose* differ from other relative pronouns?
5. Explain to someone who hasn't taken this course why restrictive modifiers are called *restrictive* and illustrate with your own examples.
6. In standard edited English, what are the two conventional ways to signal that a relative clause is nonrestrictive?
7. What's a test for NP equivalence or NP functions?
8. Why are gerundive and infinitive phrases not called clauses?
9. What's wrong with telling people to "put main ideas into main clauses"?
10. How do subordinate clauses differ structurally from relative clauses?
11. Name the coordinating conjunctions.
12. What is the two-part test for distinguishing between subordinating conjunctions and logical relators?
13. Why must clauses that are related through logical relators not be joined to other clauses with commas?
14. Is the rule referred to in question 13 a rule of English grammar? Why or why not?

FURTHER STUDY AND DISCUSSION

1. You have no doubt heard the absent (suppressed or deleted) subject of a command (like *Sit down*) referred to as "understood *you.*" In Discovery

Activity 8-11 you were asked to render a judgment about the probable grammatical relationship between infinitives and other parts of sentences. Regarding the sentence *It was too hot to handle,* does the notion of an understood subject help your analysis? Can you suggest an understood subject for the infinitive *to handle?* What other understood items would you have to include if you posit a hypothetical subject for *to handle?* Does the notion of hypothetical sentences (as used in reference to passive/active sentences in Chapter 5 and to the indefinite relative clause in this chapter) seem to you to be a useful tool in grammatical analysis? Does it make sense to include in an analysis of a sentence something that isn't even in the sentence? In a well-developed paragraph, comment on this issue in any way you like.

2. In some textbooks, relative claues are called "adjective clauses." Why do you think this is so? Do you consider "adjective clause" an appropriate name for this structure? Why or why not?

9 | The Sound System

A grammar of a language describes the "organization of the noises" of that language. There are many noises that humans can make with their speech organs; but each language uses only a limited number of vowel and consonant sounds, and each language puts limits on the particular combinations of sounds that can be used. This chapter will provide an inventory of the sounds that make up the American English language, and a system for the transcription of those sounds—information that is vital to your understanding of the English spelling system, of dialect differences, and of language change.

SOMETHING ABOUT SOUNDS

The most obvious feature of natural human languages is that their medium is the sound produced by the larynx and oral cavity. The human vocal apparatus is capable of producing a wide range of sounds, all of which are meaningless in and of themselves, in isolation from one another. You can see for youself: pronounce the sounds usually represented by the letters *f* or *s* or *n*; then pronounce the sounds represented by *e* or *o*. You are using sounds that occur in English, but you are not speaking English. The miracle of language is this: it uses meaningless noises to make meaning.

In order to "make meaning," each language has a set of noises and a set of rules for combining them. By combining the meaning*less* noises represented by the letters above, we can produce meaning*ful* noises: the words *fee, foe, see, so, knee, (k)no(w)*. With a small number of sounds and a small number of operations for their combination, we can make an infinite number of meaningful noises—our words, phrases, and sentences. English uses approximately thirty-six distinct vowel and consonant sounds. Some languages use more and others use fewer. Hawaiian, for example, uses only twelve basic speech sounds, seven consonants and five vowels. It doesn't matter. Speakers of Hawaiian can say as much about anything as speakers of any other language. Just as our counting is not limited by the small number of digits we use because the digits can be permuted to infinity, our talking is not limited by a small number of sounds because sounds can be combined and rearranged indefinitely.

The mathematical analogy is not perfect, of course. There are literally no limits on combinations and permutations of digits, but every language does place limits on the permissible combinations and permutations of the sound segments. In English, for example, we can find the sound sequence represented by *mb*, but only accidently, as it were, when two adjacent syllables bring it about, as in the word *combine*. English does not permit a syllable to begin with that sound sequence, and when English speakers try to speak a language that does allow it, they find it almost impossible to pronounce. Try *mbira*, for example. The Spanish language does not permit a syllable to begin with the combination *sp*, and when Spanish speakers learn English they have the same difficulty with words like *speak* (which they may pronounce "espeak") as we have with *mbira*.

Except for phonologists, speakers generally are not conscious of the phonological rules. Yet it is obvious that if we are speakers of English we know them, because we pronounce English sound sequences accurately and recognize inaccuracies as manifestations of a "foreign accent." We may not be conscious of individual sound segments, which, being meaningless, are seldom uttered in isolation from one another. And because we live in a literate society, we may tend to confuse sounds, the noises we make with our mouths, with letters, the marks we make with our pens. You may be surprised, for example, that the letter *x* actually represents a combination of two sounds, "k" and "s" (*tax* sounds like, or is *homophonous*, with *tacks*). Conversely, many two- and three-letter combinations represent single sounds. Consider, for instance, the *ph* of *phone* and the *tch* of *watch*.

In this chapter, we will discuss the sound system of English by analyzing meaningful sound sequences (words) into their meaningless component parts. To do this, we will concentrate on what we hear when we pronounce words rather than what we see when we spell them out on a page.

When you were only six or seven years old, you learned the alphabet: twenty-six symbols and their names. You learned how to write the symbols and even learned what sounds they generally correspond to. The trouble with the alphabet, however, is that it has only twenty-six symbols for representing or transcribing about thirty-six distinct **vowel** and **consonant** sounds. In order to transcribe (represent) the sounds of the language accurately, we use a special system of "spelling" the sounds—especially the vowels.

The system, called a **broad phonemic transcription**, is based on a phonetic alphabet that uses a distinct symbol for each distinctive sound. At first these strange new "spellings" may seem difficult. With a little practice, though, they should become familiar and easy. We'll start by using only those consonant sounds whose symbols are exactly like corresponding alphabet letters, but will add some vowel symbols that have different values from those you are accustomed to in ordinary spelling.

Phonemic transcriptions are always surrounded by virgules (or slashes), to distinguish them from ordinary spellings: transcription of the word *pet*, for example, is /pɛt/. In order to avoid confusion, always make your phonemic symbols exactly as given: do not substitute an /e/ for an /ɛ/ or the reverse. Here are five vowel symbols and their phonemic values:

/i/ has the value of the vowel of *beet, meat, mete*
/ɪ/ has the value of the vowel of *bit, sit, quit*
/e/ has the value of the vowel of *bait, bay*
/ɛ/ has the value of the vowel of *bet, said, breath*
/æ/ has the value of the vowel of *bat, math, ask*

This system is called broad transcription because a single symbol can represent a range of sounds, instead of just one sound. The sounds represented may not in fact be exactly the same in all environments. The vowel sound in *ban*, for example, is not exactly like the one in *bat*, and the vowel of *bank* is even more different. All of these vowel sounds, however, are treated as if they were exactly alike: /bæt/, bæn/, and /bæŋk/. Later on, we will discuss the reason for this deviation from the principle of a distinct symbol for each distinct sound.

As you do Discovery Activities in this chapter, you can expect your transcriptions to differ from those of your classmates and instructor, and certainly from the author's, which are based on a dialect spoken in South Philadelphia.

DISCOVERY ACTIVITY 9-1

1. Transcribe the following words, using the symbols above for the vowel sounds, but ordinary alphabet letters for the consonant sounds. The first few have been done to provide models. Work across the page, not down the columns.

seat /sit/	Pete____	greet____	steam____
sit /sɪt/	pit____	grit____	hid____
sate /set/	pate____	great____	play____
set /sɛt/	pet____	fret____	said____
sat /sæt/	pat____	frat____	plaid____
nag____	mean____	tape____	rip____
fate____	fat____	fit____	trap____
date____	debt____	feet____	scene____
bet____	been____	bee____	bay____
pin____	pink____	plan____	plank____

2. Now reverse the procedure. For each of the phonemic transcriptions below, give the ordinary spelling of the word:

/mit/____	/ple/____	/hit/____	/hɪt/____
/mɪt/____	/plid/____	/plet/____	/flæt/____
/met/____	/flit/____	/flɪt/____	/min/____
/mɛt/____	/sɛnd/____	/sɪnd/____	/sænd/____
/mæt/____	/mɛs/____	/gɛs/____	/list/____

Now we will add six vowel symbols and some of the consonant symbols that have values that are different from corresponding alphabet letters. Here are the symbols and their values:

/ə/ (called *schwa*) has the value of the vowel of *but*, *some*, the value of the vowel in unstressed *the*, the value of both vowels in *above*

/a/ has the value of the vowel of *pot*, *squash*, and *far*

/ɔ/ has the value of the vowel of *bought*, *taught*, and *for*

/o/ has the value of the vowel of *boat*, *stow*

/ʊ/ has the value of the "oo" of *look*, *would*, and *pull*

/u/ has the value of the "oo" of *boot*, *spook*, *pool*, *Luke*

/ŋ/   has the value of the "ng" in *sing, sang, sung*
/j̆/   has the value of the "g" in *gem, gym, gin*
/k/   has the value of the "ck" in *stack, stock* and the value of the "c" in *cat, can*

Speakers of some dialects do not recognize a difference between /a/ and /ɔ/ in all environments. If you speak a dialect where pairs like *don/dawn* and *cot/caught* are homophones, you may not even hear the difference when other speakers pronounce these pairs. But if you can distinguish between *boy* and *by/buy* and the others in the following series, you may be able to train yourself to hear the *cot/caught* distinction.

buy	/bay/	boy	/bɔy/
ardor	/ardər/	order	/ɔrdər/
star	/star/	store	/stɔr/ (*cf.* stower /sto ər/ or /sto wər/)

Another way to train yourself to hear this distinction is to try to pronounce the word *morning* without the *r*, like someone from the South. The result should sound something like "mawnin," or /mɔnin/. Now compare that to the vowel sounds in *moaning*, /monin/, and *farming*, again without the *r*, hence /famin/.

DISCOVERY ACTIVITY 9-2

Fill in the blanks below with a key word for each of the phonemic symbols given.

/i/ _____		/ɔ/ _____	
/ɪ/ _____		/o/ _____	
/e/ _____		/ʊ/ _____	
/ɛ/ _____		/u/ _____	
/æ/ _____		/ŋ/ _____	
/ə/ _____		/j/ _____	
/a/ _____		/k/ _____	

The symbols /i/, /e/, and /u/ all represent "long" vowels, while the /ɪ/, /ɛ/, and /ʊ/ represent "short" vowels. The symbol /ŋ/ is the only one needed at the end of words like *sing* (/sɪŋ/) because the sound usually represented by the letters *ng* is actually a single sound, just as the sound usually spelled *ck* is a single sound. Note that "c" is represented by a /k/ or /s/; there is no "c" in the phonemic system.

DISCOVERY ACTIVITY 9-3

Using the phonemic symbols, transcribe the following words. Say the words aloud and work across the page, not down the columns.

pack___	get___	jet___	stay___
crop___	crap___	crape___	creep___
cook___	kook___	luck___	Luke___
foe___	far___	for___	fat___
fate___	feat___	fit___	phone___
fun___	fin___	stuck___	stick___
steak___	stack___	streak___	strum___
boot___	but___	boat___	bought___
not___	naught___	nut___	none___
nun___	nap___	nape___	grain___
sung___	clung___	wing___	string___
star___	store___	stair___	stir___
fist___	mist___	cyst___	kissed___

You may have had some difficulty in deciding how to transcribe the vowel sounds in syllables that end in r. As you have seen, vowels are notoriously variable, perhaps the most noticeably varied feature of regional differences in pronunciation. In addition, in anticipation of the sound represented by the letter r, the quality of the vowel just before it is often affected or **colored**, because final r has a vowel-like quality of its own. Finally, the vowels are affected in different ways because of regional differences in pronouncing the sound represented by final r itself.

In some varieties of English, a final r is pronounced /ə/, and you may find that a word like *stair* can best be transcribed as /steə/ or /stæə/. The system of broad transcription we are using does not provide enough symbols to enable us to make fine distinctions, so we will work with approximations. For example, we can approximate the sound of the vowel +r in syllables like *her, cur, stir, word,* and the final syllable of *forward* by transcribing that combination as /ɚ/, or as /ə/ by itself to represent an "r-less" variety. With the help of your instructor, you can decide what symbols are best suited for contrasts like that of *for* vs. *far* if /fɔr/ and /far/ do not represent your pronunciation closely enough.

THE PHONEME DEFINED

Before we go any further with phonemic transcription, let us investigate the meaning of *phonemic*, as well as *phoneme*, the word it derives from. A **phoneme** is a segment of sound which has absolutely no meaning of its own: /p/, for example, doesn't mean anything. Notice, however, that from a given sequence of these sound segments a meaning emerges: /p/ + /e/ + /n/, for example, amounts to /pen/, a meaningful sequence, *pane* or *pain*. Notice further that if we change just one of those segments of sound, but leave the rest of the sequence alone, the meaning changes: a pain is neither a pan nor a pen. Thus, a phoneme, though meaningless itself, has the power to change the meaning of a sequence if put in place of some other sound.

This process of changing just one small segment in a sequence enables us to identify exactly which sound differences are significant, or **phonemic**, and which are not. If changing a single sound changes the meaning, we say the sound is significant, or phonemic. We know, for example, that /res/ (*race*) and /rez/ (*raise*) mean different things, and that (along with many pairs that have that contrast) enables us to establish /s/ and /z/ as phonemes in English. Pairs like *race* and *raise, pen* and *pain, dim* and *dime* (called **minimal pairs**) enable us to determine which "noises" are phonemic, and which are just variants of the "same" sound.

In the interest of greater accuracy, it's important to note that the concept of the phoneme is really an abstract grammatical construct. We can't actually pronounce a phoneme. The symbol /d/ is a kind of shorthand for *voiced alveolar stop*, a technical description of the range of sounds represented by /d/. All phonemes are named according to how and where they are articulated. The sound represented by /d/ is made by abruptly releasing air after it has been stopped for an instant by the action of the tongue against the alveolar ridge (the ridge of bone behind the teeth). But it's easier to think of /d/ as a graphic representation of "the initial sound of *done* or the final sound of *rode*," and sufficient for our purposes to do so.

Now we will add the last three vowel symbols and some consonant symbols that are different from the ordinary alphabet letters. The last three vowels are **diphthongs**, which are characteristically "complex"; that is, when pronounced, they start out as a simple vowel, then take on the sound of a second vowel. If you pay close attention, you will notice, for example, that the vowel of the word *boy* starts out as if it were an /ɔ/ and ends up like a "y" sound.

Although we use two symbols to represent a complex vowel, a diphthong like /ɔy/ as in *boy* or /ay/ as in *buy* still counts as a single phoneme, just as the diphthong /e/, as in *bay*, is a single phoneme. Because we really do pronounce many long vowels as diphthongs, some transcription systems use complex symbols for all long vowels, including, for example, /iy/ for the vowel in *bee*, /ey/ for the sound in *bay*, /ow/ for the vowel in *go*, and so on. Your instructor may want you to adopt that practice. Here are the symbols for the diphthongs and the remaining consonants for which we can't use alphabet letters.

/aw/   has the value of the vowel in *loud, cow*
/ay/   has the value of the vowel of *high, ice*
/ɔy/   has the value of the vowel of *noise*
/θ/   has the value of the "th" of *ether, thigh, thin*
/ð/   has the value of the "th" of *either, thy, then*
/č/   has the value of the "ch" of *church*
/š/   has the value of the "sh" of *sham*
/ž/   has the value of the "s" of *measure, vision*

All of the other consonant symbols that are used in phonemic transcription are exactly like ordinary alphabet letters, and their values can be deduced. For example, /skw/ represents the cluster of sounds normally spelled *s-q-u*, as in *squash*, and /tæks/ represents both *tax* and *tacks*. If you pronounce *whale* differently from *wail*, that is, with an initial /h/, you will transcribe the former as /hwel/ (not /whel/) and the latter as /wel/.

DISCOVERY ACTIVITY 9-4

1. Fill in the following blanks with a key word for each of the phonemic symbols given. Use this chart as a key to help you transcribe the words listed in the rest of the activity until you have learned the symbols and their values well enough not to need the key.

Simple vowels

/æ/ _____   /ə/ _____
/ɛ/ _____   /ɔ/ _____
/ɪ/ _____   /ʊ/ _____
/a/ _____

Long vowels and diphthongs

/e/ _____   /u/ _____

/i/ _____   /aw/ _____

/ay/ _____   /ɔy/ _____

/o/ _____

Consonants not represented by alphabet letters

/ŋ/ _____   /ð/ _____

/ĵ/ _____   /θ/ _____

/č/ _____

/š/ _____

/ž/ _____

2. Why is there no "c" in the phonemic alphabet? _____
   _____

3. How do we represent the x of *tax*? _____

4. How do we represent the *qu* of words like *quit*? _____

5. Transcribe the following:

food _____   feud _____

boot _____   beauty _____

coot _____   cute _____

6. Do you pronounce the first syllable of *Tuesday* /tyuz/ or /tuz/?

7. Transcribe the words that follow. Work across the page, not down the columns.

bay____	boy____	buy____	bough____
cat____	cot____	caught____	Kate____
catch____	ketch____	bar____	bore____
star____	store____	stare____	stay____
cry____	whacks____	wax____	tacks____
race____	rays____	trace____	trays____
mouth____	month____	moth____	myth____
then____	this____	sure____	shore____
beat____	bite____	bat____	bet____
wash____	squash____	pots____	robs____
spars____	sparse____	tense____	tens____
scares____	scarce____	ski____	sky____
ice____	eyes____	toil____	champ____
chump____	chimp____	shine____	shame____
thigh____	thy____	how____	cow____
coy____	kite____	catch____	cash____
bilk____	bilge____	chill____	Jill____
boot____	but____	bought____	put____

root___	rout___	right___	rate___
bale___	boil___	coil___	Kyle___
crowd___	loud___	think___	thing___
gem___	gum___	city___	kitty___

SYLLABLES

Thus far we have dealt mostly with words of only one **syllable**, and you may have noticed that regardless of how many vowel letters were used in the regular spelling, only one vowel symbol was used in its transcription. Thus, *pain* and *pane*, spelled with two vowel letters, are transcribed with /e/. The vowel of a syllable is generally uttered more sonorously than the rest; that means that it can be heard distinctly and usually carries farther than consonants. Every syllable has a "peak of sonority," which is generally carried by a vowel sound. In English, there are a few consonant sounds that sometimes carry the peak of sonority and are in those instances called **syllabic**. If you say a word like *bottle*, for instance, you will be hard put to identify a vowel sound in the second syllable. Because of the way it is produced, an /l/ can be sonorous, like a vowel. The same can be said of the /n/ in words like *bacon* and *button* and the /r/ in *butter*. If you do identify a vowel sound in these unstressed syllables, it is likely to be either a schwa, /ə/, or a short vowel of indistinct or indistinguishable quality, something like an /ɪ/, but less clear.

It is typical of English syllables that they are not uttered with equal **stress**, or force. In general, the vowel quality of all weakly stressed syllables, not just those with syllabic /l/, /n/, or /r/, is reduced to an indistinct or indistinguishable sound. This all-purpose vowel varies from dialect to dialect, and it doesn't matter much what symbol you use for its transcription, since no meaning difference is at stake. You could transcribe *category*, for example, as /kætəgɔri/ or /kætɪgɔri/. *Bacon* could be /bekən/ or /bekɪn/.

DISCOVERY ACTIVITY 9-5

1. Pair up with a classmate. One of you should cover up the words in column 1 and listen as the other person reads the words aloud. You should both transcribe the words. Then, exchange roles so the other

person dictates the second column, which you both transcribe. Transcribe the third column together if there's time; otherwise, finish the exercise alone.

great____	take____	scrape____
if____	trip____	rocks____
scrap____	gasp____	box____
even____	peak____	sneaker____
desk____	Fred____	debt____
love____	crumple____	mother____
who____	grew____	blue____
should____	book____	crooked____
grow____	Joe____	toe____
caught____	awful____	ridicule____
cot____	lot____	ridiculous____
order____	organ____	petite____
ardor____	squash____	potted____
star____	stare____	past____
luxury____	measure____	passed____
food____	feud____	scent____
newspaper____	husband____	sent____
sixth____	glimpsed____	prints____
close (adj.)____	close (verb)____	prince____
illusion____	opinion____	something____
crossed____	oozed____	hiccough____
ice____	eyes____	smile____

2. So far we have dealt with individual words in isolation, a very unnatural practice, which distorts the actual pronunciation used by speakers of American English. For example, most people say /lɛmigo/, not /lɛt mi go/. Convert the following to normal spelling:
   a. /am gɔnə/ kray/ _____
   b. /yə wɑnə rayd/? _____
   c. /jit yɛt/? _____
   d. /jə rili hæftə go/? _____
3. Now transcribe the following strings. Use your natural pronunciation and try to hear your normal way of saying them. Transcribe what you hear, not what you see on the page:
   a. Give me a chance. _____
   b. Never mind that. _____
   c. Wish you were here. _____
   d. You want to dance? _____
   e. Little Red Riding Hood. _____
   f. Little Red Writing Hood. _____

VOICED / VOICELESS CONTRAST

You have seen that /s/ and /z/ are phonemes because we can find many minimal pairs like /res/ (*race*) and /rez/ (*rays* or *raise*), /ays/ (*ice*) and /ayz/ (*eyes*), /klos/ (adjective) and /kloz/ (verb) where substituting /z/ for /s/ makes a difference in the meaning of the sequence of sounds. The next paragraph explains the slight physical difference between these two sounds, which also distinguishes other pairs: /p/ and /b/, /t/ and /d/, /k/ and /g/, /f/ and /v/, /š/ and /ž/, /č/ and /ǰ/, and /θ/ and /ð/.

The quality that distinguishes /b/, /d/, /g/, /v/, /z/, /ž/, /ǰ/, and /ð/ from the others is called **voicing**. All vowels have this quality, as do the **nasals**, /m/, /n/, and /ŋ/, and the **liquids**, /l/ and /r/. To understand what this means, put your fingertips on your larynx (your "Adam's apple") as you pronounce /z/ and hold it. You will feel your larynx vibrate. Now pronounce /s/, and you will feel nothing. Pronounce any vowel, nasal, or liquid, and you will feel the vibration. That is voicing, and any sound that has that quality is a **voiced** sound. Those that do not have it are called **voiceless** or **unvoiced**. Let's take a closer look at this property of the language.

DISCOVERY ACTIVITY 9-6

1. Transcribe the following pairs of words, being careful to transcribe what you hear, not what you see.

A

Singular	Plural	Singular	Plural
horse____	horses____	ditch____	ditches____
dress____	dresses____	crutch____	crutches____
rose____	roses____	edge____	edges____
quiz____	quizzes____	judge____	judges____
dish____	dishes____	mirage____	mirages____
crash____	crashes____		

B

cap____	caps____	cat____	cats____
cake____	cakes____	cliff____	cliffs____

C

robe____	robes____	rod____	rods____
cog____	cogs____	wave____	waves____

sum___	sums___	son___	sons___
song___	songs___	bale___	bales___
fear___	fears___	sky___	skies___
sofa___	sofas___	day___	days___
candy___	candies___	ski___	skis___

   a. Pronounce the singular forms in (A). List the final phonemes of those singular forms: _____

   b. Give the phonemic transcription of the plural affix as it sounds in all the plural forms of set (A): _____

   c. Pronounce all the singular forms in (B) and list the final phonemes that occur in those singular forms: _____ Are these phonemes voiced or unvoiced?

   d. What is the phonemic transcription of the plural affix in (B)? _____ Is that a voiced or unvoiced sound?

   e. List the final phonemes that occur on the singular forms of (C). _____ Are these final phonemes in (C) voiced or voiceless?

   f. What is the phonemic transcription of the plural affix in (C)? _____ Is that a voiced or voiceless sound?

2. Now complete the following generalization, which describes what we do when pronouncing plural forms, and is therefore a phonological rule.

   a. When a singular ends in /s/, /z/, /š/, /ž/, /ĵ/ or /č/, the plural affix will actually add a syllable. The result is pronounced (transcribed) as: _____

   b. If the singular ends in an unvoiced sound not listed among those in (a), the plural affix will be pronounced (transcribed): _____

   c. If the singular ends in a voiced sound not listed among those in (a), the plural affix will be pronounced (transcribed): _____

The phenomenon illustrated by Discovery Activity 9-6 is known as **assimilation**, which simply means that two sounds that are next to one another tend to become like one another. In the case of plurals, the pronunciation of the affix is affected by the quality of the sound immediately preceding it.

Sometimes a sound will be affected by the sound following it— for example, in the pronunciation of many prefixes. The negative prefix *in-* ("not"), for example, has assimilated to the /l/ of *legal* and we have *illegal*, not **inlegal*. The same prefix has become assimilated to the /r/ in *irresponsible*, and to the /p/ in *impossible*. Assimilation occurs when two adjacent sounds are articulated rapidly in normal speech.

DISCOVERY ACTIVITY 9-7

1. For each of the following verbs, give the phonemic transcription of the stem form, the third person present tense form, and the past tense form, as illustrated in the model; then answer the questions that follow.

Stem	Third Sing. Pres.	Past
walk /wɔk/	walks /wɔks/	walked /wɔkt/
stop_____	stops_____	stopped_____
laugh_____	laughs_____	laughed_____
pass_____	passes_____	passed_____
rub_____	rubs_____	rubbed_____
wish_____	wishes_____	wished_____
shrug_____	shrugs_____	shrugged_____
create_____	creates_____	created_____
rave_____	raves_____	raved_____
wrench_____	wrenches_____	wrenched_____
need_____	needs_____	needed_____
scream_____	screams_____	screamed_____
fill_____	fills_____	filled_____
stir_____	stirs_____	stirred_____
blend_____	blends_____	blended_____
play_____	plays_____	played_____
mute_____	mutes_____	muted_____
snow_____	snows_____	snowed_____
help_____	helps_____	helped_____
float_____	floats_____	floated_____
nod_____	nods_____	nodded_____

   a. Sort out the verbs on the basis of the pronunciation of the affix for third person singular present. What three pronunciations appear? _____

   b. State the rule for pronouncing this verb affix, as you did the rule for noun plurals in Discovery Activity 9-6: _____

   c. Now sort out the verbs on the basis of the pronunciation of the affix for the past tense. You will see that this changes the grouping. What three pronunciations of the past tense affix appear? _____

2. State the rule for pronouncing this verb affix. _____

3. Are the generalizations you arrived at rules of English grammar? Why or why not? _____

The effect of assimilation may seem to create a contradiction or paradox. We have said that /s/ and /z/ are phonemic, and that changing one to the other causes a change in meaning. Yet with noun plurals and third singular verb forms, that is not the case, since both /s/ and /z/ "mean" plurality, and so, for that matter, does /ɪz/ (or /əz/). This demonstrates that native speakers ignore differences that are not significant, and treat all plurals as if they were the same sound even though they're not. The phonemic principle still works to differentiate pairs like /sparz/ (*spars*) and /spars/ (*sparse*); /tɛnz/ (*tens*) and /tɛns/ (*tense*).

DISCOVERY ACTIVITY 9-8

This activity is a preview of some of the principles you will be dealing with in the next chapter. After you have transcribed these words, try to see what sound-spelling correlations keep reappearing.

huge____	Scrooge____	badger____	ledger____
cage____	cadge____	sludge____	budge____
lack____	lace____	lacy____	lackey____
icky____	sticky____	ice____	icy____
lack____	lake____	like____	lice____
pack____	pick____	peck____	pock____
peak____	peek____	poke____	pike____
stuff____	stiff____	staff____	staves____
fill____	file____	still____	stile____
pill____	pile____	doll____	dole____
moll____	mole____	wall____	whale____
bite____	biting____	bitten____	bitter____
ripe____	riper____	ripen____	ripped____
write____	writer____	writing____	written____
pan____	pane____	pain____	peen____
pen____	pin____	pine____	pining____
occur____	occurred____	occurring____	occurrence____
cure____	cured____	secure____	securing____
rage____	rag____	raged____	ragged____
curly____	curling____	securely____	
notice____	noticed____	noticeable____	
panic____	panicked____	panicky____	
staged____	stagger____	courageous____	
serviceable____	despicable____		

Look at your transcription of the words *occurred* and *cured*, *occurring* and *securing*, *curly* and *securely*. Try to formulate some principle to account for spelling some with two *r*'s and others with one.

COMBINING SOUNDS

Languages vary widely not only in the sounds they include in their phoneme inventory but also in the allowable arrangements of those sounds. A speaker of English may find it impossible to pronounce /ŋwa/, /pfunt/, /kpadi/, or /šči/; yet they are transcriptions of actual words in other languages. These "impossible" combinations are not excluded because they are more difficult than the combinations we use; rather, they only seem difficult to us because English doesn't have them. To a speaker of Japanese, a language that doesn't have consonant clusters, English combinations like /str/ and /skw/ (as in /stre/ and /skwɔk/, *stray* and *squawk*) seem equally "impossible."

As a speaker of English you know, although you are not conscious of knowing, the **phonotactic rules**, that is, the system of rules governing such things as the allowable locations and possible combinations of individual phonemes. At the ends of syllables, for example, we may have as many as four consonant sounds, as in the case of /glɪmpst/ (*glimpsed*). Perhaps you are aware that the maximum number of consonant sounds (though not necessarily letters) that can occur at the beginning of a syllable is three, but except for phonologists, most people are not consciously aware that all three-segment initial consonant clusters in English must begin with /s/. Moreover, only the voiceless stops, /p/, /t/, and /k/, can appear in second position.

DISCOVERY ACTIVITY 9-9

1. Make a list of as many words as you can think of that begin with a three-consonant cluster beginning with /s/. Which sounds can appear in the third position? Check your dictionary to find out whether there are any you didn't think of.
2. Why do you think there are so few dictionary entries beginning with /sf/ and /skl/?
3. Some of the following are not possible English words because they violate rules about where or in what combinations a sound can occur. Write the probable spelling for those that *are* possible. Write "no" by the others.

/dlop/____   /fup/____   /rakz/____   /relz/____   /kpadi/____
/fred/____   /dudg/____   /grah/____   /zep/____   /gro/____
/sprad/____   /psit/____   /poth/____   /klet/____   /sti/____

If you were responding (out of habit) to alphabet letters rather than to the sounds represented by the phonemic symbols, you may have been fooled by some of the sequences in (3). If you check carefully, however, you will see that /dudg/, /psit/, /grah/, /rakz/, and /poth/ (along with the more obvious /dlop/ and /kpadi/) are not possible in English. Although we spell the initial /s/ of *psychology* as *ps*, and although we can have the sound sequence represented by /ps/ at the end of a syllable (e.g., *caps*), we cannot begin words with the sequence of sounds represented by /ps/. Nor can we have a sound sequence like /dg/ without an intervening vowel, although the letters *d* and *g* appear together in the spelling of the final consonant of *budge*. And although we find the letter *h* at the end of many words, we never have the sound represented by /h/ in that spot.

As the dictionary entries show, we have many words beginning with /str/, /skr/, /spl/, /spr/, and /skw/, and we even have a few like *skewer*, which begin with /sky/. But there's no /*stl/, and we find /skl/ only in a few borrowed words like *sclerosis*. The two-phoneme cluster /sf/ of *sphere* is also rare because it too is not native to English. In that sense, /skl/ and /sf/ are "impossible" combinations that have gained entry into the language through the vocabulary even though they defy the phonotactic rules excluding them from the native stock.

SOMETHING ABOUT SOUNDS: A POSTSCRIPT

This brief introduction to the grammatical subtopic of phonology has been vastly oversimplified; it provides only a superficial treatment of some of the most obvious phonological facts. Note that the study of phonology is not limited to a discovery and inventory of the vowel and consonant sounds. In English, contrasts in both pitch and stress are highly significant in expressing and interpreting meaning. Stress, for example, enables us to differentiate between *SUBject* as noun and *subJECT* as verb. Pitch, along with associated pauses, differentiates *What's that in the road ahead?* from *What's that in the road, a head?* From these examples, you can see that there is a great deal more to know about English phonology that is beyond the scope of this chapter.

SUMMARY

1. English has approximately thirty-six significant vowel and consonant sounds.

2. Significant contrasts reflected in minimal pairs like *hate*, /het/, and *heat*, /hit/, enable us to identify the phonemes of the language.
3. A phoneme is a meaningless sound which has the power to change the meaning of an utterance when replacing some other sound.
4. The quality of the vowel in an unstressed syllable is typically reduced to an indistinct or indistinguishable sound.
5. Because of assimilation, we have three different pronunciations for the plural *-s* as well as three for the past tense and third person singular present verb affixes, depending on the final sound of the stem.
6. Pronunciations like /wənə/, /gɔnə/, and /lɛmi go/ are not "sloppy English," but normal pronunciation in ordinary, rapid speech.

STUDY QUESTIONS

1. What is a phoneme?
2. What evidence or data is used to discover or establish that a particular sound is a phoneme in English? Give some examples.
3. How many phonemes are there in your speech?
4. Discovery Activity 9-7 led to the following three-point generalization:
   a. If a verb ends in /t/ or /d/, its past tense form will be /ɪd/: /kri-etɪd/ = *created*.
   b. If a verb ends in a voiceless sound other than /t/, its past tense form will be /t/: /plapt/ = *plopped*.
   c. If a verb ends in a voiced sound other than /d/, the past tense form will be /d/: /rabd/ = *robbed*.
   Is this generalization a rule of English grammar? Why or why not?
5. Here is a rule you may have been taught: "Don't say *goin* or *gonna*—the words are *going* and *going to*." Is this a rule of English grammar? Why or why not?
6. In your own words, give a definition of *assimilation* as it pertains to phonological phenomena.
7. People sometimes misspell phrases like *supposed to*, *used to*, and *happened to* as "suppose to," "use to," and "happen to." What is the probable reason for this spelling error?

FURTHER STUDY AND DISCUSSION

Because of phenomena like consonant assimilation and vowel reduction in unstressed syllables, pronunciations like "gonna," "wanna," "hafta," and "usta" are predictable and normal. Only rarely, in very careful speech, do we hear the "full forms," *going to, want to, have to,* and *used to.* As an experiment, try using the full forms as often as you can remember to do so during the course of a day. Do you find that you automatically make adjustments in other features of your speech style? Pay attention to the responses of others toward your speech. Make notes, if possible, of any comments or questions put to you about the way you're talking. Report your findings, along with any conclusions you can draw from the experiment, to your classmates.

10 | The Spelling System

If you reflect on how many cultures there are, all of which have languages but few of which have writing systems, you may want to argue that a writing system can hardly be a part of the structure of language. If it were, all languages would have one. Yet some scholars argue that where a writing system exists, it is an independent manifestation of the abstract language system, and not merely a system of representing speech. Regardless of which position you take, as an educated person, you ought to understand how the spelling system works. Moreover, discovering the rationale for some of our spelling practices can be interesting in its own right. This chapter will help you discover some of the many consistencies in the English spelling system.

SPELLING PATTERNS

In the following activities, we will be focusing on **spelling patterns**, and you will discover many correspondences between patterns of letters and the sounds they consistently represent.

DISCOVERY ACTIVITY 10-1

1. Working across the page, give phonemic transcriptions of these words:

bag___	beg___	big___	bog___	bug___
at___	Ed___	id___	odd___	up___
scratch___	etch___	which___	splotch___	crutch___
Dan___	den___	din___	don___	dun___
flag___	fled___	slid___	clod___	club___

---

2. Give the phonemic symbols for the five vowel sounds in the words above: _____

3. Are those short vowels or diphthongs and long vowels?

4. What is consistent about the spelling of all these words?

All the words in Discovery Activity 10-1 have short vowel sounds and all end in a consonant sound. All conform to a spelling pattern consisting of a single vowel letter followed by at least one consonant letter. That pattern only rarely yields long vowel sounds (e.g., *-ild* words like *wild* and *-ost* words like *most*). Even more rarely, a word with a short vowel will be spelled with two vowel letters (e.g., *give, come, done*; *bread, thread*). But most of these exceptions actually constitute subpatterns with their own internal consistency, and the sound-spelling correspondence between short vowel sounds and one-letter representation is consistent enough to constitute a kind of "first rule of English spelling": A **closed syllable** (that is, one ending in a consonant sound) whose vowel sound is short will almost always be spelled with a single vowel letter.

DISCOVERY ACTIVITY 10-2

The sound-spelling correspondence between short vowels and one vowel letter is seen in stressed closed syllables of longer words, as you can see by transcribing the following words:

antagonistic	_____	fantastic	_____
fetishistic	_____	hospital	_____
botanical	_____	hundred	_____
trumpeter	_____	nostrum	_____
umbrella	_____	reminiscent	_____

As demonstrated by Discovery Activities 10-1 and 10-2, stressed syllables that end with a consonant (closed syllables) and have a short vowel are spelled with one vowel letter.

DISCOVERY ACTIVITY 10-3

1. For each of the following phonemic transcriptions, give the ordinary English spelling. See if you can discover a letter pattern that corresponds to a different sound pattern. Work across the page, not down the columns.

/kæp/____	/kep/____	/hap/____	/hop/____
/dɪm/____	/daym/____	/slap/____	/slop/____
/kæĭ/____	/keĭ/____	/fɪl/____	/fayl/____
/dal/____	/dol/____	/pək/____	/pyuk/____

    a. What two changes did you have to make in spelling to correspond to the change in sound from short vowel to long vowel or diphthong? Look especially at *cadge/cage*, *fill/file*, and similar pairs.

    b. How many vowel letters does it take to spell long vowels and diphthongs in stressed, closed syllables?

2. For each of the following phonemic transcriptions, give the ordinary English spelling or spellings:

/pæn/_____	/pen/_____	_____
/stæk/_____	/stek/_____	_____
/pɛt/_____	/pit/_____	_____
/bɛt/_____	/bɪt/_____	_____
/pɪk/_____	/pik/_____	_____
/bɪt/_____	/bayt/_____	
/gat/_____	/got/_____	
/rad/_____	/rod/_____	_____
/bət/_____	/but/_____	
/kət/_____	/kyut/_____	
/kat/_____	/kot/_____	_____
/fɛnd/_____	/find/_____	

All the words in Discovery Activity 10-3 are closed syllables; that is, their final sounds are consonants, regardless of their spelling. Since a consonant sound is last, the final *e*, when present, might at first glance appear to represent nothing; hence, the myth of the "silent *e*." You can see, however, that the *e* is no different from the second vowel letter of all the other pairs of letters used to spell long vowels; without it, the words would have short vowels: both *cote* and *coat* spell /kot/, but *cot* spells /kat/. In other words, we need two vowel letters to spell long vowels and diphthongs in closed syllables.

DISCOVERY ACTIVITY 10-4

    1. For each of the following, give the ordinary spelling:

/lætər/ _____	/letər/ _____
/rəfərd/ _____	/ɪntər fird/ _____

/strɪpt/ _____   /straypt/ _____
/slapt/ _____   /slopt/ _____
/kətər/ _____   /kyutər/ _____

2. How many consonant letters intervene between the two vowel letters in the words with short vowels?

3. How many consonant letters intervene between the two vowel letters in words with long vowels?

4. Add the suffixes indicated to each of the following words and adjust the spelling accordingly:

ride + -en _____   ride + -ing _____
admit + -ance _____   contrive + -ance _____
grit + -y _____   grime + -y _____
pomp + -ous _____   fame + -ous _____
occur + -ing _____   secure + -ing _____

5. What two adjustments did you have to make in spelling the short-vowel words?

6. Which short-vowel word is an exception?

7. Why is *pompous* an exception?

8. What adjustment did you make in spelling the long-vowel words?

9. Why do we drop the final -e on long-vowel words when adding these particular affixes?

10. Make a generalization about spelling the words in (1) and (4), relating spelling to sound.

11. Some words seem to break the spelling rule about double consonants after short-vowel syllables. For example, it is not necessary to double the consonant in *bigoted, programing, stenciled,* and many others. Can you guess why? If not, look back at the discussion following Discovery Activity 10-2; then pronounce these words aloud.

   a. What condition is not met in the words that appear to defy the rule?

   b. Give the full spelling rule for when to double and when not to double consonants when adding suffixes.

DISCOVERY ACTIVITY 10-5

1. Supply the correct letters to represent the long *a* sound in the following words:

excl____m   refr____n   portr____   pl____   b____t
p____d   r____sin   dec____   dism____   rel____
prev____l   f____th   afr____d   w____t   tr____l

2. Under what conditions did you spell the vowel with the letters *ay*?
3. Under what conditions did you spell the vowel with the letters *ai*?
4. The preceding Discovery Activities have dealt with letter patterns for spelling vowel sounds, but there are also letter patterns that are used for consonant sounds. Transcribe the following words:

staff____	class____	bell____	crack____
stiff____	chess____	spell____	sick____
bluff____	miss____	skill____	neck____
scoff____	fuss____	dull____	clock____

   a. What is the prevailing spelling practice for /f/, /s/, /l/, and /k/ when they appear at the end of one-syllable, short-vowel words?
   b. Consider words like *fun, fan, sun, sin, love,lug, cat, cut.* Are the sounds /f/, /s/, /l/, and /k/ normally spelled with two letters at the beginnings of words?
   c. Why is the abbreviated nickname for a professor sometimes misspelled with two f's when *professor* has only one?
   d. Reflect on your responses to the questions in (3) and (4). When more than one spelling is possible for a particular sound, what factor other than the quality of the sound itself influences the choice of spelling?

5. Add the indicated suffixes to the following words:

solemn + -ity	_____	hymn + -al	_____
sign + -al	_____	bomb + -ard	_____
column + -ar	_____	paradigm + -atic	_____
malign + -ant	_____	autumn + -al	_____

   a. What happened to the so-called silent letters when you added suffixes?
   b. What do the silent letters represent in words like *solemn, sign, bomb, malign*? That is, why do you think they are there?

6. Transcribe the following words:

bath	_____	bathe	_____
booth	_____	soothe	_____
wreath	_____	wreathe	_____

   a. Pronounce the words above and listen carefully to all the sounds. Aside from its function as an indicator of vowel quality, what else does the final e tell you about pronouncing the words in the second column?
   b. In addition to its diacritical functions as an indicator of sound qualities, the final e has a morphological function in the words

above. What is it? (Hint: What form classes do the words belong
to before and after adding e?)

7. You have seen that the plural -s spells the /ɪz/ of *horses*, the /z/ of
dogs, and the /s/ of *cats*. If the plural -s, the e of *bathe*, and the
silent letters in question 5 don't represent specific sounds, what do
they represent? What purpose do they all serve?

8. Transcribe the following words:

cell, call, cull _____

cite, cote, cute _____

cyst, cast, cost, cussed _____._____

certain, carton, curtain _____

cynical, conical _____

city, catty _____

cylinder, calendar, colander, cullender _____

cigar, cougar _____

deception, decapitation _____

decimal, decade _____

decide, decode _____

  a. Make a generalization about the two spelling patterns involving
  the letter c, relating it to the sounds represented by that letter.
  (Hint: When did you transcribe /s/, when /k/?) Notice that this
  question is not related to vowel *sounds* although it involves
  vowel *letters*.

  b. Why is *panicky* spelled with a k, when *panic* isn't?

9. Assume that all of the following are bonafide words in English and
that all of them mean different things. Transcribe them:

jone, noan, phone, shoan, wrone, thoan, sown,

joan, known, foan, shone, roan, choan, bone

  a. Each "word" in (9) above has how many phonemes? ____

  b. How many different initial phonemes are established by this
  list?

  c. Give the three spellings of /o/, each consisting of two letters,
  represented in the words above.

  d. What vowel sound would be represented if only the letter o
  were used?

  e. What is the rationale for saying that there are no silent letters
  in English spelling? (Hint: See your responses to questions 5, 6,
  and 9.)

10. Give the pronunciation (phonemic transcription) of the following:

A

| sing____. | singe____ | bing____ | binge____ | flang____ |
| lung____ | lunge____ | pong____ | sponge____ | flange____ |

B

fudge____	·budge____	judge____	huge____	refuge____
badge____	cadge____	cage____	ridge____	oblige____
dodge____	doge____	edge____	collegiate____	

a. What is the function of the final e in (A)? Notice that in these words, final e has nothing to do with the internal vowel sound.
b. What is the function of the letter d in (B)?
c. Why does the final e affect the vowel sound in *cage, huge,* but not in *lunge, flange*?
d. Note that *collegiate* has an *i*, not an *e*, after the g. Is there any "so-what-ness" to that?
e. You have seen that the vowel letter of an affix will do the job of the so-called silent e, which can be dropped from *fame* and from *secure* to make *famous* and *security*. Why, then, must it be kept on words like *courageous*?

IN DEFENSE OF ENGLISH SPELLING: G-H-O-T-I DOES NOT SPELL *FISH*

Many people are quick to point out the "inconsistencies" of English spelling. Some people even enjoy a parlor game that challenges them to invent wildly improbable spellings like "psoloquoise" for *circus*.† Oddly enough, few teachers have pointed out that English spelling is *not* inconsistent, perhaps because even they believe the myth of inconsistency. In fact, the English spelling system is highly systematic. If it were not, there would be even fewer good spellers than there are, since few people would be able to commit all the spellings of individual words, one by one, to memory. Certainly there must be many more regularities than irregularities.

Dispelling the Spelling Myth

Over twenty years ago, a research team at Stanford University determined that the correct spelling of English words can be predicted 90 percent of the time when all relevant factors, including morphology and syntax, are taken into account along with pho-

---

†*Circus* is pronounced (transcribed) /sərkəs/:
ps = /s/, as in *ps*yche, /sayki/
olo = /ær/, as in c*olo*nel, /kərnəl/
qu = /k/, as in pi*qu*ant, /pikənt/
oise = /əs/, as in porp*oise*, /pɔrpəs/

nological information. Their findings suggest—contrary to the common belief that the English spelling system is wildly inconsistent, whimsical, irregular, even random—that there are far more regularities than irregularities and imply that it may be the common perception of the spelling system, rather than the spelling system itself, that is at fault.

The research team was not unmindful of the shortcomings and real problems in the English spelling system. Ideally, an alphabet should be phonemic; that is, it should have a distinct symbol for each distinct sound in the language. But the English alphabet has fallen short of that ideal from the moment it was adapted from the Latin alphabet, which was not designed to represent the sounds of a Germanic language. Furthermore, we have seen that English has about thirty-six distinct sounds, but only twenty-six letters to spell them with. Obviously, there cannot be a one-to-one correspondence between individual sounds and single-letter representation. Moreover, the inventory of sounds used in the English language has changed since the alphabet was adopted, but the spelling of many words had already been established before completion of some major changes in pronunciation, so that some current spellings (like *laugh* and *rough*) represent now forgotten pronunciation.

Despite these complications, there is a high degree of regularity in the system; otherwise, how would anyone learn it? But paradoxically, many people have less difficulty with "hard words" and "exceptions" than they do with perfectly predictable spellings like *occurrence*, perhaps because they don't know what to base their predictions on. The Discovery Activities in this chapter are designed to call attention to the variety of factors that may affect the spelling of a word in our system.

Letters Don't Make Noise

First of all, we need to realize that unlike a phonemic symbol, an alphabet letter by itself can't represent (much less "make" or "have") a sound. Letters are all equally silent until we put them into a context with others. We should rid ourselves of the notion that the letter *a*, for example, "represents at least eight phonemes," as one text claims. Rather, the letter *a* represents no phoneme at all until we put it between *h* and *t*, or between *squ* and *sh*, or in front of *bout*, or in some other particular environment. The letter combination *at*, on the other hand, does consistently represent or spell the sound sequence that makes rhymes of *hat*, *cat*, and so forth. The *at* combination is only a single example of a much more general spelling pattern which is consistently used to spell short vowels in thousands of syllables. Examples can be drawn from consonant spellings as well. Discovery Activity 10-5, item 8, shows that the letter *c*, for example, spells no sound at all until you combine it with *e*, *i*, or *y* to represent /s/, with *a*, *o*, or *u* to represent /k/, with *h* to spell /č/, and so forth.

Secondly, the choice of which spelling to use for any particular sound will depend to some extent on the specific location of that sound within a syllable or word (initial, medial, or final), and to some extent on the nature of adjacent sounds. You saw in Discovery Activity 10-5, for example, that although we have several spellings for long *a*, we are not at liberty to choose at random from among them; rather, we are constrained by the location of the sound. In the case of /č/, which may be spelled *ch* or *tch*, our choice depends on whether the preceding vowel is long or short: compare *each/etch*, *speech/stitch*. Similarly, the /k/, usually spelled *ck* at the end of a one-syllable word with a short vowel, is spelled *k* at the end of a one-syllable word with a long vowel, which is itself usually represented by a two-letter combination: *peck/peek/peak*, *stack/steak/ stake*.

The two-letter combination for spelling the long vowel, in the case of words like *stake*, is the combination of the vowel letter *a* and the so-called silent *e*. The letter *e* is neither more nor less "silent" than the *a*. All letters are "silent" until they enter into combinations with one another, and in this case it is the combination of *a* and *e* that spells the long vowel of *stake* (and of *steak*) not the *a* alone. In short, the *e* has a vital function as a diacritical mark in such words and should not be treated as if it were an unnecessary appendage.

A consequence of "*non*-silent *e*"that should be made explicit is that a short vowel needs to be "protected" from the influence of a second vowel letter. Thus, *written*, which has a short vowel, must be spelled with two *t*'s, while *writing*, which has a long vowel sound, needs only one. Discovery Activity 10-4 emphasizes that there is a consistent correspondence between stressed short vowel syllables and the two-consonant letter sequence and the same consistent correspondence between long vowel syllables and the one-consonant spelling: *cadge/cage, better/meter, ripper/riper, slopped/ sloped, drudge/huge*. In words that result from affixation, the vowel letter of the affix performs the same function as the silent *e*, which it replaces. In a few words (*hoeing, canoeing*), we retain the *e* in spite of a constraint against the sequence *eing* in order to avoid the sequence *oing*, which could be misinterpreted as a single syllable, as in *boing*. A letter sequence like *eed* might be misread as a separate long vowel syllable in its own right (note *refereed*); therefore, we usually drop the *e* before adding the past tense affix *-ed*. On the other hand, when we add an affix beginning with a consonant letter to long-vowel syllables, we must keep the final *e* in order to preserve the long vowel: *secure, securing, secured*, and *security*, but *securely*. If the *e* were dropped before adding the *-ly*, the result would have to be pronounced like *curly*.

What about those words that end in a short vowel syllable but don't require a double consonant before the suffix? These apparent exceptions can be accounted for and predicted if we consider the influence of stress. It is typical of English that unstressed syllables have a reduced, short vowel. Thus, words like *bigoted, programing*, and *trumpeter* don't need a second consonant to assure the short vowel sound in the final syllable of the stem because those syllables, not being stressed, will automatically be read with short vowel sounds. Yet the tendency to put in an extra consonant letter after a short vowel is so strong that many words can be acceptably spelled with either one or two consonant letters: *traveler/traveller*. Stress placement can also affect the spelling of consonant sounds: compare the spelling of /k/ in *attic* and *attack*.

Finally, paying attention to pronunciation can help in predicting correct spelling. Table 10-1 provides advice for choosing between *ie* and *ei*.

Spelling Is More than Sound

Thus far, it may have seemed as if the sound system were the only factor to consider in English spelling, but many spellings are more consistent with the morphology of the words than with their sounds. A phonemic transcription of *stubbornness*, for example, would clearly show that there is only one /n/ between the last two syllables. Nevertheless, we retain the two *n*'s to reflect the fact that the word consists of *stubborn* plus *-ness* and not *stubborn* plus *-ess*. And as you have seen, the pluralizing *-s* spells the notion "this is a plural," rather than the actual sounds we make, for we don't make the same sound for all the plurals that are spelled *-s*.

Closer attention to derivational morphology might also help to prevent misspellings like "accidently" for *accidentally*. In deriving adverbs, a good policy is to conform to systematic sequences like *logic/logical/logically* and disregard pronunciation. The *-ally* com-

TABLE 10-1 Choosing between *ie* and *ei*

If you have difficulty with *ie* and *ei* words, it may be because you're not paying enough attention to the sounds of the words in question. Here are some suggestions for separating *ie* and *ei* words.

1. Say the word out loud. If the word has a long *e* sound, it will be spelled with *ie* except after the letter *c*.
   priest, niece, piece, *but* receive, ceiling.

2. Learn these seven words. They are the only common ones with the long *e* that violate the rule given in (1).
   either   financier   seize   weird
   leisure   neither   species

3. Say the word aloud. If the word has a long *a* sound, it is likely to be spelled with *ei*.
   beige   freight   skein
   Moreover, except for the *-ceive/-ceit words*, the *ei* combination is likely to be followed by *g*, *gh*, *gn*, or *n*.
   beige   neigh
   feign   skein
   (*Veil* is the only exception that comes to mind.)

4. If the word in question has neither the long *e* nor the long *a* sound, look it up in the dictionary. There's no way to predict *heifer*.

bination is so common for adverbs that even *basic, specific,* and *drastic,* which have no *-al* form, become *basically, specifically* and *drastically.*

We must also consider syntactic information when deciding how to spell a word. Many of our spelling choices must be made not on the basis of sound but on the basis of syntactic function, which in English is usually determined by the position of a word relative to others in phrases. Sets of homophones, for example, will become less troublesome if you take syntax into account. If you remember that the word *your* is most often followed by words like *book, future, audacity,* or *father's moustache* (that is, nouns and noun phrases) while *you're* is most often followed by forms ending in progressive aspect *-ing*, you will increase the likelihood of choosing the right spelling. See Table 10-2 for some rules regarding use of apostrophes in words like *you're.*

So the next time someone mentions George Bernard Shaw's suggestion that *fish* be spelled *g-h-o-t-i* because *gh* spells /f/ in

TABLE 10-2   Using the Apostrophe

1. Use an apostrophe in contractions at the point where letters have been left out.
   you're = you [a]re   it's = it [i]s, it [ha]s
   they're = they [a]re   who's = who [i]s, who [ha]s

2. Use an 's for possession (genitive case) with singular nouns and indefinite pronouns.
   John's son   my *father's house*   *nobody's business*

3. Use only an apostrophe to show possession with regular plural noun forms. Make your noun plural first, then add the apostrophe.
   the Martins' house   babies' temperatures   dogs' tails

4. Use an 's to show possession with irregular plurals.
   women's rights   men's wear   children's hour

5. Do not use an apostrophe for possession with determiners. They have "possession" built into their meaning. Pronouns with apostrophes are actually contractions (see [1]).
   your book   its illustrations
   their summer home   whose house burned down

---

laugh, o spells /ɪ/ in *women*, and *ti* spells /š/ in *nation*, you may want to point out that *gh* spells /f/ only after *ou* or *au* and only at the end of a syllable, that *ti* spells /š/ only in combinations like *tion*, and *o* spells /ɪ/ in exactly *one* word—*women*.

SUMMARY

1. Contrary to common belief, English spelling is not inconsistent. While it is true that some sounds can be spelled in a variety of ways, the choice from among them is highly constrained, not only by phonological factors but by morphological and syntactic factors as well.
2. Spelling is not based entirely on sound.
3. Even when sound is the basis for a particular spelling, phonological features other than the quality of the sound itself are relevant to correct choice. Additional phonological features, including stress, must be considered.
4. Phonological factors that influence spelling include:
   A. The phoneme:
       1. the sound quality of the vowel or consonant itself

2. the location of the sound in a syllable or word (initial, medial, or final)
3. the quality of the other sounds in the environment (whether adjacent vowel is long or short)
   B. Stress on a syllable can determine the spelling of its phonemes (e.g., whether to spell /k/ *ck* or *c*).
5. Non-phonological factors that influence spelling:
   A. Morphology
   The structure of the morphemes, rather than the resulting sound, determines many spellings (e.g., *misspell* vs. *dispel*).
   B. Syntax
   The syntactic function, determined by position, will dictate the spelling in the case of homophones (e.g., *their* vs. *there*).

STUDY QUESTIONS

1. Cite two factors to account for many of the apparent spelling irregularities in English.
2. What is a diacritical mark? If you can't infer the answer from the context of this chapter, consult your dictionary; but answer in your own words.
3. Explain in your own words why the *l* of *palm* and *calm* constitutes a diacritical mark whether or not it also represents a separate sound. (Hint: What happens when it's not there?)
4. Name two non-phonological factors that are relevant to spelling, and explain in your own words and with original examples how or why they are relevant.
5. Why does *misspell* have two *s*'s while *dispel* has only one? If you cannot deduce the answer from the context of this chapter, check your dictionary.
6. Explain the rationale for saying that the final *e* of a word is not a silent letter. Notice that it is not enough to say that it's a diacritic. What other function(s) can it have? (Hint: Compare *lapse* and *laps*. Since they're homophones, the *e* obviously isn't a diacritic in this case.)
7. What's the "first rule of English spelling"?
8. Why do we keep the final *e* in *securely* but drop it in *security*?
9. Suppose we had only one spelling for the homophones *pear*, *pair*, and *pare*. How would you know which word was meant?
10. If someone misspells *their* as "there," how do you know it's misspelled?
11. What do questions 9 and 10 illustrate about spelling?
12. Why don't *plastic*, *music*, and *attic* have a *k*, as *attack* does? Notice that this question has nothing to do with vowel sounds.

FURTHER STUDY AND DISCUSSION

Despite the discussion in this chapter you may still have some grievances against English spelling or some serious objections to the position presented here. Even if you are convinced, you may still have some stories to tell about your own experiences learning (or failing to learn) the system. Write a well-developed paragraph about something to do with spelling and you.

11 | Using Your Dictionary

You are probably so used to hearing the expression "look it up in the dictionary" that is may not have occurred to you that there's really no such thing as *the* dictionary. Like other books, dictionaries are made by a variety of publishers and designed to fulfill a wide variety of needs. It should come as no surprise, therefore, that all dictionaries are not alike. In order to get your money's worth out of the dictionary you own, you will have to know its peculiarities. This chapter will help you get acquainted with dictionaries in general and with your particular dictionary so that you can make good use of it for the rest of the term and throughout your college career. As you work through the Discovery Activities, keep in mind that the words we will explore are not notable in themselves, but were chosen to exemplify the methods used by dictionaries for conveying the relevant information.

SPELLING

DISCOVERY ACTIVITY 11-1

1. Copy out all of the spellings your dictionary reports for each of the following words:

cabala, catsup, curb, cullender, develop, domicile, judgment, parakeet, surprise

2. Read the information in the front of your dictionary regarding variant spellings; then answer the following questions for each of the words listed in (1):
   a. How many correct spellings does your dictionary give?
   b. Does your dictionary indicate that one spelling is preferred, or does it count the variants as equal? What method, device, or symbol does your dictionary use for conveying that information?

c. Do variant spellings reflect or imply variant pronunciations for any of the words? How is that information conveyed?
3. Does your dictionary report *alright* as an alternate spelling of *all right*? With or without comment?
4. Compare your answers with those of your classmates who use different dictionaries. Do the dictionaries all report the same information about number of spellings?
5. Look up the entry for *subtile*. Is it a variant of *subtle*? If so, why is it not listed as such in the entry for *subtle*?
6. Look up *moustache* and *soubriquet*. Are definitions given at those entries? If not, why?

PRONUNCIATION

DISCOVERY ACTIVITY 11-2

1. Copy out the pronunciation symbols exactly as given in your dictionary for as many of the following words as your instructor assigns. (If more than one pronunciation is indicated, copy all variant pronunciations.)

banal, calliope, ennui, erudite, eschatological, impious, internecine, irreparable, nuclear, oenophile, patina, pineland, quixote/quixotic, rodomontade, sesquipedalian

2. Consult the information about pronunciation in the front of your dictionary; then answer the following questions for each word listed in (1):
   a. How many pronunciations does your dictionary give? Does your dictionary differ from other dictionaries in the number of pronunciations it reports?
   b. Does your dictionary indicate or imply that some pronunciations are to be preferred, others restricted, disapproved, or condemned? Do your classmates' dictionaries agree with the judgments of yours?
   c. Compare your pronunciation symbols with those of classmates who used different dictionaries. Point out as many differences as you can spot (e.g., different letters, symbols, or diacritical marks for vowel or consonant, different kind or placement of stress mark).
   d. Pronounce all the assigned words as your pronunciation guide directs. Despite the variety of dictionary symbols, you should be pronouncing the words pretty much the way your classmates are

pronouncing them. If you notice differences in pronunciation, what accounts for them?

3. Is a pronunciation given at *colorblind*? If not, can you determine why?

4. Many people pronounce *mischievous* as "mis-chee-vee-ous." Does your dictionary or any of those used by your classmates report that pronunciation? What does this imply about that pronunciation or about the attitude of the dictionary editors toward the pronunciation?

5. Look up the following pairs of words, and copy out the pronunciation symbols. Then answer the questions.

cot/caught, don/dawn, pin/pen

   a. Does your dictionary indicate different pronunciations for *cot* and *caught*? If so, is someone who pronounces them exactly alike mispronouncing them? If a dictionary indicates no difference in pronunciation, is someone mispronouncing them who pronounces them differently?

   b. Some people pronounce *dawn* and *don* exactly alike; others distinguish between them. Which group uses correct pronunciation?

   c. Does your dictionary indicate different pronunciations for *pin* and *pen*? Is it mispronunciation to pronounce them both as "pin"?

HOMOGRAPHS AND MULTIPLE ENTRIES

DISCOVERY ACTIVITY 11-3

1. Look up the following words and note the number of entries for each:

crash, frank, grave, pay, peaked, staff

2. Read the information about entries in the front of your dictionary and answer the following questions:

   a. Why are some words entered more than once? Be specific.

   b. Is the same reason for multiple entries given in the dictionaries used by your classmates?

   c. Compare your findings on the number of entries with those of your classmates. If other dictionaries have fewer or more entries for any word than yours has, can you suggest a reason?

   d. Check all the entries for *grave*. Which one is pronounced differently from the others?

   e. What is the difference between *homograph*, *homophone*, and *homonym*?

STATUS AND USAGE LABELS

DISCOVERY ACTIVITY 11-4

1. Look up any six of the following words, and copy out any status labels:

hassle, damned, louse, nocent, snotty, critter, jazz, feisty, hippie, ain't, mad, soapy, goober, soupy, stink

2. Read the information about usage or status labels in the front of your dictionary; then answer the following questions about the words in (1):
   a. When a status label is used, does it apply to all senses or definitions of a word?
   b. Do the labels for any of the words differ in classmates' dictionaries?

3. How does your dictionary define *colloquial*? Does your dictionary use *colloquial* as a status label?

4. What is the difference between *archaic* and *obsolete*?

5. Does your dictionary include usage notes in addition to status labels for any of the words you looked up?

6. Read the entire entry for *irregardless*. Does your dictionary comment on the status of this word? Does your dictionary differ from any of those used by your classmates?

7. Read the entire entry for *finalize*, including any usage note(s) following the entry itself. Does your dictionary comment on the status of this word? Does your dictionary differ from your classmates' dictionaries?

8. Is *how come* defined in your dictionary? How is it labeled?

9. Does the inclusion or exclusion of an expression like *how come?* affect your attitude toward the expression? Does the inclusion or exclusion affect your attitude toward the dictionary?

10. What usage information do you find in or following the entry for *like*?

11. Does the treatment of *like* in your dictionary differ from treatment in other dictionaries? Does the treatment of *like* in your dictionary affect your attitude toward that usage or toward that dictionary?

12. If it would not offend you to do so, look up some words that you consider vulgar, obscene, or taboo. How does your dictionary deal with such words? Do your classmates' dictionaries vary in this respect?

13. Does your dictionary enter words generally considered racial or ethnic slurs? How are they treated? Does the treatment of such words affect your attitude about the words or the dictionary?

14. Does your dictionary have separate entries for *chairman*, *chairperson*, and *chairwoman*?

INFLECTIONS AND "PART OF SPEECH" LABELS

DISCOVERY ACTIVITY 11-5

1. Look up the following nouns and copy out their plural forms:

focus, thesis, medium, horse, stiletto, octopus, crisis, country, kudos

2. Read the information about grammatical functions ("part of speech" or word class labels) and inflections at the front of your dictionary; then answer these questions:
   a. How many plural forms are reported for each word in the list?
   b. Does your dictionary think it unnecessary to spell out *babies* because it is predictable from our spelling rules, or does it consider plurals spelled *-ies* irregular?
   c. At the entries for *datum* and *medium*, does your dictionary comment on the use of *data* and *media* as singulars? Is *kudos* identified as a plural?
   d. Does your dictionary differ from those of your fellow students in its treatment of any of the words on the list?
3. Does your dictionary have separate entries for *walk* as noun and *walk* as verb? Does your dictionary have separate entries for *eccentric* as adjective and *eccentric* as noun?
4. Does the treatment in your dictionary of words with more than one grammatical function differ from the treatment in your classmates' dictionaries?
5. Does your dictionary indicate comparative forms (e.g., *taller*) and superlative forms (e.g., *tallest*)?
6. Look up the following verbs and copy out and label all the past tense and all the perfective (past participle) forms; then answer the questions:

drag, sneak, weave, dive, burst, sink, walk, search

   a. How does your dictionary distinguish past tense forms from perfective forms?
   b. Which perfective forms are also listed as main entries? Why?
   c. Does your dictionary comment on the status of any of the forms? For example, if *drug*, *snuck*, or *busted* are reported as forms of *drag*, *sneak*, or *burst*, are they labeled in any way or are usage notes given?
   d. Does your dictionary differ from those of your fellow students in its treatment of any of the verbs?
7. Look up the entries for the following words, make a note of the grammatical functions listed, and answer the questions.

dog, fun, parent, party, sober

a. How many grammatical functions does each of the words have?
b. Do any of the functions of the words above carry status labels or usage information?
c. Many people use *fun* as an adjective (*She's a fun person to be with*) and some even inflect it for degree: *It was funner than . . .* Does your dictionary report this usage?
d. Does the fact that *fun* is (or isn't) reported as an adjective affect your attitude toward the usage? Does it affect your attitude toward your dictionary?
e. Can you suggest any reasons for failure to report this use of *fun*?

DEFINITIONS AND ETYMOLOGIES

DISCOVERY ACTIVITY 11-6

1. Consult the information about definitions and etymologies in the front of your dictionary. Then look up the following words and answer the questions.

commode, corn, magazine, take, get, lexicon

a. How many definitions or different senses are given for each of the words?
b. In what order are various meanings of a word listed in your dictionary?
c. Compare your findings with those of your classmates. Does the order of definition differ from one dictionary to another? What determines the order of definitions in the dictionaries used by your classmates?
2. Why is it important for you to know the order of definition?
3. What is an etymology?
4. Look up the following words and copy out the etymological information. Be prepared to interpret this information in a way that will convince your instructor that you understand all of it.

Example:
Our contemporary word, *dreary*, evolved from the Middle English form, *dreri*, which had the same meaning as it has now. The Old English *dreorig* derived from the noun, *dreor*, meaning "blood," and at first meant "bloody" or "gory" but came to mean "sad." The related verb form, *dreosan*, meaning "to drip" was also related to the noun *dropa*, "drop," and to forms in Old High German, in Gothic, and in Greek.

buxom, chauvinist, crucible, lewd, pilgrim, supercilious, touch

a. Compare the etymological information in your dictionary with what your classmates have found in theirs. Point out any differences you find. Can you explain the differences?
b. Has any of these words changed its meaning since it entered the English language? How can you tell?
c. Are there some words for which no etymology is given? Why?
d. Do the etymologies for any of the words surprise you? If so, which ones, and why?
e. Do the etymologies help you understand the current meaning or use of any of the words?
5. What is a combining form? What did Chapter 2 call combining forms?

MISCELLANEOUS

DISCOVERY ACTIVITY 11-7
1. It is unlikely that you will find *pseudohuman* in your dictionary. How does your dictionary help you determine the meaning of the word?
2. You are unlikely to find *liveliness* entered alphabetically in your dictionary. Where will you find it, and why?
3. What is the difference between: *catholic* with a lowercase c and *Catholic* with a capital C? Between *republican* and *Republican*? *Impressionistic* and *impressionistic*? *Exodus* and *exodus*?
4. What is the conventional way to divide the following words at the end of a line? What accounts for the difference in where to divide?

regrettable, kissable, spelling, admitting

5. Does your dictionary contain a style manual or handbook section covering conventions of punctuation, capitalization, bibliographic form, and other manuscript conventions?

The Discovery Activities you have completed in this chapter were designed to acquaint you with the many services our modern dictionaries perform and to increase the likelihood that you will use yours efficiently and often, for it can be a source of enjoyment as well as instruction. As you have seen, your dictionary does much more than define words. Besides reporting the spelling, pronunciation, grammatical function, meaning, and, in some cases, relative acceptability or social status of words, our dictionaries contain historical information that not only enhances our understanding of the current meanings, but also provides information that is interesting in itself.

Chapter 1 made the point that a language is not merely a collection of words, but a system of rules for creating sentences. Yet the grammatical system presupposes an inventory of words (and, of course, combining forms like *pseudo*, *mini*, and the like). Recent grammatical theory, after years of almost total concentration on syntax, has restored the lexicon to a prominent place in the study of grammar. In a "Postscript" to Peter Sells's 1985 book, *Lectures on Contemporary Syntactic Theory*, for example, Thomas Wasow not only maintains that "acquiring a language . . . reduces largely to learning the meanings of words" but goes so far as to claim that "sentence structure is a projection of the semantics of words." If that is the case, study of the dictionary should be central to any study of grammar.

THE DICTIONARY AS DICTATOR

In November 1987, when Random House brought out the second edition of its unabridged *Random House Dictionary of the English Language (RHD-II)*, Christopher Porterfield, a *Time* reviewer, characterized the book as "an eminently practical, everyday reference." Yet he went on to lament that it seemed, "unfortunately," to be "swerving back toward *Webster's*" in adopting a less prescriptive stance than the first edition had taken. "And because many people wrongly consider the past tense of sneak to be snuck (instead of sneaked)," he complained, "the word has been promoted from 'chiefly dialect' in *RHD-I* to full respectability here" (as if "dialect" implied lack of respectability in the first place). This kind of complaint, so reminiscent of the attacks made in the early sixties on *Webster's Third New International Dictionary*, tells us more about Porterfield than about the dictionary: first, he doesn't like *snuck*; and second, like the journalists who trashed *Webster's Third*, he doesn't understand how a language works and what modern dictionaries are about.

Language change is rarely started, prevented, or held at bay by fiat. Nor do people usually consult a dictionary to find out the past tense of *sneak*; rather, a dictionary "consults" the people to find out the past tense of *sneak* and reports that the general practice is to use either *snuck* or *sneaked*. Unlike a shoe, which remains a shoe and doesn't become a hammer no matter how often it's used to pound nails, a word becomes what its users think it is. When *snuck* is perceived by large numbers of native speakers to be the past tense form, it is the past tense form. Dictionary editors do not arbitrarily "elevate" a word to "full respectability." Rather, they gather millions of bits of evidence of how words are actually used by speakers and writers, and report their findings. In one of the few favorable reviews of *Webster's Third*, Ethel Strainchamps pointed out in the St. Louis *Post Dispatch* that today's lexicographers have "accepted the obvious truth that a linguistic error ceases to be one when it has been embraced by the majority," and although "error" is a misnomer, the point is well taken.

The popular and persistent notion that it is both possible and desirable for dictionary editors to decide what should be in the language goes back a long time. In the preface to his 1755 *Dictionary of the English Language*, Samuel Johnson reflected that widely held attitude when he said that "every language has its improprieties and absurdities, which it is the duty of the lexicographer to correct and proscribe." But although he thought it his duty to correct and proscribe, Johnson soon became aware that his earlier, more ambitious plan to "fix our language, and put a stop to those alterations which time and chance have hitherto been suffered to make in it without opposition" was an "expectation which neither reason nor experience can justify."

In the end, Johnson settled for a more modest but perhaps equally futile goal: "It remains that we retard what we cannot repel, that we palliate what we cannot cure." Although Porterfield does not go so far as to equate linguistic change with "decay and corruption," as Johnson did, he does adopt Johnson's position that we should defend against it, and quotes John Ciardi in support: "Those who care have a duty to resist. Changes that occur against such resistance are tested changes. The language is the better for them—and for the resistance." It is not clear how we could decide whether that is true. Despite resistance, the change from *sneaked* to *snuck* is all but complete; yet the remaining resistors obviously do not think the language is "better."

Is the language better for *caught*? If so, how? On what grounds can you establish its superiority to *catched*? Resisted by the likes of Milton, Bunyan, Pope, DeFoe, and Samuel Johnson himself, who all used *catched*, the irregular form (*caught*) nevertheless won out over its rival. If the irregular *caught* (an interloper whose etymological legitimacy is highly questionable) is somehow superior to *catched*, then why isn't the irregular *snuck* (which is attacked on grounds of etymological illegitimacy) preferable to *sneaked*? If there's something inherently superior in the sound of *caught*, why don't we have, instead of *hatched*, *latched*, *patched*, and *snatched*, "haught," "laught," "paught," and "snaught"? What does *caught* have to recommend it that *snuck* doesn't? How is our language "better" for having it, and is it "better" or "worse" for having *snuck*, which has been resisted by so many for so long?

Attitudes like those expressed by Porterfield, no matter how widely held, reveal ignorance of the nature of language. Moreover, they are based on misconceptions about what dictionaries are for, how they are made, and how they are generally used. Yet such attitudes persist. As early as 1857, Richard Trench defined a dictionary as an inventory of all the words in a language and insisted that the lexicographer's proper duty was to record the language as "an historian," not to criticize or pass judgment on the words. He suggested that those who wished to advise others on the propriety or impropriety of specific words or phrases should not write dictionaries, but usage handbooks (although he did not call them that) and could not imagine why anyone "should consent in this matter to let one self-made dictator, or forty, determine for him what words he should use, and what he should forbear from using." Trench's vision of a dictionary that would include every word in the language, along with a comprehensive and objective report of its history, ultimately became a reality in the *Oxford English Dictionary*, the first edition of which was begun in 1858 and completed in 1928. A new edition has recently been published, and there is even an edition on computer discs.

STUDY QUESTIONS

1. What is the name of your dictionary, its publisher, and its date of publication?
2. Name five types of linguistic information besides definition that you expect to find in a good desk dictionary.
3. Why is it important for you to read the entire entry when you look up a word in your dictionary?
4. Does your dictionary go beyond the function of reporting how words are in fact used? Look at its introduction or preface for an explicit statement about the editors' attitude toward prescribing usage.
5. What is the difference between prescription and proscription, that is, between the words *prescribe* and the term used by Samuel Johnson,

proscribe? (Consult your dictionary; then, in your own words, interpret those definitions that are relevant to the discussion in this chapter.)

6. Look up the word *fix*. Which sense of the word is intended in the citation of Samuel Johnson?

7. Write a well-thought-out paragraph beginning "The thing that most surprised me about dictionaries was . . ." or "It never occurred to me that a dictionary . . ." Use lots of concrete examples to illustrate your claim.

FURTHER STUDY AND DISCUSSION

What is your position on the descriptive/prescriptive or report/instruct issue? Do you agree that a dictionary's function is to report usage without further comment? Or do you believe that people need or want, and therefore should get, advice from their dictionaries on how they should speak and write? If you want to know more about this controversy, look for James Sledd's book, *Dictionaries and That Dictionary*, (Scott, Foresman, 1962), in your college library.

12 | Variation in English

In Chapter 1 we explored the notion that native speakers know the rules of their language even though they are unable to say what those rules are. If you reflect for a moment, you will realize that native speakers' unconscious knowledge encompasses far more than the grammatical rules enabling them to construct and understand words, phrases, and sentences. Every speaker of English, for example, knows not only that *Have you been waiting long?* and *Been waitin' long?* are different ways of asking the "same question" but also which version would be considered appropriate on an occasion where the other would be out of place. That is, speakers understand not only the linguistic meaning of an utterance, but its social significance.

In addition to the ability to switch from one style to another in response to the appropriate level of formality or degree of intimacy, some people can even switch from one dialect to another. That is, some people know how to use more than one "accent," just as bilingual speakers use more than one language, and can even use a range of styles in each. Moreover, all of us understand more dialects than we can actually speak. This ability to recognize, identify, understand, and use different styles and dialects provides evidence that all varieties of a language are governed by similar rule systems. In the last twenty years, scholars in a wide range of disciplines have been studying those systems and how they interact in actual use, and a large body of research about variation in language has been accumulating. This chapter, which looks at varieties of American English, will introduce some concepts of language variation.

CASUAL OR INFORMAL ENGLISH

You may have the impression that **casual or informal English** is "less grammatical" than formal English or that you just "relax" the rules when you speak casually. Not so. The rules governing things like contraction, ellipsis, and the alternate pronunciations that characterize informal usage are of the same kind and just as strict as those governing formal English.

DISCOVERY ACTIVITY 12·1

1. The following sentences all have *tag questions*, a device sometimes used for confirming, sometimes for challenging, a statement. For the following sentences, give equivalent sentences in a slightly less casual style:

Example
Goin' t' town, aren' cha? <u>You're going to town, aren't you?</u>

   a. Been workin' hard, haven' cha? _____
   b. Fightin' a lot lately, aren't they? _____
   c. Expectin' a lot, aren't they? _____
   d. Expected by eight, isn't he? _____
   e. Singin' in the choir, isn't she? _____

2. What two grammatical functions are "missing" from the informal sentences?
3. Would any of these sentences be grammatical in any variety of English if they lacked only the subject—for example, *Are going to town, aren't you?*
4. Write a slightly less casual version of the following sentences:

Example
Aren't goin' to town, are ya? <u>You aren't going to town, are you?</u>

   a. Haven't been workin', have ya? _____
   b. Haven't been fightin', have they? _____
   c. Hasn't seen anythin', has she? _____
   d. Aren't expectin' much, are they? _____
   e. Isn't expected yet, is he? _____

5. What grammatical function did you "restore" in this set?
6. Explain why the sentences in (4) are grammatical although only their subjects are missing while those in (1) would be ungrammatical if their subjects were all that was missing. Can you formulate a rule or find a condition that accounts for omitting subject + auxiliary as opposed to subject only?
7. Write slightly less casual versions of the following:

Example
You see the fight last night? <u>Did you see the fight last night?</u>

   a. She make it to class on time? _____
   b. Charlie call you about that matter? _____
   c. Your parents lend you the car? _____
   d. The test come out all right? _____
   e. Sam and Sue eat lunch yet? _____

8. What grammatical function is "missing" from this set of questions?
9. What various sorts of things happen if you eliminate both the subject and the periphrastic auxiliary *do* from the sentences in (7)? (Check each sentence.)

You can see from Discovery Activity 12-1 that in one set of questions we can do without the subject + auxiliary, in another set we can do without the subject but must have the auxiliary, and in a third set we can do without the auxiliary but must have the subject. If we try to eliminate the "wrong" grammatical function from some questions, we will wind up not with something informal, but with something ungrammatical or with a changed meaning. The rules governing these kinds of **elliptical questions** are quite complex. Only in those cases where the subject and auxiliary can be contracted together to form a unit like *you're, you've,* or *he's* can both be eliminated. We can't contract things like *isn't, hasn't,* or *aren't* to a subject (**he'sn't, *you're'nt,* etc.); therefore, questions with negatives can drop only the subject and must retain the auxiliary. Periphrastic *do* can be eliminated from many questions, but *do* + subject can be eliminated only when the subject is *you.* That is, if we eliminate the subject from *She make it to class on time?* the question will be understood to mean *Did you make it on time?* and if we eliminate the subject from *Charlie call you about that matter?* we get something ungrammatical or uninterpretable, or a different meaning (perhaps *Shall I call you about that matter?*).

Although the activity oversimplifies the situation and does not provide sufficient data or evidence for you to discover the complete rule governing the structure of questions in the informal style, you can see that casual or informal English is just as strictly governed as formal English. Even without knowing exactly what controls or constrains "dropping" of various components, you can see that we can leave out a sentence component only under restricted conditions, and are not free to dispense with or substitute just any element in any environment. Regardless of dialect or degree of formality, some utterances are legitimate, grammatical English utterances and others clearly are not. In short, informality cannot be equated with ungrammaticality.

DISCOVERY ACTIVITY 12-2

In addition to the syntactic differences, how else would (or do) the informal questions in Discovery Activity 12-1 differ from your more formal versions?

You probably didn't need to do a Discovery Activity to be aware that we all tend to pronounce certain sounds differently when speaking casually than we do when we're being careful, and spelling conventions like *cha* and an apostrophe instead of the letter *g* are established spelling conventions for representing informal style. But notice that stylistic variables like the alternation between *-in'* and *-ing* are strictly constrained; that is, although we hear *clingin' vine*, we will not hear **clin'in' vine*. In general, the more relaxed, casual, or intimate the conversation, the more often *-in'* will occur in the place of *-ing*, but no matter how casual, the replacement can occur only in completely unstressed syllables. So even though the relative frequency of *-in* increases, you will never hear **clin'in' vine* or **swin'in' sin'les*.

DISCOVERY ACTIVITY 12-3

This collaborative activity, recommended by sociolinguists Benji Wald and Timothy Shopen, is reminiscent of a ploy used by the famous sociolinguist, William Labov, to gather data for his study of the influence of social factors on pronunciation. First, decide on an alternation, like *-in'/-ing*, that you think is a stylistic variable. Then, in situations where you have heard very well what has been said, ask the speaker to repeat what was said (ask, "What?" "Pardon me?" "Could you please say that again?," etc.). Listen carefully for differences between the original and the repetition. As soon as you can, make notes about the identity of the people who were speaking, their relationship to one another, the social occasion, the topic of conversation, and anything else you think relevant. When you and your classmates have gathered twenty examples each, organize the data and try to draw some conclusions about the differences you recorded. What kinds of differences did you record? Can you suggest explanations for the differences?

REGIONAL DIALECTS

It is a commonplace that language is always changing. Yet change is seldom noticed by speakers within any group, who must all make more or less the same changes in order to continue to communicate with one another. So despite the changes, we can understand and be understood by friends, children, grandchildren, and many generations of descendents before we experience the dreaded "breakdown of communication" so dear to the hearts of pop grammarians.

Linguistic change over centuries can result in breakdown of communication, that is, a loss of mutual intelligibility, between the speakers of different varieties of a language, especially if they have little need to communicate with one another. From our twentieth-century vantage point we can see that Italian, Spanish, Portuguese, French, and Rumanian were at one time different regional varieties of Latin, spoken by groups of people who settled in widely separated areas of the Roman Empire. Different changes took place in each location, and as the changes accumulated over the years, the varieties came to resemble one another less and less as differences began to overshadow similarities. Where there were previously just varieties of a single language, there are now separate languages, each associated with a different political entity, or country.

But political boundaries do not always coincide with linguistic ones. In Italy, speakers from widely separated regions who want to communicate must rely on knowing a second, mutually intelligible, variety of Italian (usually the standard dialect) in addition to their regional one, since differences are so marked as to inhibit mutual intelligibility. Yet we say that they all speak dialects of Italian. Notwithstanding such anomalies, we can say in general that **dialects** are simply varieties of a language whose speakers not only count themselves as speaking the same language but who also understand one another despite systematic differences in vocabulary, pronunciation, morphology, and syntax.

Although English has undergone different changes in various places around the world, the varieties have retained sufficient *structural* similarity to continue to count as varieties of English, rather than as languages in their own right. Thus, we speak of "British English," "Australian English," "American English," and so on, despite noticeable differences, especially in vocabulary and pronunciation. Each of these varieties can be further subdivided into **regional dialects.** For example, despite the mobility of the American population and the ubiquity of national advertising that exposes all of us to the same linguistic examples, regional differences persist, mostly in pronunciation, but also—surprisingly—in vocabulary. Everyone speaks a dialect—notwithstanding the tendency in all of us to think that it's the other person who "talks different."

DISCOVERY ACTIVITY 12-4

1. For each of the following, give the term you are most likely to use or would expect to hear spoken in your home region.
   a. Window coverings that roll up
   b. A drink made with milk, flavored syrup, and ice cream
   c. Carbonated soft drinks
   d. Container used for mop water
   e. The paper container for carrying groceries from the store
   f. The sandwich made on a large roll and containing a variety of cold meats and cheese
   g. The elastic band for holding things together
   h. The kind of footwear worn for protection from rain and snow
   i. A limited-access, high-speed road without traffic lights or cross-roads
   j. The space between opposite-direction traffic on such a road
   k. The strip of grass between the sidewalk and the curb
   l. The device to which a firefighter attaches a hose to get water
   m. The amusement park ride on tracks that goes up and down at breakneck speed
   n. The call that children use to interrupt a game of hide and seek or kick the can to call in all the players without penalty
   o. The term used for unauthorized absence from school
2. Compare your responses in (a–o) with those of your classmates; then answer these questions:
   a. Do the differences surprise you, or were you already aware of them?
   b. What other vocabulary items can you think of, whether or not from personal experience, that reflect regional differences? (Consider, for example, household, farm, or industrial equipment, fences and buildings, stores and markets, places to park, places to eat, games and recreation, plants, animals, insects, food items.)
   c. Do the differences correlate at all with differences between urban, suburban, and rural life, with large geographical regions of the country, or with something else?
   d. Do some classmates lack terms for things others consider quite common and ordinary? (Consider the items listed in (2b), for example.)
   e. Are all of the terms entered in a standard desk dictionary? Do any of them carry labels identifying them as dialectal?

In general, differences in morphology and syntax are not a reflection of regional variation, but of level of education and social class, but a small number of grammatical variations persist, without stigma, as **regionalisms**.

DISCOVERY ACTIVITY 12-5

In each of the following, identify the expression you use or are most likely to hear in your home region (or supply it if it's not listed). Assume equivalent meaning for all the choices given in each set.

1. the floor needs swept, the floor needs to be swept, the floor needs sweeping
2. we stood in line, we stood on line
3. quarter to eleven, quarter 'til eleven, quarter of eleven, quarter before eleven, ten forty-five
4. sick to your stomach, sick at your stomach
5. he isn't at home, he isn't home, he isn't to home
6. she dived into the river, she dove into the river
7. this is as far as I'll go, this is all the further I'll go
8. I'm waiting for you, I'm waiting on you
9. he hadn't ought to do that, he oughtn't to do that, he shouldn't do that
10. he may be able to do it, he might could do it

When you hear people speaking, you can often guess what part of the country they're from by their pronunciation, or accent. Thus, *accent* is the nontechnical term commonly used for *regional dialect* in the United States. Radio and television network newscasters, however, often use a way of speaking that erases or neutralizes easily identifiable or noticeably regional pronunciations, and a kind of "Network Standard" has come into being. Let's turn to Discovery Activity 12-6 and explore this neutral "dialect."

DISCOVERY ACTIVITY 12-6

Choose a network news program and listen carefully to the anchorperson for at least a week. Then answer the following questions:

1. List as many different words as you can, with as much context as you can recall, that the newscaster does not pronounce the way you do.
2. Sort the words into groups on the basis of the particular phoneme being pronounced differently.

3. Are you aware of difference in pronunciation of any of the consonant phonemes? If so, which ones?

4. In particular, does the newscaster pronounce *r*'s differently from the way you do? Can you isolate or specify the particular environment(s) where the difference occurs?

5. Which of the newscaster's vowel sounds differ from yours? What is the nature of the difference? That is, do you hear diphthongs or long vowels where you have simple vowels? The opposite? Both?

6. Can you find any pattern or system to the differences? That is, if the newscaster pronounces the first person pronoun, *I*, differently from you, does the distinction hold in all environments containing the sound (long *i*, or more precisely, diphthong /ay/)? If not, what are the specific environments that call forth the difference?

7. Can you infer from what you hear whether the newscaster has contrasts where you do not, or lacks contrasts where you have them? That is, can you infer from what you hear whether or not the speaker would be likely to distinguish pairs like *don/dawn*, *pin/pen*, *pool/pull*, *store/stower*?

8. If you speak an *r*-less dialect, that is, one that pronounces *source* and *sauce* almost as homophones, how might you teach someone from an *r*-full dialect to pronounce words your way? What strategies might you adopt if you wanted to imitate the *r*-full pronunciation of Network Standard?

9. If you speak a dialect that has the *r*, what strategies might you adopt if you wanted to imitate your *r*-less classmates? What strategies might you suggest to someone who wants to learn to pronounce words your way?

10. Assuming you do not already speak Network Standard, summarize the changes you would have to make in your speech in order to imitate it.

Although Discovery Activities 12-4 to 12-6 call attention to regional differences that may appear to you to be quite extreme, American English as a whole is actually far more homogeneous than many other languages. But despite this relative uniformity of the language in general, more variety is tolerated in standard English than in the standard dialects of other languages.

Moreover, no single regional variety has been identified as the standard variety. Rather, speakers of all regional varieties, regardless of their accent, are in general perceived as speakers of standard or nonstandard English largely on the basis of easily identifiable grammatical features. In each region of our country, persons of high status and prestige, especially if they are longtime residents, are likely to speak with the local accent but comply with morphological and syntactic norms or rules they share with high-status speakers from other regions. For example, consider the speech of John F. Kennedy, Lyndon Johnson, Richard Nixon, Jimmy Carter, and Ronald Reagan, who all spoke standard English with a different regional "accent."

Nevertheless, sociolinguistic studies have shown that a wide variety of speakers regard the "unregional" Network English as the prestige variety and therefore perceive any accent, including their own, as undesirable. Some researchers have reported a trend among college students to shed their regional accents to protect themselves against the possibility of negative stereotyping that might be attached to the use of any regional variety. Others, however, deny that anything approaching homogenization is taking place and assure us that regional varieties are in no danger of dying out. The fact is that there have always been some people who have made a conscious effort to change their way of speaking and others who have not only been content to keep their accent, but are proud of it. Chances are, things will remain that way.

SOCIAL VARIATION

Variation in language is not merely a matter of geography, of course. Language varieties not only indicate speakers' geographical origins, but also reflect differences in educational background and social status. Although a good deal of research has been done on urban social dialects, very little has been done to define or describe Standard American English beyond saying that it is the language of the educated. To find a detailed description of Network English, which at least some linguists seem to equate with Standard American English, you may need to consult a handbook for actors or television and radio announcers, not a linguistics textbook.

Just as we identify formal and informal styles by the relative frequency (as opposed to total absence or presence) of features like -in as opposed to -ing and deletion of auxiliaries, we identify standard and nonstandard dialects by the relative frequency of features like don't vs. doesn't, and there is a tendency for formal style and standard dialect to converge. That is, speakers of nonstandard varieties of English are aware of the stigma attached to certain forms. These include, for example, double negatives, he don't, and reduction or omission of final consonants, and research shows that such speakers tend to use fewer of them in situations they interpret as requiring more formality.

Although stigmatized forms such as *I ain't got none* and *it don't* are no less grammatical and no less comprehensible than the "approved" variants and hence do not impede communication, they have usually been counted as "errors" or "mistakes" rather than simply as alternates, even by those who use them. In the past, schools used to try not merely to teach students to read and write standard English, but also to eradicate such disapproved forms from speech, probably because it was believed that nonstandard speech was an impediment to literacy. We now know that it isn't necessary for people to abandon their original dialect in order to acquire an additional one. Regardless of spoken dialect, anyone can learn standard written English without making a concomitant change in speech habits. It now seems clear, moreover, that whether or not they are also literate, those who are not motivated to speak the standard variety will resist any attempts to force them to do so, while those who are motivated to use it can often do so without instruction.

SUMMARY

1. All varieties of language are governed by rules.
2. The style of a speaker's language varies in measurable ways according to the speaker's perceptions of level of formality, degree of intimacy, topic of discussion, relative authority of the participants, and many other situational factors.
3. Dialects, whether regional or social, are varieties of a language whose speakers can understand one another despite systematic differences in phonology, morphology, and syntax. In the United States, regional dialects exhibit differences mostly in pronunciation, while social dialects display differences in morphology and syntax as well.
4. Differences, whether in style or dialect, are not mistakes, but evidence of variable forms and rules.

STUDY QUESTIONS

1. Explain to someone who has not taken this course how we know that all varieties of language are governed by strict rules.
2. What distinguishes stylistic difference from dialect difference?

FURTHER STUDY AND DISCUSSION

Write a brief paper discussing your own experiences with language variety. When, for example, did you become aware that not everyone talks alike? What can you recall of early school experiences relating to your language or that of your classmates? Are you from a region with fairly uniform speech, or are you from a region with more diversity? Did you form opinions about others based on their manner of speaking? Have you ever been self-conscious about your accent? Did you have any experiences with students coming into your neighborhood from outside the region? Did anyone comment about the way they spoke?

13 | Standard Edited English

Thus far we've been dealing with English in general, assuming that certain basic structures are common to most, if not all, regional and social varieties and that our description reflects the shared features. Of course, there isn't any such thing as "English in general." Any use of language is by particular persons on actual occasions for specific purposes. People do not need to be instructed in the use of their native dialects, because they are in full (albeit unconscious) control of the rules governing that use. But not everyone has control of the conventions governing the type of *written* English demanded in the academic world. This chapter will acquaint you with some of them.

SUBJECT-VERB AGREEMENT

One of the defining characteristics of standard English, especially the written varieties, is **subject-verb agreement**. Failure to observe this convention tends to arouse the disapproval of teachers, editors, graduate school admisssions committees, and employers. Even those who normally have subject-verb agreement in their dialects, however, sometimes violate the convention because of uncertainty about which phrase or word in the subject NP is the headword, which controls the verb form. Turning a sentence into a yes/no question is an excellent way to isolate the complete subject, but only the first step toward identifying the specific part that should control the verb form.

DISCOVERY ACTIVITY 13-1

1. Convert each of the following statements into a yes/no question by shifting the first auxiliary element to the position in front of the complete subject.

Example
The incoming students whose last initials start with A through M should line up in front of the registration table.
Should the incoming students whose last initials start with A through M line up . . . ?

    a. Esmerelda and Charlie were fighting over custody of the record collection.
    b. The dean of Arts and Sciences was making a tour of the campus.
    c. All the families in that middle-class neighborhood have bought vacation homes in the inner city.

2. Convert each of the following statements into a yes/no question by inserting the appropriate form of *do* and adjusting the form of the main verb.

Example
That timorous young woman upstairs *has* a very vicious Doberman.
Does that timorous young woman upstairs *have* a . . . Doberman?

    a. The king of Greenwich Village always fights hard for his turf.
    b. The dean of Arts and Sciences tours the campus at midnight.
    c. Each family in that middle-class neighborhood buys a vacation home in the inner city.

3. Underline the verb form you had to adjust in each sentence.

Finding the Headword

Once you've identified the complete (expanded and modified noun phrase) subject in any sentence, ask yourself what single word within that string could substitute for the whole thing. If, for example, the expanded NP is *the dean of Arts and Sciences*, the NP *the dean* could do the same grammatical job that the expanded NP does, *of Arts and Sciences* being a modifier or complement. That is why the verb must be *tours* and not *tour*. This is not an entirely foolproof method, as the following example from a student paper will illustrate:

A large quantity of peanuts have been eaten.

When asked what single word in the noun phrase would substitute for the whole thing, the student immediately picked *peanuts* instead of *quantity*, and argued that it was the peanuts (and not something called "a quantity") that had been eaten. Logical, but still perceived as a violation of standard usage. What you need to see is that the headword of the subject NP will not be inside a prepositional phrase. In the example, *peanuts* can't be the head-word because it's the object of a preposition and thus only part of a modifier (or complement) of the headword, *quantity*. Grammatical structure, not logic, must determine the verb choice, which must be *has been eaten*.

DISCOVERY ACTIVITY 13-2

1. Underline the complete subject of each of the following:

Playing chess and checkers can really eat up your time.
Chess and checkers can really eat up your time.

2. In which of the sentences above could you substitute *it* for the complete subject?
3. In which of the sentences above could you substitute *they* for the complete subject?
4. Rewrite the sentences without the modal auxiliary, using the third person singular form of the verb in the one that allowed substitution of *it*.

Problems sometimes arise with NP substitues like *playing chess and checkers* because it is easy to overlook the fact that the gerund, *playing*, is the head in this situation. Discovery Activity 13-2 shows that if we can substitute a singular pronoun (*he, she, it, this*) for the expanded NP or NP substitute, the subject is singular and the verb should be third singular. If, on the other hand, we can substitute *they* or *these*, the subject is plural:

Playing chess and checkers (*this activity* = it) *occupies* all his time.

Chess and checkers (*these games* = they) *occupy* all his time.

The *it* versus *they* test doesn't work, however, when the subject is a compound using *or*. With *or* and *nor*, the noun closest to the verb controls the number:

Neither his parents nor the teacher *understands* his lackluster performance.

Neither his teacher nor his parents *understand* his lackluster performance.

But Discovery Activity 13-2 suggests a construction to use if you're unable to determine which word or words should control the verb choice or if the "correct" choice doesn't seem comfortable (as sometimes happens in cases with *or*). You can use a modal auxiliary because modals have only one form regardless of the number of the subject:

> Neither his parents nor the teacher *can* understand his lackluster performance.

Remember that indefinite pronouns like *everybody* are singular forms despite their plural meaning, and that *each* signals a singular NP as well. Many subject-verb agreement errors result from failure to keep this in mind. Standard usage requires <u>*Each of the members*</u> <u>*contributes* two hours of work</u>. The plural form, *members*, might appear to mean "members as a group" contribute a total of two hours of work, but the sentence actually means "each member as an individual" contributes two hours of work.

Another source of agreement errors is the use of sentences with *there*. In speech, many people are accustomed to saying "there's" regardless of number. But in writing, when the headword of the main NP is plural, the convention is to use *there are*:

> Where there's a will, there's a way.

> Where there *are* obstacles, there *are* also opportunities.

DISCOVERY ACTIVITY 13-3

1. All of the following sentences contain subject-verb agreement violations of some kind, some of which can be corrected merely by cutting out unnecessary words. Revise in any way you like to eliminate breaches of agreement conventions, bearing in mind that "correctness'" by itself does not constitute "good English" or good writing.
   a. The session staff, the university, and Morgantown is pleased to be your host.
   b. A complete list of reading assigments follow.
   c. Impressionable kids see this and think using these drugs are O.K.
   d. The design on these two putters are about the same.
   e. A great deal more variety of woodwind instruments are found in the Symphonic Band.

f. Objectivity and communication of factual material is the goal.
g. Colloquial patterns has a way of getting into our writing.
h. Where there's children, there's trouble.
i. Each of the fields in a given core have similar evidential methods.
j. The togetherness and enjoyment we get out of our culinary experiments makes up for the bad taste.
k. Perhaps the plague of computer reports which characterize our country are more benign portents of things to come.
l. Even at four A.M. there's usually lights on.

2. Explain what's wrong in the following tricky sentence.

The tours our office provide are an essential element of our public relations efforts.

3. Strict adherence to the subject-verb agreement rule would "outlaw" the following sentences, all of which were written by well-educated writers. (Subjects and their verbs are italicized.) Discuss these "incorrect" verb choices with your instructor and classmates. Are they defensible? Why or why not? Shouldn't writers have the option of breaking the agreement rule when it seems justified? What conditions seem to justify breaking it?
a. A great *mass* of Americans, especially in the urban centers, *are* locked in a permanent condition of poverty.
b. In most abortion clinics, though, there is only minor harassment as a steady *procession* of anxious women *arrive* to undergo what some doctors call "the procedure."
c. A *total* of 650 truckloads *were* taken out before the road was closed.
d. A wide *variety* of theoretical positions *have* been blocked out.
e. A limited *number* of scholarships *are* still available.
f. A growing *number* of people *are* offended by sexist language.
g. There *are* still an undetermined *number* of people under detention.

4. How is the following sentence different from those in (3)? Does the choice of verb form seem more or less constrained in this instance than in those in (3)? Why?

The limited *number* of scholarships *requires* us to be very selective.

IRREGULAR VERBS

You may recall from Chapters 4 and 5 that English has a small number of **irregular verbs** whose past tense and perfective forms do not conform to the general pattern used for the majority of verbs. In many spoken varieties, these forms have tended to fall together, and a single form serves for both of them, just as is the case with regular verbs. Sometimes the simple past is adopted, and we hear "We've drank it all." Sometimes the perfective is adopted and we hear "I seen it." In still other cases, an entirely new form emerges. In any case, speakers are sometimes unaware that they are using forms that are not accepted in standard edited English. The following Discovery Activity was designed to alert you to some of the verbs that create problems.

DISCOVERY ACTIVITY 13-4

1. Supply the standard past tense form or the perfective (-*en*) form of the irregular verb given in parentheses. Don't assume you know the standard form. Look up the verb in your dictionary, where correctly inflected forms for standard edited English are given. Make a note of any of the verbs that have more than one past tense or perfective form. Be prepared to give a rationale for your choice in those instances.

a. The child was crying because his balloon had (burst) _____.

b. The child cried when his balloon (burst) _____.

c. When I got home from school, I (lie) _____ in the sun for an hour.

d. He has (lie) _____ in the sun so long he looks like a prune.

e. We have already (drink) _____ the well dry.

f. Mrs. Fosnick has (bear) _____ Mr. Fosnick's hardships long enough.

g. He (fling) _____ the child over his shoulder and (run) _____ down the stairs to the street.

h. They (lead) _____ the horse to Dr. Pepper but they couldn't make it drink.

i. They have (lead) _____ lives of noisy desperation.

j. His team, the Westover Wombats, has been (beat) _____ so often that he now says he has (lay) _____ his last bet.

k. He (lay) _____ a blanket over the sleeping child.

l. When my parents told me something, it only (sink) _____ in as "We told you so."

    m. After the fight, he got up and (sneak) _____ out of the room.

    n. This legislation has (speed) _____ up the process of getting a loan.

    o. After the accident, the driver (speed) _____ away from the scene.

    p. Despite the lawyer's advice, he (plead) _____ guilty.

    q. I've already (show) _____ you my best work.

    r. Have you ever (swim) _____ the Hellespont?

    s. He (dive) _____ into the river.

2. Although the past tense and perfective forms of *fly* are *flew* and *flown*, we say that a ballplayer "flied out" or "has flied out," not "flew out" or "has flown out." Why?

3. Use your dictionary to complete the paradigm below for each of the verbs.

Stem	Third Sing. Pres.	-ing	Past	Perfective
fall	_____	_____	_____	_____
fell	_____	_____	_____	_____
lie ("recline")	_____	_____	_____	_____
lay	_____	_____	_____	_____
rise	_____	_____	_____	_____
raise	_____	_____	_____	_____
sit	_____	_____	_____	_____
set	_____	_____	_____	_____

4. Write out a brief definition of each of the verbs in your own words. Do not copy the dictionary definitions.

5. What semantic feature distinguishes the two words in each of the following pairs?

fall, fell; lie, lay; sit, set; rise, raise

    Merely saying "transitive vs. intransitive" will not suffice for an answer. What is the specific meaning relationship between the members of each pair?

6. On a separate sheet, copy out the sentences below, using the standard forms. Simply underlining a form will not be acceptable. (Practice in writing out the context and the correct form is important.)

    a. Her fur coat was (laying/lying) on the floor and she was (laying/lying) on the couch.

    b. He (lay/laid) a towel on the sand and (lay/laid) the child on it.

    c. He (lay/laid) down on the couch an hour ago and I think he has (laid/lain) there long enough.

    d. She was (laying/lying) her best tablecloth on the floor!

e. He used to (lay/lie) bricks but now he (lays/lies) rugs.
f. It was (sitting/setting) on top of the filing cabinet.
g. (Sit/set) this on the filing cabinet.
h. He (set/sat) his belongings on the floor.
i. He (raised/rose) the flag.
j. He (raised/rose) from the floor.
k. He has (raised/risen) a lot of money.
l. He has (raised/risen) through the ranks.

SUBJUNCTIVE FORMS

You may be among those for whom irregular morphology causes no problems, yet be unacquainted with the grammatical feature known as the **subjunctive mood**, which has all but disappeared from most of the spoken varieties, but continues to be a convention of standard edited English. The following Discovery Activity will help you understand the subjunctive.

DISCOVERY ACTIVITY 13-5

In each of the following pairs of sentences, the syntactic structure is the same for (a) and (b), but the verb forms are different. As a result, (a) and (b) do not mean the same thing. For each sentence, first identify the verb forms in both clauses. Then, as precisely as you can, explain what each sentence means, using words or sentence structures that are different from the originals.

1. a. If John is here, I don't see him.
   b. If John were here, I'd see him.
2. a. If John was here, he didn't speak up.
   b. If John had been here, he'd have spoken up.
3. a. Ms. Smith insists that Mr. Smith stays in bed all day.
   b. Dr. Jones insists that Mr. Smith stay in bed all day.

Discovery Activity 13-5 illustrates two of the conventional uses of the subjunctive verb forms to express conditions that are perceived by the speaker or writer to be impossible or contrary to fact (or at best, highly unlikely), as well as for future events the speaker perceives as desirable, or necessary, to bring about. The **indicative** form, *If John is here,* leaves open the possiblity that John might be here, though we aren't sure. Similarly, *If John was here* leaves open the possibility that he was here, even though we aren't sure. *Ms. Smith insists that Mr. Smith stays in bed* states a matter of fact. The use of *were* to talk about the present and *had been* to talk about the simple past, however, is a way of saying that the proposition expressed by *John is/was here* is contrary to fact, not so, or untrue. To say *if he were* is to say *I'm certain he's not* and to say *if he had been* is to say *I'm sure he was not*. In the sentences about the Smiths, Ms. Smith is testifying to what she believes to be a matter of fact, that is, that Mr. Smith in fact *does stay* in bed; Dr. Jones, on the other hand, is prescribing what she believes to be necessary or desirable for the good health of Mr. Smith, that is, that Mr. Smith *should stay* in bed.

Some speakers have abandoned the use of these forms, relying on other linguistic features in addition to situational context to convey their meanings, and it is possible that this usage (except, perhaps, for conventional expressions like *I wish I were rich* and *I move that the meeting be adjourned*) will disappear from speech entirely. Nevertheless, some people cling to the notion that only these forms are capable of expressing the concepts in question. In the academic world, especially in writing, you will be expected to observe this convention. Here is a summary of the forms and their most common uses:

1. For ifs and wishes in present time, use a past tense form:

If I knew (= " I do not now know"), I'd tell you.

I wish John were (not "was") here (= "he is not here") to confirm the story.

I wish I had (= "I do not now have") some money.

2. For ifs and wishes in past time, use a past tense form of *have* and a perfective form of the verb:

If I *had known* (= "I did not know then"), I'd've told you.

I wish John *had been* here (= "he was not here") to confirm the story.

3. The convention allows *would have* and its contracted forms only in the clause that follows the *if* or *wish* clause, not in the clause itself:

If I had known (not *if I would have known*), I would have told you.

I wish John had been (not *would have been*) here to confirm the story.

4. Use an uninflected (stem) form in *that* clauses after verbs of ordering, commanding, compelling, insisting, or requiring:

I demand that he see (not *sees*) the dean.

I move that the meeting be (not *is*) adjourned.

DISCOVERY ACTIVITY 13-6

1. In the following sentence, the use of the subjunctive, *were*, is probably an instance of overcorrection. The indicative form, *was*, should have been used. Try to explain why.

One morning my three-year-old son came into our bedroom about six o'clock, asking if it were time to get up.

2. Can you explain the difference in meaning implied by the contrasting verb forms in the following sets? In each case, what is the speaker implying?
   a. If you study, you'll do well in tomorrow's test.
      If you studied, you'd do well in tomorrow's test.
      If you studied, how come you didn't do well?
      If you had studied, you'd have done better.
   b. If you play your cards right, you'll make a bundle.
      If you played your cards right, you'd make a bundle.
      If you had played your cards right, you'd have made a bundle.

SEQUENCE OF TENSES

Even though you saw in Chapter 4 that there is not a one-to-one correlation between time and tense, standard edited English observes a convention called **sequence of tenses**, which is based on temporal sequence in the real world. The following Discovery Activity will illustrate the adjustment of verb forms to show whether two past events were contemporaneous or sequential.

DISCOVERY ACTIVITY 13-7

1. Examine the italicized verb phrases in the following sentences; for each remaining verb phrase, specify the tense and aspect, as illustrated.

Example
were lying has a past tense of *be* and progressive aspect of *lie*.
   a. We *were lying* when we *called* our parents from Tommy's and *told* them we *were* at the teen center.
   b. We *were lying* when we *arrived* home and *told* our parents we *had been* at the teen center.

2. In (a), was the lying over the telephone happening at the same time as the putative attendance at the teen center? That is, didn't the speaker say over the phone, *We are at the teen center* or *we're calling from the teen center*?

3. In (b), could the lying have happened at the same time as the putative attendance at the teen center? That is, could the speaker have said, in this case, *we are at the teen center*?

Discovery Activity 13-7 provides a model for tense sequence when talking about events that occurred in the past. If two events occurred at the same time, we use the same form for referring to both events, but if one preceded the other, we use the perfective for the earlier of the two. In general, you will not be misunderstood if you make "errors" in sequencing the tenses, just as you are unlikely to be misunderstood if you say "I wish he was here." Nevertheless, many readers, especially in the academic world, expect writers to observe conventional tense sequencing.

DISCOVERY ACTIVITY 13-8

1. This activity is an opportunity to test yourself and to practice the usage conventions connected with verbs. Rewrite the following sentences to conform with the conventions regarding subjunctive forms and sequence of tenses. Assume a formal level of writing but don't overcorrect, and consider more than one option. If the standard form sounds unnatural, can you find a way to express the idea that sounds more natural yet doesn't violate the conventions?

Example #1
Through all seven years, the student usually has the same teacher, which makes school seem boring. The only consolation was that everyone got A's.

Possible revisions

Through all seven years, the student usually has the same teacher, which makes school seem boring. The only consolation is that everyone gets A's.

Through all seven years, the student usually had the same teacher, which made school seem boring. The only consolation was that everyone got A's.

The day I found out the meaning of "frustration" was the day I had been accused of shoplifting though I was perfectly innocent.
(This should read " . . . the day I was accused . . ." The form "had been" is unnecessary, because the day she found out and the day she was accused were one and the same.)

Example #2
He looks as if he was about to die.
Possible revisions
He looks as if he is about to die.
He looks as if he were about to die.

a. At the time of his death, Dr. G. was Professor Emeritus of English, having retired in 1972. He resided at Tanner, where he lived on a farm as a boy. (Hint: How could he "live on a farm as a boy" at the time of his death?)
b. Archie confessed to his friend that he was unhappy because he never rode a horse or played a ukulele. He was miserable because a couple of his dreams (however trivial they may be) never came true.
c. I found equipment that looked as if it came out of the Middle Ages.
d. When I found out I was chosen for the job, I almost had a stroke.
e. I thought capital punishment was abolished.
f. If I was from a different state, I would have to pay more tuition.
g. Most clients believed they got bigger refunds than if they did their own returns.
h. If Charlie would have won, I would have protested.
i. The game would be childishly simple if that was all you had to do.
j. On the previous Tuesday we played Parkersburg in the semi-finals, so this wasn't something new to us.
k. But if we started with the traditional, then introduced the new math while children are still young enough to understand the basics, perhaps by the time they're in high school they may understand the new way of doing arithmetic.
l. The closing scene fades out on Michael as he was reminiscing about his past.

m. This would still not have been sufficient reason to have caused her to do such a thing. (This one is tricky. No example has been given, so you'll have to puzzle out what's wrong. Can you do it?)

2. Paraphrase each of the following to demonstrate the difference in meaning or suggest different contexts for their use:

He looks as if he is about to die
He looks as if he were about to die.

PRONOUN-ANTECEDENT AGREEMENT

Some usage handbooks on standard edited English espouse **pronoun-antecedent agreement**, that is, a requirement that pronouns agree in person, number, and gender with their antecedents. But when the subject is an indefinite NP (*the average American*) or pronoun like *everybody*, it may seem more natural to use *they/them/their* because the meaning or reference is plural even if the form is singular: *Everyone has a right to speak their mind.* The prohibition against the plurals *they*, *them*, and *their* after singular antecedents has weakened, especially since the National Council of Teachers of English has voiced its approval, and some writers have been defying it for a long time anyway. For example, in *Linguistics and Composition* (Georgetown University, 1975) Louis Arena used "anyone . . . their": "Lees doubted that a knowledge of grammar would help anyone to increase their writing skills." Some of your professors, however, may still insist that you observe the rule, although it is unlikely that even the most persnickety would object to the plural pronoun in *The doors opened and everyone pushed as though their lives were at stake.* But if you must "correct" what some perceive to be an error, instead of bringing the pronoun/determiner into line with the singular antecedent, try recasting the sentence altogether. You can often make the antecedent plural and give a plural *they*, *them*, *their* its natural role: *When the doors opened, the fans pushed as though their lives were at stake.* Certainly you wouldn't want to say "everyone pushed as though his life was at stake."

It is no longer considered a good policy to use masculine singular forms when the referent includes or could include females, but some readers find the *his/her* and *his-or-her* alternatives annoying. Often, you can simply strike out a pronoun or determiner: *everyone has a right to privacy*, not *to their privacy.* Or you can use an entirely different type of syntactic structure. Instead of *If a CEO knows what he or she is doing, he or she will take bold steps*, you can say *A CEO who is alert will take bold steps* or *CEOs who are alert . . .* , which both avoid the problem by using a relative clause instead of an *if* clause. Another alternative is to use plural antecedents, including the first person plural, instead of singular indefinites. Instead of *When someone hears about a spouse who has been beaten, they wonder why he or she doesn't leave home*, you might try *When we hear about spouses who have been beaten we wonder why they don't leave home*.

DISCOVERY ACTIVITY 13-9

Without resorting to sexist language, *his or her*, or *his/her*, rewrite the following sentences so that they conform to agreement rules for person, number, and gender. Do not mechanically change only the pronouns/ determiners; try a variety of different grammatical structures in place of those used.

Example
Frowned upon: Everyone has *their* own way of talking.
Considered sexist: Everyone has *his* own way of talking.
Considered awkward: Everyone has *his or her* own way . . .
Possible solutions: Everyone has a *unique* way of talking.
                       No two people talk alike.

1. We have all heard someone say that they are sick and seen them an hour later looking hale and hearty.
2. A poor person can think of little else but where his next meal is coming from and how he can get the money for it.
3. There are those who say that if the student misses class often he will not benefit from his education.
4. Scarr's study shows that the adopted child will average in the upper half of their class even when the child's intelligence doesn't correspond to their adoptive family's educational and economic level.
5. An analysis shows why each magazine appeals to their particular audience.
6. Everyone had the chance to share their thoughts and to learn from one another.
7. A person who is too outspoken is bound to get themselves in trouble.
8. There are many reports of a person being injured or in danger and their dog coming to the rescue.
9. No one likes having something forced on them.

10. When you come upon somebody who you believe has had a heart attack the first thing you should do is find out if they have an airway through which to breathe.

APPROPRIATE PRONOUNS

In Chapter 7, we discussed the significance of the terms *subject* and *object* as syntactic relationships between NPs and verbs, and in Chapter 3 you learned that an NP or pronoun following a preposition is its object. Also in Chapter 3, we discussed the forms for subject, object, and possessive pronouns and how to distinguish the latter from determiners. Now we can add *who* to the list of subject pronouns and *whom* to the object pronouns and note that pronouns also come in **reflexive forms** with *-self* and *-selves* (*himself, ourselves, themselves*) whose usage in standard edited English is more restricted than it is in spoken varieties, where these forms show up in a wide range of functions.

Use a reflexive in the subject position only for emphasis: *The president himself awarded the medal.* A reflexive can be an object, generally when it's coreferential with the subject: *He cut himself while shaving.* In standard edited English, it is not used as part of a compound subject or object: instead of *They appointed Charles and myself* and *Charles and myself were appointed*, most of your professors will expect you to write *They appointed Charles and me* and *Charles and I were appointed.*

Usage decisions, including the choice of pronoun, are often rhetorical, not grammatical, since alternate forms may be grammatically, but not socially, equal. Wise rhetorical decisions presuppose an accurate perception of the grammatical relationships and a clear understanding of the grammatical principles being invoked. The argument against locutions like *Harry and her were sweethearts* goes like this: In speaking of Harry and Emma, you probably do not say, **them were sweethearts*, but *they were*. Because the pronoun *her* comes from same subset as *them*, the argument goes, it should not be chosen for a function where *them* wouldn't be chosen. Similarly, since you do not say *between we* and you know that *I* and *we* belong to the same group, you should understand the prohibition against *between you and I.*

The proscription of constructions like *I resented him giving them my name* will also make sense if you understand that the gerund, *giving*, is the grammatical object of *resent* and needs to be introduced by a determiner, despite its form class, because it is functioning in an NP. According to this analysis, **him giving* does not constitute a legitimate NP any more than does **him gift*.

But perhaps the most troublesome choices of all surround the relative and interrogative pronouns. We have already noted that standard edited English does not welcome *that* in nonrestrictive clauses (although there is no concomitant prohibition against *which* in restrictive clauses). Formal usage also restricts use of *which* and *that* to non-persons, reserving *who/whom* for persons, even though many of us use *that* in speaking: *There's the man that told Harry to buzz off.*

Many inexperienced writers have difficulty with the choice between *who* and *whom*. In contemporary English, this formal contrast is not functional; that is, we infer subject or object from syntax, not from the form of the pronoun, and nowadays most people use *whom* only when it comes immediately after a preposition: *He's a person to whom you can speak candidly.* If the object appears at some distance from its preposition, we hear *Who did you talk to about that matter?* Those who want to observe the most formal and conservative practice realize that standard edited English requires *who* in subject functions and *whom* in object functions. They may have no difficulty in recognizing *whom* as an object (the *m* reminds us that it's the equivalent of *him* and *them*) yet have difficulty in trying to discover whether the pronoun is in a subject or object relationship to other sentential elements. To determine the function of a relative or interrogative pronoun, all that is necessary is to reverse the embedding process outlined in Chapter 8 (and reviewed in Discovery Activity 13-10) and thus reveal the function of the NP that the pronoun replaces.

DISCOVERY ACTIVITY 13-10

1. Create a relative clause from the second member of each of the following pairs by replacing the italicized NP with *who* or *whom*; then embed it in the other sentence.

Example
a. It's hard to let bygones be bygones when dealing with persons.
b. We feel *they* (="those persons") have wronged us.
It's hard to let bygones be bygones with persons who we feel have wronged us.

a. Sidney decided to visit Esmerelda.
He hadn't seen *her* (= "Esmerelda") for quite a while.
b. Because he was shy, he wouldn't attend a party where there
would be many people.
He didn't know *them* (= "those people").
c. Nor would he attend a party where there would be people.
They (= "those people") might be serious thinkers.

2. The author of the original sentence about letting bygones be bygones actually chose the inappropriate *whom*—an overcorrection.
What do you think prompted that?

3. In each of the following, write the appropriate pronoun (*who/
whom*) for the formal level of standard edited English:
    a. I have no doubt about _____ was hiding in the closet.
    b. They caught the person _____ I think was guilty.
    c. Not only must the historian of science decide _____ should
    be studied, but also what activities are scientific.
    d. I have no doubt about _____ will be elected.
    e. I have no doubt about _____ they will elect.
    f. The person _____ I most respect is the one _____ I see
    working hardest.
    g. The person _____ I most respect is the one _____ is
    working the hardest.

MODIFIERS

In actual use, basic sentences are highly unusual. They are
merely the skeletons for the greatly expanded and heavily modified
sentences we actually speak and write. In general, speakers automatically put modifiers where they belong without having to think
about what they're doing. In writing, however, we tend to use
longer, syntactically more complex sentences than we do in speaking and must take time for conscious decisions about constructing
and placing modifiers so that they do not mislead readers.

Just as we can see the skeleton of a basic sentence in a relative
clause, we can "recover" the underlying structure of other modifiers
to make sure that grammatical and logical relationships are in
harmony in the result. Failure to do so can result in unintentionally
humorous sentences like the following from a medical advice column in a local newspaper: "After recovery from a testicular transplant, his wife got pregnant." Clearly unintentionally, the sentence
says that the wife had a testicular transplant. There being no
mention of who really had the transplant, the modifier is said to

"dangle." Poorly positioned modifiers can also be misleading, as is the case with *consistently*, which might modify either *studies* or *makes progress* in the sentence "The student who studies consistently makes progress." Note that the confusion cannot be cleared up by inserting commas into a sentence that does not otherwise call for them.

DISCOVERY ACTIVITY 13-11

1. Revise the following sentences, either by changing the position of any **misplaced**, awkwardly placed, or ambiguous **modifier** (whether it's a single word, a phrase, or a clause) or by rewriting other sentence elements.

Example
He does not think that cloning is a threat to society and says that clones are hardly different from identical twins as a basis for his belief.

Possible revision
He does not think that cloning is a threat to society and says, as a basis for his belief, that clones are hardly different from identical twins.

   a. Action for Children's Television believes that the ads are deceptive and make children crave things that are hazardous to their health such as sugared cereals and candy.
   b. The story is about a Union soldier in the Civil War named Fleming.
   c. He stayed in the library studying almost until his eyeballs fell out.
   d. The suspect made it clear that he knew his rights and his responsibilities to the police.

2. Revise the following sentences, most of which contain **dangling modifiers**; that is, no NP in the clause being modified has the same referent as the implied subject of the modifier. There is no single "right way" to revise these sentences.

Example
If deported, the U.S. government will have to bear the cost of returning the illegal aliens.

Possible revision
The U.S. government will have to bear the cost of relocating any illegal aliens who are deported.

   a. After removing the windshield from the truck, the children were pulled free and harnessed to rescuers.
   b. Following a mass escape from West Virginia Penitentiary nearly three years ago, 14 inmates of the prison faced a stack of criminal charges, including John Arthur Keenan.

c. While working in a hotel dining room, a famous producer encouraged her to continue her quest for fame and fortune in show business.

d. The judge found Austin in contempt of court after being two hours late for the trial.

e. Added to the darkness and thickness of the smoke, Guthrie probably could not find his way out of his own house, said police captain Smith.

f. The kitchens boast a prestigious list of volunteers. The mayor of Kingwood and a local surgeon fried homemade sausage on Thursday afternoon, followed that evening by the Catholic priest.

POSTSCRIPT ON USAGE: NOTHING OUTRIGHT BARBAROUS

Perhaps you have been led to believe that there is a set of rules constituting a prescription for "correct English." It may therefore come as a surprise to you to discover that the term *standard edited English* can be applied to a wide range of practices and that highly respected writers, teachers, and language scholars do not always agree about the rules. Some people are criticized, for example, for "incorrectly" using *since* to mean "because." Yet Wilson Follett, the conservative (and respected) author of *Modern American Usage*, declares that "no warrant exists for avoiding this usage, which goes back, beyond Chaucer, to Anglo-Saxon."

Disagreement about usage can occur simply because language is always changing. Pop grammarians and self-appointed guardians of linguistic purity often insist that an older usage is the only correct usage, that a more recent usage is unacceptable, and that others are "misusing" *unique*, *imply*, or *disinterested*. In some cases, disputes arise when there is precedent for two or more competing forms used by writers of unquestioned merit and equal prestige. Moreover, varieties of English are used all around the world and something that is "good English" in one place may not be equally acceptable elsewhere. In fact, judgments about usage are often a matter of personal taste.

"Well," you may be saying, "if the experts can't agree about what's right and what's wrong, how am I supposed to know?" Perhaps the best advice is this: when you write, try to anticipate your readers' reactions to your language. If you are not sure about the appropriateness of a particular construction or if handbooks tell you that it's the appropriate form for standard English but it sounds strange or unnatural to you, find an alternate way to express the idea, or consult your instructor or someone else whose judgment you respect. Pay close attention to the language of writers whose style is widely praised. With practice, you will develop the confidence to make choices without the authority of others—this book included.

In "Politics and the English Language," George Orwell gives a list of his rules for writing clear English prose and then admonishes his readers to break any of his rules "sooner than say anything outright barbarous." If you pay attention to your language choices, you may soon develop the sophistication to judge whether you've said anything outright barbarous, and to amend what you've written—within or without the rules, as you decide.

STUDY QUESTIONS

1. According to the conventions of standard edited English, there's a subject-verb agreement error in the sentence below. Do you think it is justified? Write a well-thought-out paragraph discussing why or why not.

   The first group of people propose that we should keep using the conventional I.Q. tests.

2. What is the headword of an NP, and why is it important to know?
3. Explain the uses of the subjunctive forms in English to someone not in this course. Be sure to give some original examples.
4. Explain to someone who has not taken this course what a dangling modifier is. Use examples not provided in this chapter.
5. In formal English, what controls the choice of *who* vs. *whom*?

FURTHER STUDY AND DISCUSSSION

It may have come as a surprise to you to learn that usage rules are not immutable, eternal truths, but matters of personal opinion and taste. You might like to read *American Tongue and Cheek: A Populist Guide to Our Language* by Jim Quinn (1982, Penguin), a nontechnical book about usage which cites many examples of violation of usage rules in the works of famous and respected authors.

Over the years, fashions in language propriety have changed, and some usage rules previously enforced with great vigor have been abandoned or have become less strenuously enforced. Among them are the prohibition against *different than* rather than *different from*, the insistence on *number* and *fewer* rather than *amount* and *less* with count nouns, the requirement that *whom* be used in all object functions, the condemnation of prepositions in sentence-final position, and proscription of *between you and I* and *feel badly*.

In a well-developed paragraph, argue for dropping or retaining some usage rule, whether covered in this chapter or not. In your opinion, is the rule sensible? Unreasonable? Valid? Useful? Useless? Exactly what purpose does it serve? Is there any evidence that the disapproved forms are less precise, less logical, or less comprehensible than those that are approved?

14 | Historical Backgrounds of Contemporary English

Although the English language is always in a state of flux, most of us (with the possible exception of poets and linguists) are usually unaware of changes in progress. At any given moment, although changes are occurring in phonology, morphology, syntax, and (perhaps most noticeably) in vocabulary, speakers and writers go on using English much as they've always done, for purposes ranging from the mundane to the sublime, as if the language were immutable. For most of us, the language we use *is* the language; it's the only one we're aware of.

But languages, like the people who use them, have histories. We study the history of English for several reasons. In the first place, the history of English, like any other history, is interesting in its own right. Secondly, acquaintance with earlier stages of the language can shed light on contemporary forms of English that might otherwise seem confusing or puzzling. And finally, knowing something about earlier stages of the language enhances our understanding and enjoyment of the literature of the past.

CHANGE IS NOT CORRUPTION

The only thing constant in language is change. But no matter how (or how much) a language changes, it always works. That is, speakers can always say what they mean and listeners understand, and our language always remains adequate to our communicative needs. Hence, change is neither for better or for worse. In short, "change" is a neutral term, implying neither improvement nor deterioration. Certainly it does not suggest anything like "corruption."

VOCABULARY CHANGES

Although changes are constantly at work in all parts of English, those that have occurred in the lexicon seem to hold the most fascination. When we look back, we can see that some words have disappeared, new ones have been borrowed or invented, and almost all have changed their meanings. *The Oxford English Dictionary (OED)* (twelve volumes published between 1888 and 1928 and several supplements published since 1933) contains a comprehensive record of what we know about the words in the English language. The *OED* also provides implicit and explicit information about the grammar of earlier stages of English. Discovery Activities 14-1 and 14-2 were designed not only to single out particular words to illustrate various types of meaning change, but also to acquaint you with the *OED*.

DISCOVERY ACTIVITY 14-1

Read the "General Explanations" section in the beginning Volume I of the *OED*. Then complete this activity.

1. Look up the word *phenomenon* and explain or interpret the following parts of the Identification:
    a. Pl. -*a*.
    b. *Sing.* 7 phain-, 7-9 phæn-, 7- phenomenon
    c. (*B. erron.* 8-9 -omena).
    d. Why is there no "part of speech" label?
2. Interpret the following parts of the Morphology (*Form-History*):
    a. a.L. (post-cl.)
    b. a. Gr.
3. Look now at the Signification (*Sematology*):
    a. What is the earliest written evidence of the use of *phenomenon* to mean an "exceptional or unaccountable fact or occurrence"?
    b. What is the most recent citation for sense 1? Sense 2?
    c. Has sense 3 driven out senses 1 and 2? Check a recent dictionary to find out whether the word is still used in those senses.
4. In the Quotations, what attitude is implied by the author of the 1877 quotation under sense 3?
5. Explain why *a phenomena* as a singular and *phenomenas, phenomena's,* and *phenomenae* as plurals are all considered errors, but *phenomenons* as a plural is not stigmatized.
6. Look up *anecdote*. Interpret all of the following from the Identification:

a. a. Fr. *ancedote*, or ad. its source, med.L. *anecdota* (see sense 1), a. Gr.

b. Look carefully before you answer this: What was the meaning of the Greek word that Latin adopted?

c. What was the meaning of the Greek word that formed the base of the word the Latin language adopted?

Discovery Activity 14-1 was designed to get you started, and the words were chosen almost at random. Nevertheless, they do illustrate some of the processes of **vocabulary change**. From the *OED*, you can see that the Greek word for *anecdote* came to mean "unpublished" by the simple expedient of adding a negative prefix to the word meaning "publish" (that is, by the ordinary morphological process of derivation, comparable to what we do in English with prefixes like *un-*). The Latin equivalent took on the meaning "a short story of a single event" because the "unpublished" memoirs of Justinian appeared as a series of such brief tales. It may take a bit more imagination to see how *phenomenon*, meaning "a thing that is observed" came to mean "something extraordinary," but many changes are quite transparent and easy to see in process, just by reading through the *OED* citations. Moreover, you will see from the following Discovery Activity that we can discern certain types of change occurring in one word after another.

DISCOVERY ACTIVITY 14-2

1. You may need to consult your desk dictionary for current meanings of words referred to in this activity.

   a. What is your understanding of the word *crafty*?

   b. According to the *OED*, when did *crafty* first begin to be used in the pejorative sense it now has?

   c. Now consult the entry for *craft, sb.*[1]. According to the *OED*, when did it begin to be used "in a bad sense"?

   d. Read senses 2 and 3 (including subdivisions) and the quotations for *craft*. What uses of this word probably contributed to the change in meaning of *craft/crafty* from something praiseworthy to the opposite?

   e. How does the chronology of quotations support your response to question (d)?

   f. What is your understanding of the noun *marshal*? What is the first sense of *marshal, sb.* reported by the *OED*? What is the second sense reported? Do the dates of the quotations imply that senses 1 and 2 were contemporaneous or sequential?

g. What is your understanding of the verb *starve*? What is the first sense of *starve, v.* reported by the *OED*? Is the current sense more specific or more general than the earlier sense?

h. What is your understanding of the noun *hazard*? What is the earliest sense of *hazard, sb.* reported in the *OED*? Has the meaning of *hazard* become more specific or more general?

2. Look up as many of the following as your instructor assigns and say whether the meaning has been pejorated, as in *crafty*; elevated, as in *marshal*; specialized, as in *starve*; or generalized, as in *hazard*. Are there some that don't fit into those specific categories of change? Which of the words have undergone more than one type of change, simultaneously or in succession? Which ones retain older meanings alongside newer ones?

article	disease	go	lord	reek
butcher	err	gossip	lust	smirk
corn	fond (adj.)	grandiose	meat	stool
crave	frock	lewd	notorious	villain
deer	fulsome	liquor	ordeal	virtue

3. Can you suggest any other ways that meaning change comes about and give some examples to illustrate? Think about the following, for example: How does *brilliant* come to mean "smart"? Why is the bottom of a mountain the "foot"? What is a "chain store"? Don't limit yourself to answering just these specific questions; consider any words in your vocabulary.

4. Spelling in the following quotations from Shakespeare's *Julius Caesar* has been modernized. For each italicized word below, write a contemporary equivalent; then, consult the *OED* (where these are all cited) in order to confirm—or correct—your guess.

a. For let the gods so *speed* me as I love
   The name of honor more than I fear death.

b. That you do love me, I am nothing *jealous*.

c. Him and his worth and our great need of him
   You have right well *conceited*.

d. Is Brutus sick, and is it *physical*
   To walk unbraced and suck up the humors
   Of the dank morning?

e. Thou, like an exorcist, has conjured up
   My *mortified* spirit.

f. Now, whilst your purpled hands do *reek* and smoke,
   Fulfill your pleasure.

   g. Believe me for mine honor, and have respect to mine honor, that you may believe. *Censure* me in your wisdom, and awake your senses, that you may the better judge.

5. Before looking up the words in question 4, did you assume their contemporary meanings were the correct ones for these quotations?
6. Look at the *OED* entries for as many of the following words as your instructor thinks necessary. Pay close attention to the variety of forms reported in the Identification and to the Old English and Old Saxon forms in the Form History, and look especially at the inflected forms in the citations. For at least one noun and one verb, make careful and faithful copies of all the forms; in addition, jot down the information you will need in order to answer the questions about the specific words assigned.

Nouns

bath	finger	lord	sister
bridge	fire	love	star
brother	fish	milk	summer
child	food	month	sword
cradle	game	mother	thief
daughter	goat	mouse	tongue
day	god	name	tooth
death	gold	night	whore
ear	heart	nose	winter
earth	house	rain	wolf
eye	land	ring	
father		room	

Verbs

beat	eat	ride	sleep
break	learn	say	speak
come	live	sing	tell
drink			write

   a. What was the original meaning of each word (signification or definition, not etymological glosses)?
   b. Has that meaning been retained?
   c. Is it the central or most common meaning of the word today?
   d. If the original meaning is not central or common, how close do you consider it to the current meaning?
   e. Suggest some reasons why the meanings of these particular words have remained relatively stable over the years.
   f. What was the Old English inflectional affix for the infinitive form of verbs?

g. What symbols do you think correspond to the sounds we now spell *th*?

h. Which forms do you think are immediately recognizable as a form of the word you looked up?

i. Which forms do you think are least like their contemporary descendents?

j. What centuries count as Old English? Middle English? Early Modern?

MORPHOLOGY AND PHONOLOGY

You can see from Discovery Activity 14-2 that although the meanings of many common English words have remained relatively stable over many years, we can't say the same about their forms. In earlier stages of its history, English had an extensive inflectional system. Nouns, for example, were inflected not only for number, but for grammatical case. That is, nouns exhibited formal contrasts that correlated with specific grammatical functions like subject or object, which we now signal by syntactic positioning. Verbs were also highly inflected. Among the extinct inflections is the *-an* affix that marked infinitive verb forms in Old English.

Besides the loss of many inflectional contrasts, reflecting **morphological changes**, radical changes in some of the stems have resulted from a variety of **phonological changes**. The word *lord*, for example, was once a compound word, *hlafweard*—roughly, "guardian or keeper of the loaf," that is, "of the bread." Over the course of time, this word lost not only its initial sound (the letter *h* was not silent) but also the *v* sound then represented by the letter *f* and the sound represented by the letter *w* as well.

Furthermore, because many alphabet letters no longer have the values they held for the West Saxons, from whose texts we get most of our evidence of Old English, some words still look like their ancestors but no longer sound like them. For example, *nama*, the Old English equivalent of *name*, rhymed with today's pronunciation of *mama*. Conversely, some words that look different from the old forms actually haven't changed as much as the spelling might lead us to believe. The word *yellow*, for example (not included in Discovery Activity 14-2) may not look much like *geolu*, but it still sounds a lot like its tenth-century ancestral form.

DISCOVERY ACTIVITY 14-3

By the late 1300s, when Chaucer wrote *The Canterbury Tales*, many previously irregular verbs had become regular, many inflections had been lost, and only vestiges remained of others. In these lines from the Prologue, *-n*, a vestige of Old English *-an*, *-on*, or *-en*, appears on some of the infinitives and third person plural verb forms, but not all. The verb *help* had not yet become regular (the perfective form was still *holpen*). Complete the translation into contemporary English.

Original	**Translation**
And smale foweles maken melodye,	And small birds make melodies
That slepen al the nyght with open eye	That sleep all night with open eyes
(So priketh him Nature in hir corages);	(Nature so spurs them in their hearts)
Than longen folk to goon on pilgrimages,	Then folk long to go on pilgrimages
And palmeres for to seken straunge strondes;	And palmers to seek foreign shores
To ferne halwes, kowthe in sondry londes;	To distant shrines known in sundry lands
And specially from every shires ende	_____
Of Engelond to Caunterbury they wende,	_____
The hooly blisful martir for to seke,	_____
That him hath holpen whan that they were seeke.	_____
Bifil that in that seson on a day,	_____
In Southwerk at the Tabard as I lay . . .	_____

1. List all the infinitives, with and without the *-n*: _____
2. List all the third person plural verbs, with and without the *-n*: _____
3. How is it possible to distinguish infinitives, third person plurals, and perfectives from one another when their forms are all so much alike? Specify the various grammatical signals that have replaced the formal contrasts.
4. What is the Middle English form for *them? their?*

We can see from Discovery Activity 14-3 that Chaucer's Middle English looks very similar to modern English. But looks can be deceptive. At the time Chaucer wrote, the language had already undergone extensive changes in its morphology, with concomitant adjustments in syntax. It had lost many of its inflections and had come to rely instead on rigid word order and on function words like prepositions to signal grammatical relationships and functions. But English had not yet experienced the extensive phonological revolution known as the Great Vowel Shift (which we will discuss in the following section of this chapter). So although Chaucer's morphology and syntax were quite like ours, the sounds of his English were not. It is not apparent from the spelling, but *eye*, for example, would have sounded something like "eeyuh," phonetically represented (in square brackets) as [iyə], not [ay]; *maken* would have sounded like "mocken," that is, [makən], not [mekən]; *slepen* would have rhymed with "capon": [slepən], not [slipən]. Chaucer's *nature* was not "naitchur," as it is today, but "nah-toor" or "nah-tyoor," with stress on the second syllable. The final *e* on *ende, wende, seke* ("seek") and *seeke* ("sick") was not a "silent" letter, but a syllabic remnant of an affix, now only a weakly sounded schwa, [ə], making these two-syllable words.

SOUND vs. SPELLING

When, shortly after Chaucer's time, people began to change the way they pronounced long vowels, spelling standardization (of sorts) had already been instituted by printers; although the sounds of English changed after Chaucer, some of the spellings that reflected Middle English pronunciation did not. So today we continue to use some Middle English spellings, which, by the way, are considerably different from earlier spellings partly as a result of the many revisions made by French-speaking scribes during the period after the Norman invasion. Thus, even though Middle English speakers still pronounced Old English *bru* as [bru], rhyming with today's *goo*, they were beginning to spell it *brow*, as we do today, or "browe."

Even though they changed some spellings, Middle English speakers pronounced many of their vowels very much as speakers of Old English had done. But in the fifteenth century, speakers began to change the way they pronounced stressed long vowels. The **Great Vowel Shift** resulted in the creation of two new diphthongs, [ay] and [aw], not present in Middle English. Observing rhymes, among other indicators, we can tell that some sound shifts were complete by Shakespeare's time and some continued into the seventeenth and even eighteenth centuries.

DISCOVERY ACTIVITY 14-4

1. Give the ordinary spelling or phonetic symbols (in square brackets), as indicated by the blanks. (Note: only one of several possible Middle English spellings is given for most words.)

Old English		Middle English		Modern English	
Spelling	**Sound**	**Spelling**	**Sound**	**Spelling**	**Sound**
a. ridan	[ridan]	ryde(n)	[ridə(n)]	ride	[rayd]
fyr	[fir]	fyr	[fir]	fire	_____
mil	[mil]	myl(e)	[mil(ə)]	mile	_____
min	_____	myn(e)	[min(ə)]	_____	_____
hwil	[hwil]	hwyl(e)	[hwil(ə)]	while	_____
hwit	_____	hwit	_____	_____	_____
b. cwen(n)	[kwen]	cwen	[kwen]	_____	[kwin]
fet	[fet]	feet	[fet]	_____	[fit]
_____	[sped]	sped(e)	[sped(ə)]	_____	_____
he, we	_____	he, we	_____	he, we	_____
c. cu	[ku]	cu	[ku]	_____	[kaw]
hus	[hus]	hous	[hus]	_____	_____
mus	[mus]	mus	_____	_____	_____
clud	_____	cloud	_____	_____	_____
d. rot	[rot]	root(e)	[rot(ə)]	_____	[rut]
mona	_____	moon	[mon]	_____	[mun]
sona	[sona]	soon(e)	_____	_____	_____
foda	[foda]	fo(o)d(e)	[fod(ə)]	_____	_____
e. stan	[stan]	stoon	[stɔn]	stone	[ston]
rad	[rad]	rood	[rɔd]	road	_____

| bat | [bat] | boot | [bɔt] | _____ | _____ |
| _____ | [ham] | hoom | _____ | _____ | _____ |

2. Summarize the changes illustrated in (1):
   a. OE [i] became Mod. E. _____
   b. OE [e] became Mod. E. _____
   c. OE [u] became Mod. E. _____
   d. OE [o] became Mod. E. _____
   e. OE [a] became Mod. E. _____
3. Give transcriptions (your pronunciation) of the following words: blood, flood, hoof, hooves, roof, rooves (or roofs), root, soot, book, brood, brook, food, good, hood, rook, broom, foot.
4. All of the "double o" words listed in (3) had the long o sound [o] in Old and Middle English. According to the information in (1), what vowel sound would you expect these words to have in contemporary English? Can you suggest some reason(s) for the discrepancy between the expected and actual pronunciations?
5. You may have noticed that *seke* and *seeke*, homophones in Middle English, have become *seek* and *sick*. Note also *creek/crick, sleek/slick, breeches/britches,* and the common pronunciation of *clique* as /klɪk/ or /klik/. In parts of Appalachia, *fish* and *dish* are pronounced as if they were "feesh" and "deesh." Can you guess what all this implies?

Discovery Activity 14-4 shows how some of the discrepancies have arisen between sound and spelling in today's English. The spelling of the "double o" words goes back to a time when they all had the same vowel, [o]. This vowel shift typically ended at [u], as in *food*, but in words like *book* and *good* the vowel went on to further change, "relaxing" to become [ʊ], at least in most dialects. In *blood* and *flood* we see yet one more step in the process, with the vowel articulated differently and sounding something like "uh," phonetically [ə]. A smiliar sort of vowel instability is obviously at work on the [i] vs. [ɪ] contrast, as evidenced by *creek* vs. "crick" in contemporary English.

Spelling practices have tended to obscure certain morphological changes as well. Long after speakers had adopted the familiar /s/, /z/, and /ɪz/ (all spelled -*s*) as the regular inflection for third person singular present tense, many writers continued to spell it -*(e)th*, according to a mid-seventeenth-century book on spelling. Thus, both *rose* and *roweth* represented the sounds of [roz], now spelled *rose* and *rows*. *Knox* and *knocketh* were homophones, pronounced exactly as we pronounce *Knox* and *knocks*, namely, [naks]. Except in the case of *hath* and *doth*, Shakespeare usually used the new spelling, but the King James Version of the Bible, written at approximately the same time, retains the archaic -*(e)th*.

SYNTACTIC CHANGES

Compared to the phonological and morphological changes that have occurred in English, **syntactic changes** have been less radical, and the fundamental syntactic structure of the language has remained relatively stable for many centuries. Although Old English prose writing relied more on coordination and less on subordination than contemporary English does, the basic structure of the clause was then, as it is now, subject-verb-complement. Although word order was more varied than today's and certain arrangements that could occur then are no longer possible, contemporary scholars emphasize that each particular syntactic pattern was highly constrained and that word order, at least in prose, was not as "free" in Old English as it may at first appear.

Changes in inflectional morphology had syntactic concomitants, of course. When words bore inflectional "labels" specifying their grammatical functions, the ordering of phrases could, at least theoretically, be left open to choice. But when the grammar ceased to differentiate between, for example, *hine* and *him*, and syntactic position became the means of identifying grammatical roles like direct and indirect object, word order became more rigidly fixed and it became necessary to use more function words, especially prepositions, to make grammatical relationships clear. Notice, for example, that we must mark the indirect object with *to* when we put it at after the direct object rather than immediately after the verb: *She gave Charlie/him the bill* vs. *She gave the bill to Charlie/him*.

DISCOVERY ACTIVITY 14-5

Study this Old English sentence from the Gospel of St. Luke, with each word glossed:

Sægst þu, mæg se blinda þone blindan lædan?
Say you, can the blind the blind lead?

1. Copy the Old English NP subject of "lead": _____

2. Copy the Old English NP object of "lead": _____
3. In addition to the inflectional contrast between *blinda* and *blindan*, what distinguishes subject NP from object NP in OE?
4. Write a contemporary version of the sentence: _____
5. In the contemporary version, what grammatical device distinguishes subject and object NPs?

Using the example as a "glossary," translate the following Old English sentences into contemporary English:

Example

Se man offsloh þone beran: the man killed ("slew") the bear

þone beran offsloh se man: _____

Se man þone beran offsloh: _____

þone beran se man offsloh: _____

Offsloh þone beran se man: _____

Offsloh se man þone beran: _____

Discovery Activity 14-5 illustrates the practice in Old English of inflecting not only the major form class words, but the function words as well, as you can see from the contrast between two forms of the demonstrative, *se* and *þone*. The sentence from the Bible, where noun inflections have been attached to *blind-*, an adjective stem, also illustrates that the process of conversion has always been a productive grammatical device in our language. In contemporary English, we can still convert words from one class to another by inflecting, for example, a noun as if it were a verb (*we bottled all the wine*) or an adjective as if it were a noun (*throw away your empties*). In fact, now that phrasal position has taken precedence over inflection as an indicator of function, we can do some function shifts without even bothering with the inflections. We do not say, for example, **the poors are always with us*.

Although it would have been theoretically possible to make six different arrangements of the phrases in the "man and bear" sentence, such freedom of choice was seldom invoked. Complete inversions like the following, which was probably influenced by the syntax of the Latin from which it was translated, are in fact rare in prose composed in Old English: *ealle his þing gegaderode se gingra sunu*, "the younger son gathered all his things." The most common pattern for declarative clauses in Old English was the same subject-verb-complement order we use today: *Brittene igland is ehta hund mila lang and twa hund brad, and her sind on þis iglande fif geþeode*, "Britain island is eight hundred miles long and two hundred broad, and here are in this island five languages." Deviations from SVX occurred, but were highly constrained. For example, when the object was a pronoun it often preceded the verb: *he hine geseah*, "he saw him." If a clause began with an adverb or a negative, the verb could precede the subject and complement: *þa sealde se cyning him sweord*, "Then gave the king him [a] sword"; *Ne can ic noht singan*, "Not know-how I nothing [to] sing," that is, "I do not know how to sing anything." In certain dependent clauses, the verb could even come last: *(God geseah þa) þæt hit god wæs*, "(God saw then) that it was good."

The most noticeable syntactic changes since Old English have been in the formation of negatives and questions. In Old English, it was not necessary to have an auxiliary: *Hwy forbead God eow*, "Why forbade God you?" that is, "Why did God forbid you?" The archaic question and negative forms persisted into Shakespeare's time, overlapping with the newer pattern. In *Julius Caesar*, we find *What means this shouting?* (without *do*) only two lines above *Aye, do you fear it?* and *You love me not* followed immediately by *I do not like your faults*. Although some of these occurrences could be due to exigencies of meter, instances can be drawn from prose as well.

The syntax of the verb phrase has undergone startling changes, not in the order but in the inventory of possible elements. Although *have* and *be* were both used as auxiliaries in Old English, *be* as an auxiliary was reserved almost exclusively for passives; verb phrases with *be* + *-ing* were rare, and remained so until after Shakespeare's time. Moreover, scholars have found no Old English verb phrases with both auxiliaries; phrases like *has been going* or *has been seen* do not occur until modern times.

One peculiarity worth mentioning is the practice, which cropped up in late Middle English and died out in the 1700s, of sometimes using *do* in ordinary, unemphatic clauses containing no other auxiliary. In the mid 1500s, we find *as Plato doth plainly teach* for "as Plato plainly teaches." In some instances, *do* seems to suggest something like "really" or "indeed": "*I do fear the people / Choose Caesar for their king*," says Brutus.

DISCOVERY ACTIVITY 14-6

Translate the italicized parts of the following passages from *Julius Caesar* into contemporary colloquial English; then explain in detail any changes you had to make in vocabulary, morphology, or syntax.

Example
Where is thy leather apron and thy rule?
What dost thou with thy best apparel on?

Translation: What are you doing with your best clothes on?
Vocabulary: Although *apparel* is still in the language, it is seldom used in colloquial English.
Morphology: The second person pronoun *thou* has been supplanted by *you*. (The second person verb inflection has also been lost.)
Syntax: We can no longer ask questions with only a main verb. But use of periphrastic *do* would result in "what do you do with your best clothes on," which does not make good sense in this context. Contemporary English conventionally uses *be* + *-ing* for "at this time, at the moment."

   a. But indeed, sir, we make holiday, to see Caesar and to rejoice in his triumph.
      (Marullus): *Wherefore rejoice? What conquest brings he home?*
   b. *Now could I, Casca, name to thee a man / Most like this . . .*
   c. *Cassius from bondage will deliver Cassius.*
   d. *If he love Caesar, all that he can do / Is to himself, take thought . . .*
   e. *The clock hath stricken three.*
   f. *Thou hast no figures* [imaginary specters] *nor no fantasies.*
   g. This was *the most unkindest* cut of all.
   h. (Cassius): Then, if we lose this battle, / You are contented to be led in triumph / Through the streets of Rome?
      (Brutus): No, Cassius, no. *Think not,* thou noble Roman, / *That ever Brutus will go bound to Rome.*

 1. Following is an excerpt from *History of Plimoth Plantation*, by William Bradford, a member of the Puritan group that came to America on the Mayflower in 1620. After you have read it through, choose fifteen lines to translate into contemporary English.

In these hard and difficulte beginnings they found some discontents and murmurings arise amongst some, and mutinous speeches and carriages in other; but they were soone quelled and overcome by the wisdome, patience, and just and equall carrage of things by the Gov[erno]r and better part, which cleave faithfully togeather in the maine. But that which was most sadd and lamentable was, that in 2 or 3 moneths time halfe of their company dyed, espetialy in Jan: and February, being the depth of winter, and wanting houses and other comforts; being infected with the scurvie and other diseases, which this long voiage and their inacomodate condition has brought upon them; so as ther dyed some times 2 or 3 of a day, in the aforesaid time; that of 100 and odd persons, scarce 50 remained. And of these in the time of most distres, ther was but 6 or 7 sound persons, who, to their great comendations be it spoken, spared no pains, night nor day, but with abundance of toil and hazard of their owne health, fetched them woode, made them fires, drest them meat, made their beads, washed their lothsome cloaths, cloathed and uncloathed them; in a word, did all the homly and necessarye offices for them which dainty and quesie stomacks cannot endure to hear named; and all this willingly and cherfully, without any grudging in the least, shewing herin their true love unto their freinds and bretheren. A rare example and worthy to be remembered. Tow of these 7 were Mr. William Brewster, ther reverend Elder, and Myles Standish, ther Captein and Military comander, unto whom my selfe, and many others, were much beholden in our low and sicke condition. And yet the Lord so upheld these persons, as in this generall calamity they were not at all infected either with sickness, or lamnes. And what I have said of these, I may say of many others who dyed in this generall visitation, and others yet living, that whilst they had health, yea, or any strength continuing, they were not wanting to any that had need of them. And I doute not but their recompence is with the Lord.

But I may not hear pass by an other remarkable passage not to be forgotten. As this calamitie fell among the passengers that were to be left here to plant, and were hasted a shore and made to drinke water, that the sea-men might have the more bear, and one in his sickness desiring but a small can of beere, it was answered, that if he were their owne father he should have none; the disease begane to fall amongst them also, so as allmost halfe of their company dyed before they went away, and many of their officers and lustyest men, as the boatson, gunner, 3 quarter-maisters, the cooke, and others. At which the m[aste]r was something strucken and sent to the sick a shore and tould the Gov[erno]r he should send for beer for them that had need of it, though he drunke water homward bound.

2. Until recently, *have/has/had* to was used to express a requirement or an obligation: *You have to be a U.S. citizen to run for office; I have to be home by six.* The expression now seems to mean "certainly" or "very probably." A newspaper recently printed, for example, "The Walmsleys *have* to be proud of their sons" rather than "must be proud."

   a. Make a list of as many innovations or changes in progress, other than new vocabulary like current slang, that you are aware of.

   b. Have you heard any comment/discussion about the acceptability of these items?

c. Do you have any feelings one way or another about the acceptability of any of the items either on your list or on your classmates' lists?

HIGHLIGHTS IN THE HISTORY OF ENGLISH

If the Romans hadn't had to withdraw their legions from outposts in Britannia in A.D. 410 in order to shore up their defenses against barbarian invasions of their homeland, there's no telling what language we'd be speaking today. Left without defenses, the Britons were subjected to repeated incursions, starting around A.D. 449, by West Germanic tribes—Angles, Saxons, and Jutes—who drove them and their Celtic language north and west into what are now Scotland and Wales, and then settled down in their place. Over the generations, the language spoken by these invader-settlers evolved into the Northumbrian, Mercian, West Saxon, and Kentish dialects of the language we call Old English.

Unlike Latin languages, but like all Germanic tongues, Old English had only two verb tenses, one for past and one serving for both present and future. Like other Germanic languages, the evolving English tongue had two types of verbs—"strong" verbs with internal vowel changes (*sing, sang, sung*) and "weak" verbs with dental suffixes, *t* and *d* (*kiss/kissed, live/lived*). In addition, English retained the typically Germanic trait of stressing the base syllable of a word rather than allowing the stress to shift to an affix, a phonological feature with important morphological implications.

The Christian Conversion

After St. Augustine arrived in 597 with a band of missionaries, it took him only a few years to convert the pagan *Angli*. The Christian monasteries created a good climate and opportunity for scholarship, and were to become centers of learning that would attract students even from the Continent. Along with Christianity, the English adopted about three hundred Latin words, most having to do with religion or learning. Perhaps because their entry into the language was through writing, many of these words have remained relatively unchanged over the centuries, among them *altar, apostol* ("apostle"), *creda* "creed," and *martyr*. Despite the pervasiveness of the Latin language as the only medium of scholarship, it contributed only to the vocabulary and had no noticeable effect on the grammar of the language.

The Vikings Arrive

The Christianized English in turn soon became the victims of marauding bands of pagan invaders, North Germanic Viking tribes originating in what are now Sweden, Norway, and Denmark, but known collectively as Danes, Norsemen, or Northmen. During the eighth and ninth centuries, the Danes came to plunder and loot the rich monasteries, but before long they began to colonize. In 878, Alfred, King of the West Saxons, fought the Danes to a draw and worked out an agreement whereby they were granted a particular territory in which to settle, and ultimately they were completely assimilated.

Ethnically and linguistically, the Vikings were close relatives of the English, whose language they probably had little difficulty understanding and could easily adopt. It is quite likely that contact with the Viking settlers contributed to a fundamental change in the structure of the evolving English tongue. Because stress in these Germanic languages was generally on the base morpheme, the one most likely to be the same or similar in English and Norse, speakers could no doubt communicate in a kind of pidgin if they ignored the inflections, thus reinforcing the natural tendency of unstressed syllables to become so weakly articulated as to be indistinguishable. Thus, over the centuries, many significant formal contrasts were lost; a concomitant to this "leveling" of inflectional affixes was a decrease in syntactic flexibility.

In addition to this probable influence on the structure of English, the Viking languages also contributed a group of easily identifiable vocabulary items. Most English words beginning with *sk* are Viking **loan words**; *skate, ski, skill, skull,* and *sky* are typical. Because the languages were so similar, it is otherwise often hard to tell whether a word came from the Danes or not. However, although it is highly unusual to borrow function words, the English did adopt the third person plural pronouns *they, them,* and *their* from the Danes, probably because it was difficult to distinguish Old English *hie* "they," from *he* "he," and *heo* "she," when the vowels were no longer pronounced distinctly. These borrowed forms did not appear in writing till the twelfth century, but must have been in the spoken language much earlier.

Alfred the Great

Alfred, the West Saxon king who defeated the Danes and began the unification of the Anglo-Saxon kingdoms, encouraged the spread of literacy and established a tradition of literary prose in English by translating and having others translate Latin prose works into English. Although poetry flourished through the eighth and ninth centuries, especially in the northern dialects, and would continue to do so into the tenth century, no native prose genres had yet appeared. Old English poetry, from *Beowulf* to the poems attributed to Caedmon, is of great artistic merit. Like most poetry of whatever time or place, however, it is highly stylized and conventionalized, and with its restricted vocabulary it does not accurately reflect the way ordinary people spoke as they went about their everyday business. Translations from Latin prose and original works in English such as the *Anglo-Saxon Chronicles*, which some scholars credit Alfred with instigating, are not merely sources of historical information; they are also linguistic artifacts of great value, which tell us as much about the history of the language as about the history of events.

After Alfred's death in 899, his heirs, the first to call themselves not merely "Kings of Wessex" but "Kings of the English" as well, provided a relatively stable government (and a climate conducive to the continued production of literature) for almost a hundred years, when a new wave of Norse attacks began. A Danish king, Cnute, eventually won the throne and then married Emma, who was not only the widow of Ethelred, the late King of Wessex, but also the daughter of a Norman Duke. Cnute contributed to the emergence of London as an important cosmopolitan city and center of commercial activity by opening the former Saxon stronghold to Danish traders and commerce with the Continent.

The Normans Arrive

After Cnute's death, the throne of England reverted to the son of Ethelred and Emma, Edward the Confessor, who had been raised and educated in Normandy, his mother's homeland. When he died in 1066 without leaving an heir, Danes and Normans both thought they had a claim to the throne, and William, the Duke of Normandy, had to defeat a Norwegian, Harald III, in order to claim it. William the Conqueror, as he became known, confiscated the large land holdings and redistributed them among his Norman followers, took over all church property and monasteries, replacing the English priests and bishops with Norman clerics, and peopled his court with Norman advisors, none of whom spoke English.

The linguistic consequences of this turn of events were profound and far-reaching. Latin was the language of ecclesiastical power and Norman French the language of secular and political power. Although there is some evidence that William tried, unsuccessfully, to learn English, those with power had no good reason to learn the language of the disenfranchised and powerless. Upper-class English people who were permitted to maintain their positions, as well as a large group of tradespeople, thought it prudent and useful to learn to speak Norman French, however, and the children of French nobles whose wives were English learned English along with French, so that there was some bilingualism almost from the start, at least in the upper levels of society.

Except for the *Anglo-Saxon Chronicles,* which the monks at Peterborough kept writing in English till 1154 (at which point most scholars set the end of the Old English period) *written* English all but disappeared for around a hundred years. William at first had new laws written in Latin and old ones translated, but laws written in French began to appear around 1150, deeds in French show up around 1210, and a body of Anglo-Norman literature began to be written. Nevertheless, ordinary people kept *speaking* English. For example, witnesses and defendants in court testified in English, through interpreters. Henry III's 1258 Proclamation to the people of London survives in an English version as well as French, implying that many among the common folk had not learned French. English was forbidden in a monastery in York, the implication being that English is what the monks were speaking, and in 1300, priests were told to explain certain church regulations to their parishoners in English.

In 1204 the French king, Philip II, seized properties in France that belonged to Normans living in England, and in the 1230s and 1240s when the English king, Henry III, brought in large numbers of knights, soldiers, and nobles from his wife's home region in the south of France, the Anglo-Norman barons became so resentful that they went to war and finally forced out the interlopers. As the enmity between England and France deepened, Anglo-Normans began to consider themselves more English than French, and many of them began to speak English.

Bilingual speakers all along had been adopting and instantly Anglicizing French words by using them in both compounds and words derived with typical English affixes: *gentle* appeared in 1225, *gentlewoman* in 1230, *gentleman* in 1275, *gentleness* in 1300, and *gently* in 1330. Although Parisian French was to replace the Anglo-Norman dialect as the prestige variety, the ability to speak French remained a mark of membership in the upper classes, and English went on absorbing and naturalizing French words, sometimes adding to the English word stock, sometimes replacing existing words. At the same time, many native words simply disappeared for no particular reason, as happens in all languages. Also during this period, many of the Old English derivational affixes ceased to be productive. For example, although we have not lost existing words like *behead* and *bedeck*, *golden* and *flaxen*, we seldom make new verbs with the *be-* prefix or new adjectives with the *-en* suffix.

Resurgence of English Writing

Despite the adoption of French for personal and business correspondence as well as for official purposes, English was neither formally banned nor actively suppressed, and there is evidence that some people continued to read surviving copies of such things as sermons that had been written in English prior to the invasion. Before long, literate people began once again to look on English as a legitimate and worthy medium for literature. Around the year 1200, the Anglo-Norman Arthurian epic, *Roman de Brut*, was rendered into English by a poet whose English retained many of the obsolescent features of Old English that were soon to disappear. One amazing item written in English around the same time as the *Brut*, but in a different dialect, was *The Ancrene Riwle*, "Rule of Anchoresses." This book, a devotional manual for nuns and cloistered women, became so popular that the usual order of things was reversed: it was translated from English into Anglo-Norman and Latin.

By the early 1300s, the tide had turned so that everyone knew English, as we can tell from the testimony of the increasing number of persons who not only wrote in English but commented on its current status and on the diversity of dialects heard throughout the country. Changes begun back in the Viking days had accelerated and dialect divisions had deepened, some scholars suggest, because the use of French, especially for instructional purposes, had militated against the development of a standard dialect of English. By the end of the 1300s, however, the prestige of London had grown, and the dialect spoken there became the standard (and, incidentally, the basis for the English we speak today). Chaucer may have used French genres (with some classical Latin and contemporary Italian influences) as his literary models, but fortunately for us, the language he used in his great works was the dialect of London.

During the years from 1066 to 1400, the structural changes that had begun back in the days of the Vikings had continued apace.

Nouns had lost all case markers except the genitive, but had developed a plural inflection that was independent of case; adjectives no longer had to be marked for number and case; some verb inflections remained, although some of their functional load had been taken over by other grammatical devices; and a single invariant form, *the*, had evolved from a group of about ten items to become the only definite article in the language. During the following years, English not only continued to lose inflections, but also underwent the Great Vowel Shift. By the 1500s, Old English seemed like a foreign language, as the following versions of the Lord's Prayer indicate.

Anglo-Saxon Koiné (*before 1000*)[1]

Fæder ure þu þe eart on heofonum; Si þin nama gehalgod.
to-become þin rice. gewurþe ðin willa on eorðan swa swa on
heofonum, urne gedæghwamlican hlaf syle us to dæg. 7[†]
forgyf us ure gyltas swa swa we forgyfað urum gyltendum. 7
ne gelæd þu us on costnunge ac alys us of yfele soþlice.

Late West Saxon (*after 1150*)

Fader ure þu þe ert on heofene, sye þin name gehalged.
to-becume þin rice. Gewurðe þin gewille. on eorðan swa swa on
heofenan. ure dayghwamlice hlaf syle us to dayg. 7
forgyf us ure geltas swa swa we forgyfeð ure geltenden. 7
ne læd þu us on costnunge. ac ales us of yfele soðlice.

Wycliffite Bible (*c. 1395*)[2]

Oure fadir that art in heuenes, halewid be thi name;
thi kyngdoom come to; be thi wille don in erthe as in
heuene; ȝyue to vs this dai oure breed ouer othir substaunce;

[1]From the *Holy Gospels in Anglo-Saxon, Northumbrian, and Old Mercian Versions*, ed. W. W. Skeat (Cambridge: Cambridge University Press, 1871–87), pp. 54–55.

[2]From *The Holy Bible, Containing the Old and New Testaments, with the Apocryphal Books, in the Earliest English Versions*, eds. J. Forshall and F. Madden (Oxford, 1850), IV, 14.

†The symbol that looks like the arabic number seven was a conventional symbol used (like our contemporary &) to mean *and*.

and forȝyue to vs oure dettis, as we forȝyuen to oure dettouris; and lede vs not in to temptacioun, but delyuere vs fro yuel. Amen.

King James Bible (1611)[3]

Our father which art in heauen, hallowed be thy name. Thy kingdome come. Thy will be done, in earth, as it is in heauen. Giue vs this day our daily bread. And forgiue vs our debts, as we forgiue our debters. And lead vs not into temptation, but deliuer vs from euill. For thine is the kingdome, and the power, and the glory, for euer. Amen.

English speakers and writers continued to borrow words and word parts from all over the world, but the majority of our borrowed words orginated in Latin. It is sometimes hard to tell whether a word came to us through French or came directly from Latin, but direct adoptions from Latin and Greek were especially numerous during the sixteenth century. Some words that had been borrowed from French or Latin during earlier times were reintroduced. For example, the Latin *cleric* was readopted to refer to clergy, the earlier adoption having drifted into the general vocabulary as *clerk*, with, of course, a different meaning. Similarly, *genteel* and *jaunty*, two Anglicized versions of the French *gentil*, were borrowed in the seventeenth century, long after the first adoption had given us *gentle*.

So English is a strange hybrid. Its early ancestors were various dialects of Germanic languages, which were affected by contact with not-so-distant cousins from the Scandinavian branch of the linguistic family tree. The English that evolved became a second class citizen in its own home when Norman French briefly superseded it as the official language. When English once again became the dominant language, it had changed markedly, not only as a natural result of the passage of time, but also as a consequence of having borrowed so much of its new vocabulary and morphology from French and Latin. Like all languages, English will go on changing. Perhaps someday this page will look like a foreign language to speakers of English.

---

[3]From the *Holy Bible, Conteyning the Old Testament, and the New: Newly Translated out of the Originall Tongues* (London, 1611).

SUMMARY

1. The history of English includes the Old English period, 449–1150; Middle English, 1150–1500; Early Modern, 1500–1700. There are no dividing lines in history itself and such dating is always arbitrary.
2. Old English, an amalgam of dialects spoken by West Germanic Angles, Saxons, and Jutes and North Germanic Danes, is known chiefly through documents in the West Saxon dialect. Much of the literature originally written in the northern dialects survives only in copies made by West Saxons because the monasteries in the north were destroyed.
3. Old English is characterized by a high degree of inflection and slightly freer syntactic order than contemporary English.
4. Middle English is the period of most drastic change: inflections were lost, syntax became fixed, the Great Vowel Shift occurred, and the vocabulary incorporated many French and Latin words and word parts.

STUDY QUESTIONS

1. What is the current equivalent to *Teutonic*, which the *OED* uses to identify the family of languages including English, Frisian, and Dutch?
2. If the Anglo-Saxons had not invaded Britain, what might be the language(s) of the island today? If you want to hear those languages today, where should you go?
3. Has Latin had any influence on English? If so, when did the influence take place and what was that influence?
4. Although languages seldom borrow function words, English did borrow a subset. What is the set, and from what language was it taken? What was the reason?
5. How do we know that people were still speaking English during the years of Norman dominance for which we have no documents written in English? Besides the evidence cited, what other reasons can you suggest?
6. What evidence do we have for sound changes like the Great Vowel Shift?
7. What is the meaning of the word *koine* used on page 259 and why was it chosen?
8. Write a brief paper about change in the meaning of words, using your work in the *OED* as support.

FURTHER STUDY AND DISCUSSION

Think about the various meanings and uses of modals, including *must*, *should*, *have to*, *ought to*, *need*; then, in a well-developed paragraph, discuss the drift in the meaning of *have/has/had to* referred to in Discovery Activity 14-6, question 2.

GLOSSARY

Affix A morpheme that must be attached ("affixed") to some other morpheme. English attaches prefixes, like the *pre-* of *prefix*, before a base, and suffixes, like the derivational *-ate* of *fixate* and the inflectional *-ed* of *fixed*, after a base.

Aspect Traditionally, a system of verb inflections correlating with features such as inception, duration, repetition, or completion of events. In English, those temporal features of events are expressed in grammatical devices outside the verb phrase as well as by verb inflection. For example, *Sit here till I call* expresses a durative aspect of the sitting event without marking the verb, as you can see by comparing it to *Sit here*. Activity 4-4 illustrates grammatical aspect as reflected not only in the two aspect inflections (*-en/-ed* and *-ing*) but also in semi-auxiliaries and adverbials.

Auxiliary One of three types of verbal elements, subordinate to or dependent on the headword in a VP, that attract the negative particle *n't* and invert with the subject to form yes/no questions.

AUX rule A formula that describes the basic structure of the verb phrase in English. The AUX rule enumerates the forms (tense and aspect inflections) and the classes (modal and primary auxiliaries) that occur before the headword (main verb) and specifies the order they take.

Backformation The creation of words by a process that is the reverse of derivational affixation, that is, by subtraction of a part assumed to be an affix. The word *edit* was backformed, for example, because the existence of *editor* led people to assume the existence of *edit* as a base (and the verb *backform* is a backformation of *backformation*).

Base (Morpheme) Any morpheme to which you can attach an affix. The words *mother* and *boy* are free bases, which accept both inflectional and derivational affixes (note *mothers* and *boys* as well as *motherhood* and *boyhood*). Nonwords such as *-duce* of *induce*, *-ceive* of *receive*, and *frag-* of *fragment* are bound bases; they combine with various derivational affixes to become words.

Basic sentence (also **kernel sentence, kernel clause**) A grammatical structure consisting of subject, predicator, and any complements required by the verb. The prototype contains no modifiers and is active, declarative, and non-negative.

Bound morpheme A morpheme that cannot appear alone but must be attached to another: *frag-* is a bound base morpheme. All affixes are bound morphemes.

Case A system (not much used in English) of altering the form of a noun, noun phrase, or pronoun to indicate its grammatical function. For nouns and noun phrases, English has a genitive form (*the queen of England's*) but no special subject and object case forms (*the queen of England* has one form whether it's subject or object). As for pronouns, despite reference to *they, them,* and *their* as "subject," "object," and "possessive" case forms, respectively, the forms often do not coincide with the named functions.

Catenative verbs Verbs such as *promise, seem,* and *want,* which take nontensed complements: *She seemed to be hurt.* This class overlaps with *semi-auxiliaries.*

Clause Traditionally, a structure consisting of a subject, a tensed or "finite" verb phrase, and any complements required by the verb. Some authorities now apply the term to any structure that contains a subject-verb-complement relationship, including the untensed structures traditionally known as gerundive, participial, and infinitive phrases.

Comparative inflection A grammatical marker, *-er,* that attaches to some adjectives and a few adverbs to indicate degree or extent.

Complement Any word, phrase, or clause without which some other structure would not be grammatically complete. For example, the adjective *fond,* used predicatively, always requires a complement, specifically, a prepositional phrase beginning with *of:* **She is fond.*

Complementizer Any word or expression that marks or signals an embedded nominal clause. Activity 8-8 illustrates the use of the prototype, *that.* (This term is not found in traditional grammars.)

Complex sentence A sentence resulting from the subordination of one clause to another by the addition of a subordinator (subordinating conjunction).

Complex transitive Describing verbs like *put, consider,* and *elect,* which have complements within their complements. Activity 7-10 introduces the complex complements that give complex transitives their name.

Compound sentence A sentence made of independent clauses, whether related by a logical relator, conjoined by a coordinating conjunction, or simply united by a semicolon.

Conjunction One of several structure classes whose function is to unite two or more clauses into a single sentence. Activities 8-13 and 8-14 deal with subordinating and coordinating conjunctions, respectively. Grammarians no longer assume two distinct, mutually exclusive sets of conjunctions but rather a continuum, pointing out that some (e.g., *for*) share properties of both the coordinating and subordinating types.

Conjunctive adverb A member of the class that includes *however* and *therefore,* whose function is to indicate a logical relationship between two clauses. Most comtemporary scholars recognize that some words, including *so* and *yet,* are midway between conjunctive adverbs and conjunctions (just as some words are midway between the two types of conjunction) in their syntactic behavior. Activity 8-15 deals with prototypical members of the class.

Consonant cluster A group of consonant sounds (sometimes less precisely called "blends") without intervening vowels. Activity 9-8 shows that no more than three consonants can cluster at the beginning of a syllable.

Conversion Creation of a new member of a grammatical class by appropriating an existing word from another class, without benefit of derivational affix (hence the alternate term *zero derivation*). A new adjective, *fun,* has recently been created by conversion of the noun *fun.* Conversions from verb to noun (*a run*) and noun to verb (*to party*) are far more common than any others.

Coordinating conjunction A function word, also called a coordinator, used to unite two or more independent clauses. The central members are *and* and *or*.

Copulative verb The traditional name for any linking verb, especially *be*.

Count noun A noun that names something perceived as a countable unit, whether or not it has an overt plural form in contrast to a singular. For example, *sheep* and *deer*, as well as *woman*, *man*, and *child*, are count nouns: *ten sheep*, *many deer*.

Derivation The morphological process of forming one word from another, usually by addition of an affix: *childhood* is derived from *child*. Activity 3-2 deals with the derivation of nouns, Activity 4-2 deals with two verb-forming derivational affixes, and Activity 6-4 deals with the derivation of adjectives and adverbs.

Derivational series A group of words illustrating the variety of form classes derivable by affixation on a single base: *act, active, activity, action, actionable; visual, visualize, visualization; logic, logical, logically*.

Determiner The grammatical function (signaling NPs) prototypically performed by *the*, as well as the several subclasses of words (including *all*, *some*, and *many*) whose members perform that function. Some scholars distinguish between function (determiner) and class (determinatives); others have adopted the term *specifier* for the function; and others have pointed out the correspondence between determiners and the logical category, quantifier.

Dialect Any variety of a language regularly spoken by an identifiable group of native speakers. Dialects are marked by differences in pronunciation, such as "caht" (/kat/) and "cawt" (/kɔt/) for *caught*; differences in morphology, such as *dived* and *dove* for the past tense of *dive*; and differences in syntax, such as *stand in line* and *stand on line*. Unlike situationally adopted stylistic variants, dialectal variants are likely to be relatively permanent or stable features of a person's language.

Direct object In the complement of di-transitive verbs, the NP that cannot be paraphrased as a prepositional phrase. *I gave you my pencil* can be paraphrased as *I gave my pencil to you* but not as **I gave you to my pencil*; hence, *my pencil*, which names the thing given—not the beneficiary—is the direct object.

Di-transitive Describing verbs like *give*, whose complements contain two NPs that are not co-referential (hence not complements of one another) but are two distinct kinds of object, a direct object naming the thing given and an indirect object naming the intended recipient or beneficiary. Activity 7-11 reveals the difference between di-transitive and complex transitive verbs.

Finite verb A term in traditional grammar, roughly equal to *tensed VP*.

Form classes Traditional "parts of speech" that participate in inflectional and/or derivational morphology and can thus be identified by their potential to take particular forms. The form classes—noun, verb, adjective, adverb—are open sets.

Free morpheme A morpheme, like *apple* or *if*, that can occur as a freestanding word.

Gender The system of subdividing nouns and pronouns into sets according to differences in their morphology (not necessarily to differences in the things they refer to). In the classical languages, the subset that included the words for *man* and *he* came to be called "the masculine kind" (*gender* means "kind" or "type") and the other sets, the "feminine" and "neuter" kinds. Languages with these subdivisions have a system of marking determiners, modifiers, and other NP elements to show agreement "in gender" (that is, agreement in form) with the subclass of the headword. In Spanish, for example, a yellow dress is *una vestida amarilla*, but a yellow bird, *un pájaro amarillo*, with the forms for *a* and *yellow* adjusted to agree with the nouns *vestida* and *pájaro*. Of course, English has words like *woman* and *man*, *she* and *he*, that divide people (and even some animals) according to perceived "natural" gender, but it has no system of grammatical gender. There are no formal properties analogous to the Spanish *-a* versus *-o* that separate groups of nouns and then require adjustment of articles, adjectives, and so on to agree with the formal characteristics of the noun.

Genitive inflection   The *'s* that is added to nouns and noun phrases to change their syntactic function. The NP *my cousin* becomes *my cousin's*, which can be used in functions that the NP can't fill: **my cousin house, my cousin's house.* Activity 3-7 deals with the many functions of the genitive.

Gerund   A verb inflected with *-ing* but not accompanied by a tensed auxiliary, filling a function typically performed by nouns, NPs, and pronouns: *Skiing is fun.* Their function as NP substitutes, not their form, distinguishes gerunds and gerundive phrases from participles and participial phrases.

Grammatical meaning (also **Structural meaning**)   The various kinds of meaning conveyed by the grammatical system, as opposed to the lexical content of the words. Discovery Activity 1-4 and Table 1-2 illustrate types of grammatical meaning and the features that convey them.

Head(word)   The essential or obligatory member of a phrase, which usually gives its grammatical category name to the phrase class. The head(word) of an NP is a noun; the head(word) of a VP is a verb. Note, however, that only a few scholars have extended the use of the term *head* to include prepositions, although the class, preposition, gives its name to the phrase.

Indefinite relative clause   A clause beginning with an indefinite word, like *what(ever)* or *anything*, that is not necessarily its subject. As demonstrated in Activity 8-9, such clauses perform NP functions: *What you did was unethical.*

Independent clause   A grammatical structure consisting of a subject, a tensed verb phrase, and any complements required by the subclass of its verb. A basic sentence is in fact an independent clause with no modifiers added.

Indicative mood   See **mood**.

Indirect object   In the complement of a di-transitive verb, the NP that can become the object of a preposition and usually refers to the intended recipient or beneficiary. *She ordered me a sandwich* can be paraphrased as *She ordered a sandwich for me*; hence *me* is the indirect object.

Infinitive phrase   A phrase whose headword is an uninflected verb stem. Because some infinitive phrases are structurally analogous to clauses (compare [*I saw*] *her catch the ball* and [*I know*] *she caught the ball*), some contemporary grammarians call these structures clauses. Activities 8-7 and 8-11 illustrate the structure and functions of infinitives.

Inflection   A system of contrasting forms for words of a particular class. In English, the system includes a number inflection for nouns, tense and aspect inflections for verbs, and degree inflections for some adjectives and adverbs. The status of *'s* as an inflection is open to question, because unlike other inflections, it attaches to phrases rather than to individual words and changes the grammatical function of the phrase to which it is attached.

Inflectional paradigm   A series of contrasting forms that defines a particular class of words. The series defining the verb is displayed in Activity 4-1.

Intransitive verb   Traditionally called "verbs of complete predication" because many members of the class can predicate alone. Activity 7-5 illustrates intransitives that require complements as well as some that don't.

Kernel sentence (also **kernel clause**)   See **basic sentence**.

Lexical content   Roughly, the part of the meaning of a word that constitutes its dictionary definition or denotation.

Lexicon   The unconscious mental dictionary that speakers acquire as they learn a language. It includes not only the lexical content or meaning of a word but also its class, its distribution, and other grammatical information necessary for its correct use. For example, in addition to the meaning of *fond*, your mental lexicon contains the information that it is an adjective; that it can occur attributively (that is, before a noun, as in *fond memories*); that when used predicatively it requires a complement (**She is fond*); and that its complement must be a prepositional phrase beginning with *of*: *She is fond of/*about you.*

Linking verb   Any of the verbs, also called copulative verbs, whose typically adjectival and nominal complements predicate a quality, ascribe an identity, or assign class membership to the referent of the subject NP of the clause. The prototypes are *be*, *become*, and *seem*.

Logical relator   See **conjunctive adverb**.

Manner adverb   An adverb such as *well* or *quickly* that refers to the way something is done. Adding *-ly* to almost any adjective will yield a manner adverb.

Middle verb   A verb whose NP complement is unlike an object in that it doesn't undergo passivization and is unlike a predicative nominal in that it isn't co-referential with the subject NP. Activity 7-9 contrasts middle verbs with those being used transitively or intransitively.

Modal   An auxiliary that has neither a third person singular present nor a progressive inflection and cannot occur as an infinitive (*I hope to be able to go*, not **I hope to can go*). Activities 4-5 and 4-6 deal with the simple morphology and complex semantics of modals. Syntactically, modals behave like other auxiliaries in that they invert with subjects to form questions and attract the negative particle.

Modifier (also **expander**)   An optional function, performed by many classes, not essential to the grammatical structure of a phrase or clause.

Mood (also **mode**)   Traditionally used to identify clause types such as interrogative, imperative, and exclamative—which are associated with nonassertion—and to distinguish them from declarative clauses, which generally correlate with assertion. But it has also been used to refer to grammatical features,

encoded in some languages in verb inflections, that reflect a speaker's perceptions about what is a matter of fact, certainty, or reality (expressed in indicative form) as opposed to what is counterfactual or nonfactual, uncertain, or
unreal (expressed in subjunctive form, especially in subordinate clauses). Of
course, English has interrogative, imperative, and exclamative clause types
(*When will the pie be ready? Please eat the pie*, and *What a lot of pie you ate!*
respectively), but as Activity 4-6 implies, we use modal auxiliaries rather than
verb inflections to express many speaker attitudes that other languages encode
in subjunctive verb forms. Activity 13-5 deals with the few instances, mostly
having to do with counterfactuals, where subjunctive verb forms still occur in
English.

Morpheme   The smallest unit of meaning. The building blocks of words, morphemes may be subdivided according to various criteria: free versus bound,
lexical versus grammatical, base versus affix. All of the activities in Chapter 2
deal with rules governing the ways morphemes combine.

Nominal clause   A clause (also called complement clause) embedded, with or
without a complementizer, in some NP function in a superordinate clause.
Activity 8-8 distinguishes nominal clauses from relative clauses.

Non-count noun   Any word, such as *energy* or *equipment*, that does not accept an
indefinite article or a plural inflection: *an equipment, *equipments.*

Nonrestrictive modifier (also **free modifier**)   A structure that is adjoined to (as
opposed to embedded in or bound to) the structure it modifies. Activities 8-3
and 8-4 distinguish nonrestrictive from restrictive relative clauses, but the
terms *nonrestrictive* and *restrictive* also apply to other types of modifiers.
Compare, for example, *A severely injured child lay on the stretcher* and *A
child, severely injured, lay on the stretcher.*

Object of preposition   The noun, pronoun, or NP that completes a prepositional
phrase. Activity 3-3 distinguishes objects of prepositions from heads of NPs.

Object of verb   Prototypically filled by an NP, the kind of complement that can
often be replaced by *me, her, him, us, them*, or *whom* and/or become the
subject of a passive version of the sentence in whose predicate it appears.

Paradigm   See **inflectional paradigm.**

Paradigmatic test   The ability to accept a particular series of inflectional forms.
The ability to show a number contrast constitutes a paradigmatic test for
nouns; to show tense and aspect contrasts, the test for verbs.

Participial phrase   Traditional term for a phrase like *strolling along the road,
having beaten the Romans*, or *driven by ambition*, whose head is inflected for
aspect but whose auxiliaries, if present, are untensed. Phrases headed by
forms in *-ing* are structurally similar to gerundive phrases but are classed with
the *-en* type because both function as modifiers, whereas gerunds function as
NP substitutes.

Participle   Traditional term for a form inflected for perfective or progressive
aspect. Verbs carrying the perfective *-en/-ed* were called "past participles";
those carrying the progressive *-ing*, "present participles."

Perfective aspect   A syntactic unit consisting of a form of the primary auxiliary,
have, and the *-en/-ed* inflection attached to the following stem.

Periphrasis   The use of function words as opposed to inflectional contrasts. English has a periphrastic (sometimes called "analytic") as well as an inflectional ("synthetic") comparison, that is, *more beautiful* as well as *prettier*.

Phoneme   A segment of sound that is significant in a language because it distinguishes one utterance from another.

Phrase   A linguistic structure of one word or more that usually takes its name from the class of word that constitutes its head and is associated with specific grammatical functions. Verb phrases, for example, generally function as predicators; prepositional phrases, as complements.

Pragmatic function   Any function, beyond the merely structural or grammatical, that enables us to interpret utterances appropriately, in context, even if the utterance is linguistically ambiguous or nonspecific. When a speaker says, "Put this on the table in the bedroom," for example, hearers assume that there's only one bedroom on the premises and only one table in that room, even though the speaker hasn't said so, because they understand not only the grammatical function of *the* (to mark NPs) but also its pragmatic function, which is to signal that the NP fully specifies or defines its referent.

Predicate   The portion of a clause comprising the tensed verb phrase and all its complements. The term comes from logic, where a proposition such as "Snow is white" is said to predicate of snow that it has the quality of whiteness. Thus *white*, an adjective, is a predicate. Traditional grammarians extended the meaning of the word *predicate* in syntax to include a verb in all cases.

Predicator   The part of a predicate filled by the tensed VP (main verb and all auxiliaries) but not including the complements required by the verb.

Preposition   The class named after a category of Latin words with analogous functions but different syntactic behavior. Typically, prepositions (*of, to, at, with, under, till, during, by* . . .) combine with NPs (called objects) and often set up temporal or spatial relationships between sentence elements. In English, the object doesn't have to occur immediately after the preposition. We can say, for example, *the thing I want to talk about*, where the object of *about, the thing*, actually precedes the preposition. Unlike their Latin counterparts, which must have objects, English prepositions can sometimes occur without an object: *The realization hasn't sunk in.*

Present participle   See **participle.**

Progressive aspect   A syntactic unit consisting of a form of the primary auxiliary, *be*, and the *-ing* inflection that appears on the stem following *be*.

Proper noun   Prototypically, a noun naming a unique entity (*Easter, Ohio, Mary*) that in its central use does not have a plural form and does not require a determiner.

Qualifier   The functional position reserved for pre-adjectival modifiers, prototypically filled by *very*, and by extension the words that take that position. Traditionally, all such words were included in the adverb class.

Relative clause   Typically, a tense-marked clause with a relative pronoun such as *who(m), which*, or *that* in first position though not necessarily in the subject function. Typical relative clauses are embedded in or adjoined parenthetically to NPs as post-nominal modifiers, but indefinite relative clauses function like NPs. Activities 8-1 through 8-4 deal with the structure of typical relative clauses, Activity 8-8 distinguishes relative clauses from embedded nominal clauses, and Activity 8-9 deals with indefinite relative clauses.

Restrictive modifier Embedded or "bound" (as opposed to "free"), restrictive modifiers describe or specify the identity of the head. Activities 8-3 and 8-4 distinguish restrictive from nonrestrictive relative clauses, but the terms *restrictive* and *nonrestrictive* can be applied to other types of modifiers. Compare, for example, *The badly beaten but still conscious champ couldn't respond to the bell* and *The champ, badly beaten but still conscious, couldn't respond to the bell.*

Semi-auxiliary A class of verbs, including "marginal modals" like *used to* and catenatives like *keep*, that are intermediate between auxiliaries and main verbs in their syntactic behavior.

Stigmatized usage Usage that is condemned because it deviates from standard varieties or from what some people perceive to be "correct." This term refers to the kind of usage impugned by the popular but inaccurate epithet "bad grammar."

Structure classes (also **function words**) Closed classes of words that do not participate in either inflectional or derivational morphology and hence cannot be identified by formal contrasts or characteristics. These include such sets as determiners, conjunctions, complementizers, and prepositions, which are essential to the structure of phrases and clauses.

Stylistic variation Linguistic variation based on such situational factors as power or authority relationships, level of formality, degree of intimacy, and purpose of the communication. For instance, very careful, precise enunciation (like *won't you* with the *t* and the *y* clearly articulated as distinct and separate sounds) in place of the normal pronunciation (roughly, *woncha*) to indicate politeness or formality (and perceived as an indication of anger or annoyance when affected or overdone) is a matter of stylistic (as opposed to dialect) variation. Choosing between *residence* and *home* is also apt to be a stylistic decision, as is a choice between *Have I not?* and *haven't I?* Compare dialect differences, which are more like permanent features of speech and less open to conscious choice.

Subject The first syntactic function in a basic sentence; optional in a command; controls number in the verb in standard varieties of English; inverts with the auxiliary for yes/no questions; is filled by *I, he, she, we,* or *they* but not, in the standard varieties, by *me, him, her, us,* or *them.*

Subjunctive mood See **mood.**

Subordinate clause A tense-marked clause conjoined by a subordinator to another clause, which it modifies and on which it is dependent. This text distinguishes subordinate clauses from embedded nominal or complement clauses largely on the basis of function and from restrictive and nonrestrictive relative clauses largely on the basis of structure.

Subordinating conjunction (also **subordinator**) The class of words that unites clauses in a complex sentence. Activities 8-12 and 8-13 introduce the subordinators; Activity 8-15 distinguishes them from the logical relators.

Superlative inflection The affix *-est*, used to mark some adjectives and adverbs for degree or extent.

Tense   An inflectional contrast in the first auxiliary or verb in a VP. Traditionally, tense referred to time periods—past, present, and future—as well as to grammatical form. Therefore, English was said to have a future tense, and (because they contribute to the ways in which we can talk about time) modal auxiliaries as well as aspect markers were considered part of the tense system. Current practice distinguishes between tense (form) and time (meaning) as well as between tense forms and aspect forms.

Transitive   Said of verbs whose NP complement can be replaced by an object pronoun, can usually be passivized, and is not predicative.

Usage   In general, any customary way of doing something; thus we can speak of "standard" or "nonstandard" usage. The linguistic usage of speakers and writers of standard English is often prescribed as the usage everyone "should" adopt.

INDEX

Terms in boldface identify those found in the glossary.